MACHINE GUNNER

MACHINE GUNNER

TALES OF
THE GRIM REAPER

ROGER FORD

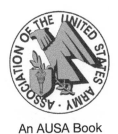

An AUSA Book

amber
BOOKS

This Amber edition first published in 2021

An AUSA Book
Association of the United States Army
2425 Wilson Boulevard, Arlington, Virginia 22201

ISBN 978-1-83886-080-6

First published in 1996 as *The Grim Reaper*

Published by Amber Books Ltd
United House, North Road, London N7 9DP
United Kingdom
www.amberbooks.co.uk
Instagram: amberbooksltd
Facebook: amberbooks
Twitter: @amberbooks
Pinterest: amberbooksltd

Printed in the United States

Contents

Chapter One

The manual machine-guns

THE COUNTRYSIDE around Richmond, capital of the State of Virginia, is dotted with battlefields – a relic of that city's former status as capital of the Confederate States of America. In the suburbs of the city itself lies the site of the battle the northerners called Fair Oaks, and the rebels came to know as Seven Pines. The battlefield site today is an unremarkable place, and the action which was so viciously fought out there on 31 May and 1 June 1862, was unremarkable enough, too, in a war whose primary characteristic was its savagery, save in one respect: above the clamour of the artillery and the rifles, the rebel yells and the shrieks of the wounded and the dying, the battle-hardened neutral observers (and there were many present that day, at a safe distance from the fierce close-quarters fighting) could perhaps have made out a new sound – a faint, faltering stutter, not unlike the noise a woodpecker makes, coming and going in short bursts: rat-tat-tat; rat-tat-tat-tat-tat . . . A new rumour was added to the awful cacophony of war at Fair Oaks, the herald of a new age and a new means of mass destruction so powerful that it was to change the very world. The machine-gun had arrived on the battlefield.

The 41,000-strong northern army of the Potomac army assembled under General McClellan for the so-called Peninsular Campaign included a battery of Ager (sometimes rendered as Alger) machine-guns, while Johnston's 35,000 Confederates had a small detachment of Williams guns. There is no evidence to show that the guns affected the outcome, whether at Fair Oaks or in the more punishing battles which were to follow. The casualty figures at Fair Oaks – around 13 per cent of each side's force killed, wounded or missing; perfectly normal during that war – indicate that nothing out of the ordinary took place. It is doubtful, even, if the generals of either side paid much attention to whatever effect the new weapon did have, since it is extremely unlikely that the primitive mechanical guns were able to fire more than a handful of rounds before they misfed – or worse, misfired – and had to be laboriously unjammed. Still, there were machine-guns there that day, and their presence lends a significance to a battle which otherwise goes almost unmarked except among historians of the US Civil War. It is worth noting perhaps that the terrain over which the two armies fought was largely woodland; if it had been open country, the lesson might have been better taught and harder learned, despite the technical deficiencies of the pioneering guns.

There were perhaps as many as a dozen different designs of hand-cranked machine-gun available to one side or the other in the American Civil War, though not a single one of them was either effective or efficient. Most significant among them was the Ager 'coffee-mill' gun which was also called the Union Gun (and, by its salesman, J. D. Mills, 'an Army in six square feet'), but there were also the Claxton, the Farwell, the Gorgas, the Lillie, the Requa, the Ripley, the Vandenbery and the Williams (some of which, strictly speaking, were

2

volley guns or organ guns). None of these was ever manufactured in other than very small numbers, though Claxton, and later a man called Accles, went on to make an inferior copy of the Gatling, which we shall discuss in a moment.

The Union Army bought a little over sixty Ager guns in total, and that was by far the most successful early model. They were single-barrelled 'revolvers', with trough-like individual chambers arranged axially around a central spindle, receiving loose rounds fed by gravity from a hopper. The resultant misfeeds, together with the doubtful regularity of the cartridges themselves, gave rise to constant stoppages and jams.

The one man we all think of in connection with the manually operated machine-gun was Dr Richard Jordan Gatling, who trained as a physician at Laporte, Indiana, but apparently never practised. He already had a string of successful inventions – mostly agricultural machines – to his name when, in 1861, he turned his attention to the field of weaponry. Like Ager, he settled on the proven revolving cylinder as a means of presenting the fresh cartridge to the barrel and hammer/firing pin for his gun, and also like Ager he experienced problems with feeding cartridges – then still waxed paper parcels containing powder and bullet – which, for the demanding purposes of the repeating gun, were inserted into heavy-walled steel tubes. These were sealed and pierced at the base, which was recessed to hold a percussion cap, the entire package being presented to the barrel by the revolving breech mechanism and functioning as a sort of disposable chamber, being expelled after the round it contained was expended and subsequently recharged. Both the Ager and the first Gatling guns adopted this approach, as did many of the others.

There is nothing to suggest that Gatling's first gun, the

prototype of which was demonstrated in Indianapolis in the autumn of 1862, was any better in general than any of its competitors, and it was not until the adoption of the composite metal cartridge, with a more-or-less pointed projectile crimped into it, and a percussion cap fitted at the base at the time of manufacture, that he was able to make any further progress. Such cartridges had been developed between 1856 and 1860, but did not come into general use for a few more years, until Colonel E. M. Boxer added the central percussion cap in 1866 (it was to be five years before Boxer's cartridges, which were wound copper tubes fixed to an iron base, gained Gatling's approval).

The one virtue of the paper cartridge was that it burned to (almost) nothing, along with the charge it contained; copper and later brass cartridge cases, on the other hand, had to be removed from the chamber after they had been discharged. To make removal easier they were rimmed at their base, and could thus be gripped by an extractor claw, and a variety of mechanisms to effect this were produced. The best solution was the bolt action, soon to be virtually universal for rifles, which ejected the spent case and loaded the next round from the magazine in the single backwards-and-forwards movement of a cartridge-follower.

Gatling's genius was to take that simple development and adapt it to the revolving mechanism of his machine-gun. In fact, he redesigned his gun completely, realizing that he could combine chamber and barrel together, assemble a group of barrels axially around a central rod and turn the whole lot, thus solving the problems of alignment he had encountered when turning a loaded multi-chambered cylinder to match up with a single barrel. A simple fixed cam moved the bolts in each chamber backwards (on their way up from the 'six o'clock' position, where the round was fired) and forwards again (on their way down from the 'twelve o'clock' position, where the by-now-empty chamber was replenished, ejection of the spent case having been accomplished by about ten o'clock) while the operator turned a handle to rotate the barrel-and-chamber assembly. It could not have been simpler, and it worked – usually – like a dream. Said Dr Gatling two years later, with no false modesty and in perfect truth: 'The gun can be discharged at the rate of two hundred shots per minute and it bears the same relation to other firearms that McCormack's Reaper does to the sickle or the sewing machine does to the common needle. A few men with it can perform the work of a regiment'[1]

There was considerable initial interest shown in Gatling's new gun, but frustratingly – for both the inventor himself and those few military visionaries who thought they could see the strategic and tactical advantages it offered – it proved to be intellectual interest almost exclusively. Gatling's first official order, for tapered-bore guns in .58-inch calibre, manufactured by McWhinney, Rindge & Co of Cincinnati, was placed by General Benjamin F. Butler, of Baltimore, Maryland, who paid a total of $12,000 for 12 guns plus 12,000 rounds of rim-fire ammunition, and used them at the siege of Petersburg, Virginia, in June 1864. Perhaps because of the inflated price Gatling set, domestic orders were scant – though the Union Navy did buy guns in small quantities – and never reached Gatling's expectations.

It was two more years before Gatling enjoyed any solid success. By that time he had refined the gun's design considerably, and succeeded in increasing the rate of fire to a reliable 300 rounds per minute (and regularly achieved twice that in his own trials), and it was now available commercially in two versions: the ten-barrelled 'light' (0.45-inch) calibre and the six-barrelled 'heavy' (1-inch) calibre (and was

5

manufactured in other calibres, too, as much to test it with different types of ammunition as for any other reason; the quality of cartridges continued to be a problem, and not only for Gatling).

Gatling abandoned his former partners in the manufacturing side of the operation, Messrs McWhinney and Rindge, about that time, and contracted with an established arms manufacturer, James Cooper of Frankford, Pennsylvania, to produce his guns. Over the second half of the decade, from 1866 (the year in which his gun received official US Army approval), he sold Model 1865 guns in considerable quantities to the US Army and Navy, and also to the British Army and the Royal Navy, as well as to the armies of Japan, Russia and Turkey, with Spain following soon after. Meanwhile the French, Swedish and Austrian governments all encouraged local research into the new genre, not all of it profitable or even original. Colt's at Hartford, Connecticut, took over manufacture of Gatling's guns in 1870, an association which was to last the rest of the inventor's life.

There has been considerable controversy surrounding the accuracy of the Gatling guns, and their true rate of fire. Much of it was due to deliberate misinformation, spread by senior officers in this or that army who absolutely refused to believe that their beautifully trained riflemen and their splendid cavalry – the traditions, in fact, which bound their lives together and made them meaningful – could be made obsolescent by a gross and ugly machine.

Concerning the true abilities of the Gatling gun, it is worth examining the results of official US Army trials conducted in October, 1873, at Fort Monroe, Virginia. A 0.42-inch Gatling gun was compared with a 12-pounder breech-loading bronze field gun, firing time-fused spherical case shot (shrapnel shell), each round containing 82 0.69-

inch diameter lead musket balls, and an 8-inch siege howitzer firing similar shot, this time containing 486 musket balls. The three guns fired at a canvas target, 9 feet high by 48 feet wide (approximately 3m × 15m), at ranges of 500 and 800 yards (460 and 730m), and each fired for one and a half minutes at a time. At 500 yards the Gatling gun got off 600 rounds, and hit the target 557 times. The 12-pounder 'Napoleon' fired seven times – and therefore launched a total of 574 musket balls – and scored 55 hits. The siege gun fired four rounds – a total of 1,944 balls – and scored 112 hits. Then the guns moved out to 800 yards, and repeated their exercise. This time, the Gatling gun scored 534 hits, the Napoleon 35, and the siege howitzer none at all. During those same trials, another Gatling gun proved its reliability by firing no less than 100,000 rounds of ammunition over a three-day period.

From the earliest days, Gatling had looked abroad for potential markets for his gun. He began a correspondence with a Major Maldon of the French Army in late 1863, and seemed to be making progress when he was asked to supply a sample weapon for testing. Overestimating his position badly, Gatling replied that he was unable to comply, but would happily fulfil a minimum order for 100 guns ... and that was the end of that. Gatling doubtless took solace from the fact that the embargo the American government soon put on the shipment of arms outside the Union would have prevented the sale from going through anyway. As evinced by their early interest in Gatling's invention, the French had very good reason to want to develop a machine-gun of one sort or another in very short order, for it had become clear that war with Prussia was almost inevitable, and even if the new weapons had not yet actually proved their worth against human targets on the battlefield, there was every reason to suppose that they would, at the first available opportunity. Thus far, the French themselves had made very little headway.

A full decade and a half earlier, in 1851, a Belgian infantry officer, Captain T. H. J. Fafschamps, had proposed a design for a volley-firing multi-barrelled gun, more an update of the organ guns which had evolved over the previous three centuries than a real machine-gun, which he called the *mitrailleuse*. Indeed, the Montigny Mitrailleuse, as Fafschamps's gun has become known, after Joseph Montigny, the engineer who refined the design and began manufacturing it, looked not unlike a small field artillery piece, though on closer inspection, its 'barrel' was actually composed of up to 37 small-bore tubes aligned around a central axis (the first version had 50, arranged in a nine-row matrix). More critically perhaps, it was to be employed like an artillery piece, much to the eventual chagrin of the French forces, who never developed any form of tactical plan for the new weapon.

There were two essential differences between the *mitrailleuse* and the various models of American machine-gun. The first lay in the way it was charged: rather than single rounds feeding into a rotating breech mechanism from a hopper or magazine, the breech-block of the Montigny, with its array of firing pins, one to each barrel, was moved in one piece to the rear by means of a long lever. The gunner then inserted a 'magazine' plate containing one round for each chamber, all ready-aligned, the breech-block was returned to the firing or battery position, and all the rounds were fired in a single volley, simultaneously – the other chief difference between it and its American counterparts. Later versions allowed the matrix of firing pins situated within the breech-block to operate sequentially by means of a cam driven by a crank handle. It was considerably slower in operation than the Gatling, but it is said that an experienced crew could get off 10–12 volleys per minute from the 37-barrelled version.

The chief drawback to the new weapon seems to have been its bulk: with ready ammunition it weighed the best part of three tons on its carriage, and took a team of six horses to move it. The situation was certainly not improved by the French High Command's insistence on siting it alongside the conventional artillery, where it was hopelessly outranged. Where it was employed rather more creatively – at the battle of Gravelotte, on 18 August 1870, for example, but also elsewhere – it proved somewhat more effective, but was still not enough to prevent a sequence of Prussian victories which culminated in the French Army being destroyed before Sedan on 1 September. That battle all but ended a war which had lasted less than five weeks and was to be the cause, successively, of the siege of Paris, revolution in France and, many would argue, the First World War itself, and everything which came after it.

If the *mitrailleuses* had been poorly used during the war, they were more effective after the insurrection which followed it, in the streets of Paris. As it became clear that the Commune was defeated, there was a general blood-letting, much of it wholesale slaughter of unarmed insurgents by troops who had remained loyal to the government. This was probably the first instance of machine-guns being used as tools of mass execution, but it was far from the last.

Among the 100,000-plus prisoners taken at Sedan (80,000 men within the fortress itself subsequently surrendered) was the French Emperor, Napoleon III, who was perhaps bitterly regretting his failure to acquire the Gatling gun the second time it was offered to him, in 1867. In that year, Paris had been the scene of a Great Universal Exhibition, at which

Gatling had shown off his Model 1865 gun, and one interested visitor was the Emperor himself. Just days after Napoleon's visit, the French Government ordered the gun removed from the Exhibition, and took it to Versailles for firing trials, many of them conducted by Louis Napoleon personally. The gun in question showed major defects – though whether just this single example or the whole production run was faulty has never been made clear – and this hardened the resolve of the War Ministry to stick to its plan to adopt the Montigny Mitrailleuse, together with a smaller, lighter, but hardly more mobile 25-barrelled version, usually called the de Reffye or Meudon Mitrailleuse, which employed 13mm ammunition developed for the newly introduced Chassepot rifle.

Despite a last-minute rush to introduce the new guns into service in 1869, only 190 of both types ever saw action in the lightning war which followed, and very few of them boasted experienced crews. There were a very few Gatling and Claxton guns in service with the French in the last two weeks of the war, but in tiny numbers only, and they achieved little, having been no better employed than the mitrailleuses. The name, which entered the French language as a generic (and the Italian, in a corrupted form, too) is the only thing left of the *mitrailleuse* today.

The Prussians, too, tried the Gatling against the Montigny, and decided they did not much care for either of them, despite the Gatling having fired the same number of rounds, in the same time, as 100 chosen riflemen and scoring 88 per cent hits against the sharpshooters' 27 per cent at a range of 800m (875 yards). In the end, they went to war without any machine-guns at all, though their Bavarian allies had a very few locally developed Feldl four-barrelled revolver-cannon which were said to be both effective and reliable.

The Swedes enjoyed a considerable reputation as metal-workers and metallurgists long before the industrial era ever began, and by the 1870s they had become a force to be reckoned with, with a powerful modern navy. Sweden even had a rudimentary 'military-industrial complex', as Americans were to call their network of bankers, arms manufacturers and the military establishment a century later, and prominent within it was the young Thorsten Nordenfelt. Nordenfelt was to be linked with the history of the machine-gun until the early years of the twentieth century – just as he was to the development of the submarine – but in both cases it was a secondary role he was to play.

The manual machine-gun which carried Nordenfelt's name was actually developed by an engineer named Helge Palmcranz, together with J. T. Winborg and E. Unge, and could almost be described as a hybrid of the mitrailleuse and the Gatling gun, having an array of fixed barrels and chambers but being gravity fed with fresh ammunition from a hopper. The movement of the breech-block, which both ejected the spent cases and fed new rounds while simultaneously first cocking and then releasing the firing pins, was lever-actuated. It was first shown to a committee of Swedish and Norwegian military personnel which met in 1870–71; their report was published in 1872, and coming, as it did, hard on the heels of the realities of the Franco-Prussian War, was to have a significant impact on the development and adoption of the machine-gun, not just in their own still-united countries, but all over Europe.

First of all, the committee established a set of criteria:

1. Rapidity of fire (which should reach the rate of 300 or 400 rounds per minute).
2. The mechanism should not be easily put out of order,

even if the rapidity of fire exceeded occasionally the normal standard.

3. The gun, with a considerable number of rounds (say 4,000), should be capable of draught by two horses.

4. The piece should be readily separated, if necessary, from its carriage; and be capable of conveyance by hand, should the place desired be inaccessible to horses. No special tools should be required for this, save a powerful screwdriver or hammer.

5. It should be furnished with automatic apparatus for giving and regulating horizontal spread of bullets, at various angles, and be capable of easy elevation, throughout a sufficient height.

6. The ammunition used should, if possible, be inter-changeable with that of the infantry.

7. Two men should be capable of performing all the duties of the piece when under fire.

8. Some sort of range-finder [the Committee recom-mended that invented by a British Artillery officer named Nolan] should always be employed with the weapon.[2]

In fact, the Swedish-Norwegian Committee was rather more demanding in its trials of rival guns than its criteria would suggest:

During the experiments carried out by the Committee, which occupied about eight days, this [the Palmcranz] mitrailleuse was stored in a damp cellar, and not cleaned between the firings. The rust appeared in no way to interfere with the working of the mechanism. 450 rounds per minute were fired from it – a magazine being emptied with a rapidity amounting to a discharge of 600 rounds per minute. The rapidity did not interfere with the regular working of the mechanism.[3]

Nordenfelt was no original thinker, but he was eager to snap up the inventions of those who were. He bought Palmcranz's patents in 1879, and immediately set up the Nordenfelt Gun and Ammunition Company to exploit them, meeting considerable early success in selling the gun in its 1-inch calibre version to the navies of Great Britain and the United States. He was nothing if not energetic – that same year he interested himself in a pioneering steam-powered submarine, too, the Revd George Garrett's *Resurgam*. His association with both Palmcranz and Garrett started out with his name being hyphenated with that of the inventor of the device in question – the Palmcranz-Nordenfelt Gun, for example – with the financier ousting the inventor as soon as the latter's technical skills were no longer required. Ironically, as we shall see later, the tables were turned when Nordenfelt linked his name with a second machine-gun pioneer; then it was his name which would disappear in short order.

That Nordenfelt should have been involved in the development of the machine-gun and the submarine at one and the same time is rather appropriate, too. The submarine was first – and perhaps more explicitly – known as the 'submarine torpedo boat', and rightly, since it was the invention of the locomotive torpedo, by the Anglo-Italian Robert Whitehead in 1866, which provided the craft with a genuinely powerful weapon. The submarine was still very much in its infancy, of course, in the 1880s, and though the real threat to shipping did come from the torpedo, it was a new generation of fast surface craft which were to launch it.

It was to heavy machine-guns like the Nordenfelt and the

Hotchkiss (and to the lighter Gatling and Gardner guns) that the task of protecting the fleet against attacks by these new 'launches' fell. Naturally, every ship of any size had to be thus equipped, as did the new intermediate class called 'torpedo-boat destroyers', not to mention the torpedo boats themselves. The machine-guns used at first were eventually superseded by weapons like the Maxim 'pom-pom', the Hotchkiss revolver cannon, and heavier 'quick-firers' still, such as the Vickers and the Elswick-Vavasseur, but those latter fall well outside the scope of this work.

The Hotchkiss five-barrel/single breech revolver was developed by an American, Benjamin Berkeley Hotchkiss, of Watertown, Connecticut, who later emigrated to France and set up manufacture there, which explains a predilection for Hotchkiss guns in the French armed services which was to continue well into the twentieth century. The first Hotchkiss – a crank-operated, multi-barrelled gun – is often described as a version of the Gatling, but in fact the operating principle was subtly different, each round being fed to a single breech, which delivered it into the chamber of each individual barrel. First demonstrated in 1873, it worked perfectly well at the slow rate demanded of the heavy machine-guns of the day, but was still considerably slower than its competitor, the four-barrelled 1-inch Nordenfelt. The latter, firing a 205-gram (7-ounce) solid steel projectile, could achieve 216 rounds per minute, while the 37mm Hotchkiss revolver, firing a cast-iron round weighing about 450 grams (1 pound) – or a rather heavier explosive-filled shell – was struggling to fire 70.

When the navies of a decade later began to demand larger calibre guns, firing heavier projectiles, both Hotchkiss and Nordenfelt switched over to single-barrelled guns of larger calibre still, though by that time both companies had also become involved in the development of the rifle-calibre automatic gun proper.

The only other manually-operated machine-gun of any note was developed in 1874 by William Gardner of Toledo, Ohio. The Gardner, a two-barrelled version of which was first officially tested at the Washington Navy Yard on 17 June 1879, where it fired 10,000 rounds of ammunition in 27 minutes 36 seconds, enjoyed a brief vogue in the 1880s, particularly in British service. It was often preferred to the Gatling for the 'small wars' so common at the time, by virtue of the lower all-up weight (about 45kg/100 pounds, including tripod) of its smaller versions. The Gardner employed a hopper-fed reciprocating action driven by a crank handle to feed a round into a just-vacated chamber, fire it and eject the spent case. Versions with up to five barrels were produced, one of which achieved a cyclic rate of 812 rounds per minute when tested by the Royal Navy. A British engineer named Robertson subsequently produced a belt-fed version, which was not adopted. Gardner later sold his patents to Pratt & Whitney, which was to become one of the giants of American arms manufacture.

It was no accident that by far the largest part of the mechanically-operated guns described so far were American in origin. There are a number of quite separate factors to account for that, some of them technological and some of them social, but most important among them was the relatively advanced state of the American machine tool industry, compared with that of Europe, and the realization in the USA that the era of the skilled hand-craftsman was drawing to a close.

American inventors were tumbling over each other in their haste to grab a slice of the fast-growing arms market. Each claimed to have ironed out the few problems remaining with the manually powered gun, but none of them made it past the start line of approval by one government or another. Some were significant to a degree in that they introduced a new element which was later perfected and universally adopted: feeding ammunition by means of a belt, in the case of the Bailey, for example, and mechanical indexing (location) of the rounds in the magazine, in the gun designed by Lowell. Gatling's gun benefited from the work of others, particularly in the introduction of the 400-round Broadwell drum magazine, by means of which it was possible to get off 4,000 rounds in ten minutes, and by a gravity-fed loading system rather more effective than the original hopper, designed by L. F. Bruce, which the Gardner gun also employed.

Even so, American engineering ingenuity and inventiveness had gone as far as it was possible to go with the manually-operated machine gun by 1880, and it was time to take the next logical step forward – the development of the automatic gun. That development actually took place in Britain, yet the dominance of American engineering creativity was still evident, for the man who was responsible for it was another American, and like Richard Gatling, a self-taught professional inventor: the redoubtable Hiram Stevens Maxim.

Chapter Two

Richard Gatling's gun goes to war

THE HISTORY of any invention has a vital strand to it beyond a description of the way it came into being and the (very often wrong) paths its developers took while trying to make it work, and that is the way the machine or process in question was employed. In the case of the machine-gun, that employment was to have the furthest-reaching consequences imaginable, for its introduction – and that of rifled breech-loading artillery, the repeating rifle and the armoured ship – coincided with (and to a great degree, enabled) the heyday of imperialism, when the industrialized European powers (and to some extent the USA) sought to take over and exploit the rest of the world. Most active among them was Great Britain, which had a head start by virtue of having by far the biggest existing Empire anyway, but a newly powerful Germany and a revitalized France, and even Belgium – or rather its King Leopold, misusing his power and acting on his own behalf as a private citizen – and belatedly Italy were all fighting to grab what was left: most of Africa, parts of Asia and odd crumbs of territory elsewhere. The Gatling gun was to play a prominent part in this orgy of imperialism.

The British Army obtained its first Gatling guns in 1869,

though there was a stout body of senior officers (and some not-so-senior ones, too) who were determined that the new weapon should be derided at every opportunity, and if possible, banished from the inventory altogether. None the less, even the most hide-bound of colonels would generally have agreed that in certain circumstances – such as repulsing the massed attack of native troops armed only with primitive weapons (a sickeningly regular scenario during the creation of empire) – the Gatling gun stood a fair chance of taking a terrible toll and thus saving the day – at least until it jammed. This was a recurring nightmare, illustrated amply in the second, and less well-remembered verse of Sir Henry Newbolt's *Vitaï Lampada*:

> The sand of the desert is sodden red, –
> Red with the wreck of a square that broke; –
> The gatling's jammed and the colonel dead
> And the regiment blind with the dust and smoke.

The machine-gun has only very occasionally figured in poetry, but when it has, the image has been a powerful one.

And since it was likely to be just that sort of circumstance the British Army would encounter in its all-too-frequent punitive raids and exploratory expeditions, it stood to reason that the Gatling gun would have an opportunity to prove its worth in action, sooner or later.

That chance came and went in 1873, in the native kingdom of Ashanti, to the north of modern-day Ghana, in west Africa. The British Government decided to send an expedition under Sir Garnet Wolseley to put down a 'rebel' army numbering around 40,000 and subdue, once and for all, a people who had never fully accepted European control since the days when their villages had been raided to supply

slaves for the markets of America and the Caribbean. Wolseley, just forty years old, but with five major campaigns
already to his credit, was overjoyed. He took with him fewer
than 4,000 British regulars and landed near Cape Coast Castle
on 2 October, with his traction engines, his 9-pounder guns,
his rocket batteries, his Corps of Engineers, with their road-
and bridge-building equipment, and a small detachment of
Gatling guns, intended for defensive deployment in stock-
aded positions, should that prove necessary.

Wolseley had higher hopes for the new weapon, but
decided, after a demonstration intended to instil 'super-
stitious dread' into a group of coastal natives singularly failed
to achieve its objective because gun after gun jammed solid
after firing just a few rounds, not to encumber himself thus
on the long march inland through dense jungle and over
swampy rivers. The absence of Gatling guns mattered not
one whit; just eighteen British soldiers were killed in action,
and the Ashanti were entirely subdued. Wolseley burnt their
capital, Kumasi, to the ground, a grateful War Office pro-
moted him, a grateful press dubbed him 'the Only General',
Gilbert and Sullivan named him the 'very model of a modern
major-general', and the rank-and-file of a cheerful British
Army accorded him a very signal honour indeed: from then
on, and for many years to come, a job thoroughly well done
was declared to be 'All Sir Garnet'.

By the time a further dozen years had passed, and the
machine-gun's performance had improved dramatically,
Wolseley was able to revert openly to supporting it, this time
in the name of the British Army as a whole: 'The British army
has now most certainly arrived at the conclusion that we
must have machine guns . . . It is still in its infancy. Its power
when in its prime will, in my opinion, astonish the world.'[1]

There is no easily accessible record of when the British

did first use their Gatling guns in action – more than likely it was in a coastal naval engagement against pirates, perhaps in the South China Sea, which were so numerous as often to go unreported in the public prints – but we know when the British Army first went into action with them. It was during the Battle of Ulundi, on 4 July 1879, during the second phase of the war against Cetshwayo's Zulus.

The early part of that war had resulted in a humiliating defeat for the British at Isandhlwana and this was most emphatically Not To Be Repeated when the two sides met again. Typically, the first reaction of Army headquarters in London was to change the commander in the field, and they despatched 'the Only General' to take over from Lord Chelmsford, but the noble Lord would have none of it. Having regrouped, he set out in search of Cetshwayo just as Wolseley landed in Durban. Chelmsford had 4,000 infantrymen and 1,000 cavalry – and two Gatling guns, on loan from the Royal Navy, together with the crews which served them. On meeting Cetshwayo's forces, Chelmsford ordered his infantry to form a hollow square, and put his Gatlings in its leading face. Made up of 4,000 infantrymen lined up in three ranks, the square that day would have been some 200 metres to a side; with rifles alone they would have been able to get off several thousand rounds per minute per side, but this was to be the Gatlings' day. The results speak for themselves. A correspondent of the *London Evening Standard* described the scene when the fighting was over: 'When we counted the dead, there lay, within a radius of five hundred yards, 473 Zulus. They lay in groups, in some places, of fourteen to thirty, mowed down by the fire of the Gatlings, which tells upon them more than the fire of the rifles.'[2]

Official reports put total Zulu losses at Ulundi at over 1,500 and British casualties at 15 killed and 78 wounded.

Chelmsford himself had a very high opinion of his machine-guns, despite some misgivings. He later wrote:

> We had two Gatlings in the centre of the front face of the square. They jammed several times in the action, but when in work, they proved a very valuable addition to the strength of our defence... Machine guns are, I consider, most valuable weapons for expeditions, where the odds against us must necessarily be great. They should not be attached to artillery, but should be considered as essentially an infantry weapon. So utilized, they might, I feel sure, be used most effectively not only in defence, but in covering the last stage of an infantry attack ... where troops have at last to cease firing and endeavour to get home with the bayonet.[3]

From then on, as Chelmsford had urged, the Gatling gun became an accepted and very welcome addition to any expeditionary force, while improvements to the gun's mechanism and greater self-control on the part of the gunners soon reduced jamming to more acceptable levels (the commonest cause of jams was over-zealousness on the crews' part, through cranking the guns too fast in their understandable anxiety to maintain as high a rate of fire as possible).

In 1877, a bitter dispute broke out between the Turks and the Russians over the Balkans. Despite claims to the contrary on behalf of the American Civil War – and even the Crimean War of the previous decade – this was probably the first truly industrialized war, with both sides employing modern breech-loading artillery (virtually all of it supplied by Krupp), repeating rifles and the machine-guns they had both been buying from Gatling since the later years of the previous decade. The Russians had actually acquired so many that

Gatling had granted them a licence to manufacture them for themselves, which they did under the name Gorloff (their then Inspector-General of Ordnance). The Russo-Turkish War of 1877 also saw systems of trenches for fighting and communications commonly used, and, at sea, witnessed the debut of the torpedo boat and the machine-guns used to fight them off. Though in these ways it foretold the shape of things to come, in its time it was an anomaly. Most of the wars up to the end of the century were colonial conflicts, limited in their scope and generally fought without 'big guns' in both the literal and metaphorical senses. There were few set-piece battles, but many small-unit actions, frequently fought against terrible human odds and, as often as not, decided by the behaviour of the Gatling or Gardner gun – though they were still far from foolproof, and never would be, particularly in the heat of battle.

The Gatlings and Gardners actually had but a short currency with the British armed forces, for they were soon replaced by the automatic gun proper. The last major land campaign in which they were used was in Egypt in 1882, first of all by naval forces sent in to secure Alexandria after Admiral Seymour's squadron had bombarded the city from the sea, and later at the battle for Tel-el-Kebir, when Wolseley's army invaded lower Egypt from Ismailia on the Suez Canal. There, in an action which lasted scarcely thirty minutes, six Gatlings – once again in the hands of naval gunners – literally swept the defending *fellahin* off the parapets and earthworks, the guns' drumming sound, which one observer likened to the tearing of calico, causing some alarm even among friendly troops.

There were Gardner guns present, too, and in the short war which followed they played a more important role than the less-mobile Gatlings. The Gardner detachment was under the command of a naval officer, Lord Charles Beresford, and he, for one, seems to have realized very early on the real benefit of the machine-gun over massed ranks of riflemen: its controllability:

> I was much impressed by the ease with which the fire of the guns could be controlled . . . in comparison with rifle fire . . . The men were very excited, the noise and general confusion preventing orders from being heard. Mounted officers rode furiously up and down the line with little effect while the bugles almost continuously sounding 'Cease Fire' seemed only to add to the noise. But the machine-guns were under perfect control, orders quietly given to 'search out that clump of bush', or 'keep your gun bearing on that corner of the wall' were carried out with the greatest regularity.[4]

After the end of the American Civil War, the government of the re-United States of America began empire-building right on its own doorstep. In 1866, the nation extended to thirty-five states, which between them occupied something over half the territory bounded by the Atlantic and Pacific Oceans, and the borders with Canada and Mexico, and the tide of expansionism was running strongly. Gatling guns were used, but only infrequently, in the long series of conflicts that followed with the various native American 'Indian' tribes. Indeed, had the weapon been more actively deployed, the lives of many American soldiers might have been saved, notably those of General Custer's Seventh Cavalry at the Battle of the Little Big Horn in 1876 – Custer had a detachment of four Gatling guns available, but left them at his base camp on the Yellowstone River.

The Indian Wars dragged on, but by 1890 the United States were largely at peace with themselves. That was not the case further south, however, where Spain was struggling to cling on to the last remnants of her huge American Empire, and it was insurrection in Cuba which drove the USA into her first real foreign war, in 1898. Most of the fighting (such as it was) took place at sea, but one aspect of the one major action fought ashore passed almost immediately into mythology, thanks largely to the participation in it of one man, Theodore Roosevelt, later to become the 26th President of the United States.

An American expeditionary force under General Shafter landed in Cuba on 24 June 1898, and a week later elements of it assaulted the Spanish strong point of San Juan Hill, commanding the port of Santiago. A volunteer regiment calling itself the Rough Riders, with Roosevelt, a self-appointed lieutenant-colonel nominally at its head, came to the fore, storming the Spanish position at the summit under fire. In support, the Rough Riders had a small detachment of carriage-mounted Gatling guns under Lieutenant John H. Parker, who took it upon himself to push the guns forward on the flanks of the attacking force, keeping up with the advancing infantry and effectively clearing a path for them. This is a very early – if not the first – instance of machine-guns being used in a mobile fire-support role. It was just as well for Roosevelt and his men, for without Parker's firepower they would doubtless have suffered even more killed than the ten per cent they did.

Roosevelt, who was no mean self-publicist, soon produced an account of his activities in Cuba, in which he wrote:

Suddenly, above the cracking of the carbines, rose a peculiar drumming sound, and some of the men cried, 'The Spanish machine-guns!' Listening, I made out that it came from flat ground to the left, and jumped to my feet, shouting aloud with exultation, 'It's the Gatlings, men, our Gatlings!' Lieutenant Parker was bringing his four Gatlings into action, and shoving them nearer and nearer the front . . .[5]

Roosevelt went on to assert that Parker 'deserved more credit than any other one man in the campaign' (well, he had saved the future President's reputation, and probably his skin, too), and had proved that the machine-gun 'could do valuable work on the field of battle as much in attack as in defence'.

By that time it had become clear that because of their weight and proneness to jamming the manually-operated machine-guns were unsatisfactory. They were rendered technically obsolete in the early 1880s by the development of the automatic gun proper – considered in detail in the next chapter – but that did not mean that they disappeared from the battlefield overnight. In fact, Gatling was still producing guns long after 1890 – and even developing new models, such as the short-barrelled, lightweight 'Bulldog' of 1893 – and the Gatling gun actually stayed in the US Army's inventory until well into the twentieth century.

The Gatling gun was popular in civilian circles, too, particularly in the land of its birth, during a long period of intensive labour unrest which seemed to many to be the precursor to an attempted workers' revolution. The first recorded sale of a machine-gun to a private individual was to the proprietor of the *New York Times*, H. J. Raymond, who bought three to protect his offices against attack during rioting against the Conscription Act of 1863, which his newspaper had supported (the guns were never brought into operation), and long before the end of the century the presence of machine-guns during civil disturbances (and particularly during labour disputes) was commonplace.

In the years just before the First World War, the Colorado coal- and iron fields were frequently the scene of pitched battles between miners and the owners' men, gleefully assisted by the National Guard, in which machine-guns were often used, but no incident was more devastating than what seems to have been a demented and unprovoked attack on 20 April 1914 on a miners' tented camp at Ludlow, in the south of the state, by National Guardsmen. The Guardsmen, together with hired thugs from the Rockefeller-owned Colorado Fuel and Iron Company, fired the camp and then turned their machine-guns on the fleeing miners and their families, killing, by some accounts, over forty men, women and children and injuring hundreds more. The Appalachian coal-mining towns of Kentucky, Tennessee and West Virginia saw Gatling guns on their street-corners, too – Gatling guns had been in evidence there since 1891, when miners in Briceville went on strike against the use of convict labour and were confronted with a machine-gun post manned by the Tennessee National Guard. Machine-guns were to stay in evidence there for decades to come, an everyday part of a striking miner's life.

Chapter Three

'A quiet, scientific gentleman living in Kent'

THE INVENTOR of the automatic machine-gun always maintained that he first started thinking about machine-guns in 1854 when, at the age of fourteen, his father Isaac described to him an idea he had had for a lever-operated, belt-fed single-barrelled repeating gun, and asked him to make both drawings and a model of the new weapon. This he did, introducing unspecified modifications of his own into the design, and showed them to a gunmaker in nearby Bangor, Maine, who said he believed that the gun would work, but that he himself did not have the tools necessary to make it. An uncle who owned a small engineering works was rather blunter; it would, he said, cost a hundred dollars to make and the result would not be worth a hundred cents. Some twelve years later, in Savannah, Georgia, on business, Maxim was introduced to a group of men at target practice with Springfield rifles, and was invited to try his hand. He was able to shoot quite as well as the best of them, he tells us modestly, though was surprised to find that the rifle gave him a very powerful kick. That kick was to reverberate around the world.[1]

It's tempting to suggest that Maxim made up the story –

it seems extremely unlikely that a young man of twenty-six born in 1840 and brought up in rural Maine, in the United States of America, had never fired a shot before – but it is actually of no matter whatsoever, for he did, at some point or other, conceive the notion of harnessing the physical energy of a gun's recoil to eject the spent cartridge, feed a new one, close the breech, release the firing pin and then continue through that cycle for as long as the trigger was depressed and ammunition was presented to the gun. It was some few years before Maxim would return to the idea, and that after an illustrious career as an inventor in the areas of electricity (particularly electric lighting and the regulation of current), and other fields. In fact, his success in rivalling the paragon, Thomas Alva Edison, so disturbed Edison's backers that they approached Maxim with an offer he probably should have refused but did not: he was to go to Europe for a period of ten years on behalf of the United States Electric Lighting Company, at a salary of $20,000 a year (£4,000 at the then-prevailing rate, but multiply that by anywhere between 50 and 100 to arrive at modern values), to report on new European developments in the field but under no circumstances to make any new electrical inventions himself.

The inspiration to switch to the design of firearms came, he said in an article in the London *Times*, from a conversation with an American acquaintance in Vienna, in 1882: '"Hang your chemistry and electricity", he was told. "If you want to make a pile of money invent something which will enable these Europeans to cut each others' throats with greater facility!"'

Presumably this prompted Maxim to resurrect the idea he had had in 1866 for a recoil-operated repeating gun, for by the time he arrived in London in 1883 he had with him a drawing for a magazine-fed automatic rifle reloaded by recoil action. Maxim was quite aware of the necessity to protect his ideas through the patent process, and soon submitted an application for an invention 'designed to utilize the kick or recoil of the rifle, or other arm, for operating the breech loading mechanism, and is constructed in such a manner that when the arm is discharged, the recoil stores up sufficient energy in a spring or springs to operate the mechanism for extracting the exploded cartridge shells, for cocking the arm, for transferring the cartridges from the magazine to the rear of the barrel, forcing them into the barrel and closing the breech.' He took care to cover a wide range of other possibilities, too, in the three-page document. Patent No. 3178, of 26 June 1883, was Hiram Maxim's passport into the world of arms manufacture, and changed his life for ever.

At this point it is worth considering, though perhaps not in great detail, the relative merits of the two slightly different recoil-actuation systems, generally known as the short- and long-recoil systems, and the basic gas-actuated system which Maxim was also soon to explore. In the short-recoil system (the one Maxim adopted), the gun's barrel and breech-block move back together over a short distance (usually less than one centimetre), the momentary delay allowing the residual pressure in the chamber to drop to a point where it is safe to open the breech without danger of rupturing the cartridge case. At this point the barrel's rearward passage is arrested, but the breech-block continues on its way, the extractor ensuring that the spent cartridge case goes with it and is expelled. The breech-block's motion compresses a spring, which reverses its travel as soon as the point of equilibrium is reached, cocking the firing mechanism and ramming the next cartridge into the chamber on the way back to the firing position.

The long-recoil system differs in that the barrel-and-breech-block assembly are driven back together rather further than the entire length of a loaded cartridge. A return spring then drives the barrel back into the firing position, while an extractor on the face of the breech-block ejects the empty case. The subsequent forward action of the breech-block then cocks the action and drives the next round into the chamber.

The simplest of the mechanisms for gas actuation is known as the blowback system; the breech-block is held closed by the action of a spring alone, with no locking lugs. On detonation of the cartridge, the breech stays closed until the pressure in the chamber overcomes the spring, at which point it flies backwards and cycles the action in exactly the same way as a recoil-powered gun. Clearly, this is a simpler solution, in mechanical terms, than the recoil-action gun, and is thus both cheaper and easier to manufacture and maintain. There have been more-or-less successful attempts to modify and delay or retard the blowback system; in the most successful propellent gas is tapped off the barrel at a point close to the muzzle, and used to act on the face of a piston, driving the assembly towards the rear, and cycling the action in the process. A simpler system relies on the breech-block having to overcome the mechanical disadvantage of an overcentre-pivoted lever before it is free to start its cycle.

Though it was recoil- and not gas-actuated, Maxim's original system (which was to form the basis of the Vickers system, too, with the linkage turned upside-down to save space), relied on an overcentre toggle lever, though this time the breech-block formed part of a complicated lock which also extracted and ejected the spent round while pulling the new one free of its belt loop, locating it in line with the chamber and then ramming it home.

By the time Maxim's first patent had been granted (there

is an inevitable delay between the application and the grant, a period in which the patent is said to be pending) he was already hard at work on the design of his first machine-gun, the 'Forerunner'. He had already clearly made the intellectual leap which allowed him to understand the real reason that the manual machine-guns of the day were unsatisfactory: that they were inherently unreliable because they were not self-regulating. Their rate of operation took no account of the actual goings-on within the chamber and barrel of the gun itself. That was their fatal flaw, not the fact that they required a strong – and entirely unnecessary – right arm to operate them. Two years later, in an address given to the British Institution of Mechanical Engineers on the occasion of his 'Prototype' having been awarded a gold medal at the International Inventions Exhibition, he described the short-comings of the manually operated guns in graphic detail:

> The workmanship of the [four main types of these] guns [the Gatling, the Gardner, the Nordenfelt and the Hotch-kiss] is exquisite. Their weak point does not lie here, but arises from another cause which would be very difficult to remedy in them. It is said by some military men that no machine-gun has ever been brought into action which has not become 'jammed' at the critical moment. Even if that be not strictly true, still the liability to accident from this cause is very great. A certain percentage of all cartridges fail to explode promptly at the instant of being struck: to use the technical expression, they 'hang fire'. Suppose that, while the handle of the gun is being worked at its highest speed, one of these sluggish cartridges happens to enter the barrel. It is struck and instantly, before it explodes, the breech is opened, and the cartridge begins to be withdrawn again out of the barrel. At this instant the explosion takes

place, breaks the shell [*sic*] in two, drives the front half forwards into the barrel and blows the rear half out of the breech and sometimes blows up the magazine. At any rate, it always drives the forward end of the cartridge firmly into the chamber of the barrel; and if the magazine does not explode, the next rotation of the crank drives a loaded cartridge into the chamber; the gun then becomes blocked or jammed, and is of no further use.[2]

He went on (this time in a brochure produced by the Maxim Gun Company, in 1887):

With hand-operated systems the speed of firing is determined and limited by the time it takes for the slowest cartridge in the entire series to explode. There may be but one cartridge in a thousand that hangs fire; nevertheless, in order that no jamming may take place, it is necessary to fire all the cartridges with sufficiently low speed to allow time for the slow cartridge to explode because it is not known when this particular cartridge is to enter the gun.

Maxim was being a little disingenuous, but since the brochure in question was a sales aid, he can perhaps be forgiven. The point he was trying to make clearly needs restating more explicitly, however: in the automatic gun, be the self-loading accomplished by recoil action or by gas pressure, the operation is self-regulating; if a round fails to fire, it stops the action of the gun, just as automatically as a successfully fired round initiates the loading and firing of the next. The gunner can then manually eject a faulty round (chambering another round and cocking the action in the process) and continue firing as before; the misfire does not result in the gun becoming jammed solid and thus useless. Maxim's insight –

and his embodiment of it – negated that last remaining reason for not accepting the machine-gun as a fully-fledged weapon of war.

Maxim was granted Patent No. 3493, on 16 July 1883, for his 'Forerunner' machine-gun, a belt-fed, recoil-action weapon using rimless cartridges of Maxim's own design and manufacture, employing an adjustable hydraulic damper to vary the gun's rate of fire. He was by no means satisfied with the design, and it served chiefly to allow him to claim patent protection on its main features. As he said: 'No one had ever made an automatic gun before; the coast was clear. Consequently I was able to take out a number of master patents, to show every conceivable way of working an automatic gun, and to get very broad claims.'

Six months later he was further to broaden his original patent base (for a gun operated by recoil action) to include actuation by means of muzzle gases with Patent No. 606, of 3 January 1884, though he never continued down that track himself. Others did, of course, and Maxim, believing their 'inventions' to be covered by Patent No. 606 and the slightly later No. 13113, became a keen litigant as a result.

The 'Prototype' followed, departing from the operating methodology of the 'Forerunner' in one important aspect: it used standard 0.45-inch Gatling–Gardner rimmed cartridges, thus introducing an essential element of standardization into the weapon (the rimless Maxim cartridges had been pushed forward through the loops of the belt which held them; now, in the 'Prototype', the rimmed cartridges were first pulled backwards out of the loop and then pushed forwards into the chamber). The 'Prototype' also had an improved hydraulic damping system.

The 'Prototype' was first fired on 24 January 1884 – Maxim recounts how he loaded a half-dozen cartridges into a belt and fired them off in less than half a second – at the workshop he had then recently set up at 57D Hatton Garden, in the heart of London's jewellery district. Its high rate of fire was equal to that achieved by the Gatlings then in use, but produced problems of its own: the barrel rapidly became overheated (the 0.45-inch Gatling, of course, actually fired only one-tenth as many rounds through any one barrel in any given time). In order to control the temperature of the barrel, Maxim surrounded it with a forerunner of the distinctive water jacket which was to become a feature of almost all future Maxim guns, though the 'Lightweight' of 1887 and the 'Extra Light', unveiled in 1895, were exceptions, albeit not wildly successful ones. To all intents and purposes, Maxim's design was finished by 1883. It was not yet perfect, certainly, but very little further actually needed doing to it, and that chiefly by way of simplifying the mechanism in order to make it cheaper to manufacture and maintain ('Do not give up until you make it so simple that it can be taken apart, examined and cleaned with no other instrument than the hands', Sir Andrew Clark, Britain's Inspector-General of Fortifications, told him). It suffered still from an inability to maintain sustained fire without stoppages, but the prime cause of that lay outside Maxim's control, in the quality of the ammunition available. 'I found that I could not obtain reliable cartridges' he wrote:

> many of them were faulty, some with only half-charges of powder, some with no powder at all; so I applied to the Government for service cartridges, and these were supplied, I, of course, paying a rather higher price for them. After a time, the Government could not understand why I required so many cartridges [he had fired off some 200,000 by then,

by his own estimates – enough to fight a small war]. I had
to explain. Finally they let me have all that I would pay for.[3]

Maxim also experienced problems caused by the sheer weight
of a belt of 0.45-inch calibre ammunition, which itself
tended to cause feed problems, and these he tried to overcome by substituting a positively-indexed drum magazine,
not unlike the Broadwell drum used on the Gatling gun in
appearance, but actually very different in nature. It proved
to be a short-lived interest for Maxim, but a very similar
system was later adopted by Isaac Lewis for the light
machine-gun which bears his name. Maxim eventually
solved this problem in a more straightforward way, by fitting
a box-like ammunition tray to the underside of the gun,
reducing the unsupported length of the belt from just over
one metre to roughly 30cm (from roughly three and a half
feet to about a foot).

A further problem involving ammunition was less easily
solved. Up until that time, cartridges were still charged with
so-called 'black powder'; that is, gunpowder: a mixture of
potassium nitrate, sulphur and carbon. It worked efficiently
enough as a propellant, but had major drawbacks: it gave off
copious quantities of smoke, thus obscuring the gunner's
view of the target, and left behind a residue which quickly
fouled the barrel. Maxim tried to circumvent the former by
devising a means of collecting the smoke and 'purifying' it
before releasing it to the atmosphere, and in the process
actually pre-invented the gas-actuation system later used by
Browning, Lewis and many others. His attempts to nullify
the defects of black powder were doomed to failure, though,
and for a while it looked as if Maxim's gun might just turn
out to be inherently flawed through no fault of its own. And

then, in 1885, in one of those instances of synergistic serendipity which so often mark the process of technological innovation, a French chemist named Paul Vielle developed a new propellant, a combination of cellulose and gelatinized nitroglycerine, which produced no smoke to speak of, and solved the problem once and for all by a much more satisfactory means.

More modifications to the basic design followed, leading to the 'Transitional' gun of 1885, and then to the Model 1887, sometimes called informally 'the first perfect gun' and in a later guise the 'World Standard' gun. Important among these changes were those required to alter the characteristics of the gun's action to take account of the different pressure curve of the new slower-burning smokeless powder and to cope with the reduced recoil produced by smaller-calibre rounds. The first small-calibre guns made were the 130 supplied to Austria in 1889 (see below), which used the 8mm × 50 cartridge (that same year the British Army adopted the .303-inch calibre Lee-Metford rifle), and Maxim produced other 'RC' (rifle calibre) guns, particularly in 7mm, 7.5mm and 8mm chamberings, for other European customers.

By the time of the 'Transitional', Maxim was able to turn more of his attention towards bringing his invention to market, and doubtless to trying to profit from it after what had been an expensive development programme. The Maxim Gun Company was incorporated on 5 November 1884, with Maxim, a businessman named Randolph R. Symon and Albert Vickers of the steel manufacturers Vickers, Sons & Co as its directors, the two newcomers putting in £35,000. A later history of the Vickers company points out that it would perhaps have been more natural for Maxim to have taken an established arms manufacturer such as Armstrong's as his partner, but Armstrong's were the British licensee of the

Gatling and Hotchkiss guns, so such an association would have had its drawbacks.

The first guns Maxim submitted to the British Army for official testing went to the Enfield proving grounds in March 1887. The specifications called for a gun weighing less than 45kg (100 pounds) and able to fire 400 shots in one minute, 600 shots in two minutes and 1,000 shots in four minutes. The three Maxims all performed satisfactorily, and after also passing sand and rust tests were purchased on the spot. Two were 27kg (60-pound) standard models, but the third was a special lightweight version weighing just 18kg (40 pounds), and fitted with a separate reservoir to augment the water jacket around the barrel. Maxim put a specially constructed belt of 3,000 rounds through this gun at a rate of 670 rounds per minute, non-stop, and this, he said, 'was the commencement of my success as a gunmaker'.

He also started looking for markets further afield. That same year he heard of trials having been conducted at Thun by the Swiss Army, to choose among the Gatling, the Gardner and the Nordenfelt, which the Gardner had won comfortably, and wrote asking for the chance to compete against the winner. That second Swiss trial was to have an interesting secondary outcome in terms of the tactics of machine-gun employment.

The object of the trial was to test the guns' rate of fire and their accuracy over 200m, 500m and 1,200m (220, 550 and 1,320 yards) and that longest range worried Maxim somewhat, for the gun he had brought with him from England was chambered for an 11mm German cartridge, whereas the Gardner was chambered for a 7.5mm cartridge which was more predictable at longer ranges. In fact his fears were groundless; on the day, the Gardner's demonstrator elected not to fire at the longest range. The Gardner, which required a crew of four, fired first, and got off 333 rounds in a little over a minute at the shortest range, Maxim replying with a similar number in less than half the time, and with considerably greater accuracy. At 500m the Gardner jammed and, in their haste to clear it, its crew spilled most of their ready ammunition on to the sand of the gun pit; they took almost four minutes to fire off their allotment, as a result. The Maxim performed as before.

Now, 1.2km is a considerable distance; the unaided eye cannot make out individual human figures at that range, and even an object as large as a family car is hardly more than a speck. Maxim's account of the third firing test of the day speaks for itself:

> The officer in command asked us to fire at a dummy battery of artillery at a distance of twelve hundred metres. At first I was quite unable to see the target, and the officer informed me that it was the blue streak that I could see in the distance. The sights on the gun had only been marked up to one thousand yards, and I therefore set them about where I thought it ought to be [for the distance] and marked it. I told Mr Vickers that if we fired off the whole 333 rounds at once, we might not hit the target at all; they might fall short, or they might pass over the top. The officers wished to see how many hits we could make in one minute. The gun-mounting was provided with two stops to limit the travel from left to right, so I adjusted these so that the gun just covered the length of the target, which might have been two to three hundred feet, and having put a belt of 333 cartridges in position, I sighted the gun for what I thought would be a little high and fired about one hundred rounds, sweeping the gun slowly round from left to right. I then changed the sight to the point that I had marked and

this time I fired rather more than one hundred shots, swinging the gun round as I fired; again I changed the sight to what I thought would be a little too low, and fired the remainder... All this was done in slightly less than a minute. After a wait of about twenty minutes, the telephone rang and we were told that we had technically killed three-quarters of the men and horses. I asked Mr Vickers if he supposed they expected us to kill the whole of them; he said he did not know, but shortly we were approached by the officer in charge, who said enthusiastically: 'No gun has ever been made in the world that could kill so many men and horses in so short a time!' and they gave us an order.[4]

The initial Swiss order was for just one gun, in 7.5mm calibre; the most important thing about it was probably Maxim's realization, while making it, that the 'World Standard' gun of 1887, designed for .45-inch and similar calibre cartridges, needed considerable modification to work with less-powerful ammunition. The Swiss Army later ordered more guns from Maxim, initially for defence of the St Gotthard Pass but later also to create machine-gun troops for each of its four cavalry brigades. Towards the turn of the century the Swiss turned to Vickers, Son & Maxim's then German agent, DWM, for their supply of machine-guns – numbered in the hundreds – and when the First World War broke out, began producing the DWM Model 1909 themselves at the Bern Arsenal, manufacturing a total of over 10,000 between 1915 and 1946.

From Thun, Maxim and Vickers travelled to La Spezia, where the Italian navy had also held a trial of machine-guns, this time selecting the Nordenfelt. There was to be no comparison shoot-out, but Maxim was simply asked to beat the record the Nordenfelt had set which, he records, was 'a very simple matter'. He was then asked to throw the gun into the sea, leave it there for three days and then recover and fire it with no preliminary cleaning. The gun performed just as well as it had when dry. They left it there and returned to London, bearing an order for 26 'World Standard' guns in 10.4mm (0.41-inch) Vetterli calibre. Similar trials in Austria later that year produced a similar result – and eventually an order for 130 more guns in 8mm calibre. Maxim returned to London and began to look round for larger workshop premises.

In confronting the Nordenfelt gun in Italy and later in Austria, Maxim had, wittingly or not, gone up against perhaps the most unscrupulous member of an unscrupulous trade: the 'Mystery Man of Europe' (as he was styled by David Lloyd George in the House of Commons), Basil Zaharoff, Nordenfelt's chief salesman. Zaharoff may have been singularly lacking in morals, but he knew a good thing when he saw one; after a desultory attempt or two at sabotaging the Maxim gun and its growing reputation (one such apparently involved bribing a Maxim Gun Co machinist to ruin the casing of a gun destined for a trial and rivet on a repair patch in such a way that the gun was bound to jam as soon as it commenced firing; another, more subtle, approach was to mix with journalists watching the Maxim firing from a distance and inform them that it was the Nordenfelt gun on trial) he set about trying to engineer a merger between the Nordenfelt Guns and Ammunition Company, the manufacturing and trading company Thorsten Nordenfelt had set up in England, and the Maxim Gun Company.

It should have been obvious to even the most committed supporter of the manually operated machine-gun that it could not compete with the automatic Maxim. It was not; and not least to Thorsten Nordenfelt himself, perhaps because he believed the lies his salesman-in-chief had been spreading so assiduously. Zaharoff's counsel prevailed, however, and in July 1887 a prospectus for the Maxim Nordenfelt Guns and Ammunition Company was issued, with the aim of raising £1.4 million in capital by means of shares and a further £400,000 in debentures. The total amount was subscribed for 'many times over' (said Maxim) in the first two hours of the offer's currency. Almost a year to the day later, on 17 July 1888, MNG&AC commenced trading, with Maxim and Nordenfelt as joint managing directors, production being shared between the Nordenfelt plant in Erith, Kent, and a site Maxim had recently acquired in nearby Crayford. Maxim finally had an engineering base which matched the promise his revolutionary new weapon showed.

While it could make machine-guns in commercial quantities – and bigger automatic cannon – the company did not make enormous amounts of money (though Maxim himself was quite well off: he was still receiving his $20,000-a-year pay-off from the United States Electric Lighting Company). According to some commentators, the failure to get the product more widely accepted was due in great measure to Zaharoff's earlier detrimental activities. The Maxim Nordenfelt contract book for 1888–89, which has survived, shows a string of small orders – two for the Imperial East Africa Company (and a third, a specially modified lightweight version, fitted with an 'arrow-proof' protective screen, presented amid much publicity to the Anglo-American journalist-turned-explorer, Henry Morton Stanley); one each for the British North Borneo Company, the Spanish Government, the Argentinian Government, the Calcutta Volunteers, the Welsh Volunteers; a total of seven for the Crown Agents for the Colonies. Larger orders included a little over 200 guns for the British War Office, 34 for the French Government, 12 for the Italian Navy, and 10 for the Australian state of New South Wales, but this was just not enough to put a company employing some 1,500 men into profit (though there was, of course, the old Nordenfelt business to be carried on, too). In fact, it was 1896 before that happened, and by then day-to-day management had been taken out of Maxim's hands and entrusted to a German-born businessman, Sigmund Loewe, brother of the man who had by then been granted the licence to manufacture Maxim guns in Germany.

By that time also, Thorsten Nordenfelt had long gone, resigning his directorship in January 1890 and selling his £200,000 holding back to the company, committing professional suicide soon after by purchasing the rights to a Swedish hybrid automatic/manual machine-gun called the Bergman, and thereby breaking an agreement to desist from armaments manufacture except on behalf of MNG&AC for the following twenty-five years, which he had signed in 1888. The Bergman gun never worked satisfactorily anyway, and Nordenfelt soon slipped away into obscurity.

There was clearly little love lost between Maxim and Nordenfelt, a situation most commentators trace to Nordenfelt's patents having become virtually valueless after the invention of the automatic gun. Dolf Goldsmith, in his very comprehensive analysis of the development of the Maxim gun (*The Devil's Paintbrush*), asserts that Maxim was unsympathetic to Nordenfelt, and dismissed his complaints and criticisms as 'the ramblings of an old man' – an interesting comment, given that Nordenfelt was actually two years younger than Maxim. It is tempting to suggest that Maxim and his partners, having got what they wanted from Nordenfelt, simply squeezed him out – a tactic the Swede had used himself with both Palmcranz and the submarine pioneer,

Garrett. Thorsten Nordenfelt died in 1920, at the age of 78, having survived Maxim by four years

Loewe proved to be an enthusiastic salesman, as well as a talented manager, and indeed, it was he and not, as is usually reported, Hiram Maxim, who liked to demonstrate the automatic gun's power by cutting down mature trees with it. He is recorded as having shown off the gun in this peculiar fashion on several occasions in the company of the Chinese Ambassador to Britain, at the house of the celebrated cookery-book writer Mrs Beeton, which Loewe had rented. His daughter later recalled that 'squads of Chinese dragging machine-guns about and firing them with more relish than discrimination were to be found at all daylight hours' in the five-acre grounds of the house, an account confirmed by the official Vickers Company history, which says: 'Loewe shared the Chinese Ambassador's pleasure in the sport of cutting down trees by machine-gun fire, and all through the summer days the glades and lawns were decorated by groups of silk-robed figures engaged in this delightful pastime.'

What the neighbours thought seems not to have been recorded.

Aristocratic fascination with the machine-gun was no new thing, of course; Maxim recorded a stream of titled visitors to the old Hatton Garden workshop, all of them eager as could be to fire the gun for themselves. The Prince of Wales, the Duke of Cambridge (then Commander-in-Chief of the British Army, so he at least had a professional, and not just what one might call a prurient, interest), the Dukes of Devonshire, Edinburgh, Kent and Sutherland all came, too, and they and their friends were doubtless responsible for a good part of those 200,000 rounds expended in testing the early guns. Maxim got tired of it, after a while, and on at least one occasion refused to let a guest blast away with two or three hundred rounds. 'My dear sir,' he is said to have said, 'this gun costs £5 a minute to fire; you provide the cartridges and I'll provide the gun!'

Later, it was to be the personal intervention of the German Kaiser Wilheim II himself (at the prompting of his cousin the Prince of Wales) which prodded the German Army into accepting the gun. 'That is the gun – there is no other', he said, after firing it (and coming close to wiping out his entire General Staff in the process; the gun in question was fitted with a device that automatically tracked it round through a pre-set arc as it was fired, and the Kaiser inadvertently set this in motion. Maxim's quick thinking saved the day, and he thereafter deleted the device, except by special order).

Chapter Four

'Whatever happens . . .'
The Maxim gun in Africa,
1890–1905

DURING THE decade which Hiram Maxim spent developing his gun, the world was relatively quiet, if only by the standards of a century when warfare in one shape or another was the norm. Units of the British Army, in particular, saw plenty of action though, in their self-appointed role as the world's policemen. The war in Egypt precipitated by the British invasion of 1882 dragged on; Serbia went to war with Bulgaria in 1885, and that same year the British sent an expeditionary force to Burma, while just to the east, France was consolidating her empire in Indo-China. But it was not until the 1890s that fresh fighting broke out in sub-Saharan Africa, and it was there, in Matabeleland, that the Maxim gun went into battle for the first time.

In 1890 the vehicle for Cecil Rhodes's own personal venture into imperialism, the Chartered British South Africa Company, cheerfully shouldered its share of the white man's burden and set out to claim for the Crown, and then exploit for itself, the region north of the Transvaal, between the Limpopo and Zambesi rivers, in what was to become Southern Rhodesia and is today the Republic of Zimbabwe. From the first, its activities were para-military; the pioneering body of 200 picked volunteers was guarded by a 500-strong contingent of the newly-formed Charter Company 'police' led by such luminaries as Dr Leander Starr Jameson and Frederick Selous (of whom more later), and commanded by a regular officer of the British Army, Lieutenant-Colonel E. G. Pennefather, of the 6th Dragoon Guards. There was the usual problem, of course: as far as the people of the region were concerned, they already had an organized society, under King Lobengula, and saw no reason to exchange his rule for any other.

Jameson was a fervent admirer of Rhodes, and was ready to go to any lengths to further his friend's ambitions in an area where his true claims were actually very shaky indeed. To put it baldly, this meant finding a way to justify decisive military action against a native king who was behaving less than provocatively. His chance came in July 1893, when Lobengula sent a large party of Ndebele to punish some Shona tribesmen for cattle-stealing. The Ndebele caught up with them near the white settlement of Fort Victoria, and commenced to massacre them, killing perhaps 400, some of them inside the white homes where they had sought refuge. Jameson lost no time in applying to Rhodes for funds to recruit a private army, ostensibly to punish the Ndebele for their act of intrusion into the white settlement, but in fact to tighten the British settlers' rather loose grip on Matabeleland into a stranglehold.

A force of about 700 volunteers, with Jameson at their head, armed with rifles, two small field pieces and five Maxims, set out from Salisbury (now Harare) and joined up with a similar-sized and similarly armed force from Victoria. They immediately turned towards Bulawayo in search of the Ndebele, who in the event did the finding, on 24 October, on the banks of the upper Shangani river. Four to five thousand native warriors, mostly armed with spears, but with a scattering of modern rifles, launched a night attack on the British camp and the Company men left perhaps 1,500 of them dead, lying three and four deep in places, cut down in swathes as they advanced towards the British position. The Ndebele could not have made a worse mistake than in underestimating the Maxims' ability to control the battlefield with intersecting fire zones, even when the target was next to invisible, as Maxim himself had first demonstrated in the Swiss trial, back in 1887. The British unanimously agreed that it was the sustained fire of the Maxim guns which had saved their lives and brought them a cheap victory, and they were almost certainly right. They wrote to Maxim Nordenfelt by the dozen to express their gratitude and bear witness to the efficacy of the gun:

> The Matabele never got nearer than a hundred yards. They were led by the Nubuzu Regiment, the King's bodyguard, who came on, yelling like fiends and rushing on to certain death, for the Maxims far exceeded all expectations and mowed them down literally like grass. I never saw anything like these Maxim guns, nor dreamed that such things could be: for the belts of cartridges were run through them [150 in each belt] as fast as a man could load and fire.[1]

The London *Daily News* concurred:

> Most of the Matabele had probably never seen a machine-gun in their lives. Their trust was in their spears, for they had never known an enemy able to withstand them. Even when they found their mistake, they had the heroism to regard it as only a momentary error in their calculations. They retired in perfect order and re-formed for a second

47

rush. Once more, the Maxims swept them down in the dense masses of their concentration. It seems incredible that they should have mustered for still another attack, but this actually happened. They came as men foredoomed to failure, and those who were left of them went back to a mere rabble rout.[2]

A Matabele account was rather less prosaic: 'The white man came again with his guns that spat bullets as the heavens sometimes spit hail, and who were the naked Matabele to stand up against these guns?'[3]

A week later the Ndebele attacked the column again, with similar result, at Bombezi, just short of Bulawayo, and after that the short, bloody war was effectively over save for a protracted pursuit of Lobengula, who eventually committed suicide. For a small enough investment – perhaps £50,000 and some fifty white lives – Jameson had driven the warlike elements out of an area of some 400,000 square kilometres, rich in farm land and natural resources, thanks largely to the Maxim gun. Each volunteer was granted 6,000 acres of choice land, much of which their descendants still hold.

The Matabele campaign was not, strictly speaking, the first time the rattle of a Maxim gun had been heard in Africa, though before that it had been a lone voice, and rather prone to stuttering. The gun Maxim presented to Stanley in 1887 found its way, via the Congo river and Lake Albert to Mombasa, on the Indian Ocean. There it fell into the hands of yet another imperialist adventurer, Frederick Lugard (whom we shall also encounter again), on his way to make a reality of the Anglo-German agreement which gave Uganda over into the British sphere of influence.

There is a school of thought which maintains that the religious missionaries who swarmed to Africa in the wake of the pioneers (and sometimes, like David Livingstone, actually at their head) did more damage to the local population than the machine-gun ever did, but in Uganda there was no such conflict; the two menaces worked hand in hand. By 1892, the region was in the grip of a sectarian civil war between tribes 'converted' by Catholic missionaries and others who had fallen under the influence of Protestantism. Lugard used his well-travelled Maxim, despite its jamming frequently, probably due to poor or non-existent maintenance, and a second which had lately arrived from the coast, to aid the Protestant Wa-Ingleza faction in their fight against the Catholic Wa-Fransas (the names the groups had adopted indicate where their so-called teachers hailed from; there was a third, the pagan Wa-Banghi, so known for their propensity for smoking cannabis), and this proved decisive.

By the third week of January, the war was effectively over, but Lugard, who was a very strange character indeed, even by the standards of that time and place, had not finished yet. On 30 January he arrived off the island of Bulingugwe in Lake Victoria. A French bishop, Mgr Jean-Joseph Hirth, head of the Catholic White Fathers, described the scene:

> It was two o'clock in the afternoon. From the road I saw fifteen boats rapidly approach the island. All of a sudden bullets began to rain upon the Royal hut, making a terrible noise in the copse that surrounded us; it was the Maxim mitrailleuse, which joined its fire to that of the boats loaded with soldiers ... We soon reached the other shore of the island; the bullets could no longer reach us. But what a sight! Just a few canoes, and a crowd of 3,000 or 4,000 throwing themselves in the water to cling to them; it was heart-breaking. What shrieks! What a fusillade! What deaths by drowning![4]

A little further east, in what was later to become Tanganyika (and is now Tanzania), the adventurers who had set up the German East African Company were to find the Maxim equally effective against Hehe tribesmen who disputed the Germans' right to pick up their share of 'the burden' by annexing nearly one million square kilometres in the name of the Kaiser; in one encounter alone, the Hehe death toll was put at over a thousand. The Governor of German East Africa, Count von Gotzen, was to discover that deadly effectiveness for himself in that same region a decade later, when the Mbunga, Pogoro and Ngoni tribes declared war on their new masters; assured by the shamans of the Maji-Maji cult that the white man's bullets would turn to water in the face of their devotion, they, too, were slaughtered in their thousands. His counterpart in German South West Africa, the infamous General von Trotha found it equally effective against the Hereros.

The Tanganyikan tribesmen should have learned from the example of their cousins in Matabeleland in 1896. They, too, had been urged on by priests who convinced them that British bullets could not hurt them, when they tried to rise in revolt against Rhodes's settlers in what has been called the first African war of independence. They killed hundreds before white supremacy was eventually restored, largely thanks, once again, to the machine-gun. It fell to Frederick Selous to lead the British settlers in this renewed fight against the Ndebele, for by that time, 'Doctor Jim' – Leander Starr Jameson, the man Rhodes had entrusted with the government of the colony-to-be after his success of 1893 – was languishing in a cell in Pretoria, waiting to be transported to London to be tried for treason. Ironically and most unusually it was over-reliance on the power of the Maxim gun, coupled with not a little complacency, which brought him to this pass.

Jameson, Rhodes and others had hatched a plot to raid into the Boer Transvaal republic and overthrow the government to benefit English-speaking settlers who had been drawn to the gold fields there. Jameson and his band of followers, supported by almost 500 men from the Charter Company's police force, armed with a 12-pounder gun and six Maxims (including some of the guns which had so effectively slaughtered the Ndebele two years previously) crossed the border from Bechuanaland into the Transvaal during the early hours of 29 December 1895, and rode for Johannesburg. On the morning of 2 January, 50km (30 miles) short of their objective, they were confronted by a large contingent of Boers led by General Cronje. Settling down to fight the engagement out, and doubtless feeling confident in the ability of their machine-guns to decimate the Boers at long range, Jameson's men were soon surrounded and under heavy fire. They replied with their rifles, the field piece and the Maxims, and were doubtless horrified to hear the machine-guns seizing up, one after the other, jammed due to overheating following a failure to keep them supplied with cooling water. Outnumbered and outgunned, Jameson surrendered and marched with his men into captivity, repudiated by his country. He himself was tried under the Foreign Enlistment Act, and spent some time in a British prison; most of his men were released forthwith, and at least 200 of them soon returned to Matabeleland as part of the column sent to relieve the besieged settlers there. The Maxims, repaired, were later to be turned on their erstwhile owners during the Boer War.

The Jameson Raid was a considerable blow to British pride, but it paled compared to what had been going on 3,000 miles to the north, in the Sudan, ever since the Mahdi's Dervishes had stormed Khartoum and killed Gladstone's 'hero, and the hero of heroes', Charles 'Chinese' Gordon, in January 1885. In 1896 the British Government finally summoned up the political will to avenge his death, and chose General Kitchener, Sirdar of the Egyptian Army, to do it. It took some time for Kitchener to bring the Dervish forces to battle, but when he did, the superior firepower he was able to deploy, particularly his Maxim guns, told an epic tale – and took an epic toll: time after time, 'a visible wave of death swept over the advancing host'. At Atbara, on 8 April 1898, the combined British and Egyptian forces encountered a slightly superior Dervish army and killed over 5,000, for the loss of a tenth of that number killed and wounded in their own ranks, the Maxims on the flanks opening fire at 1,650m (1,800 yards) and firing 'with great effect and without accidents to the guns' until the very end. Says one eye-witness report:

> The sights of the guns were hardly ever used to aim by. An officer would estimate the approximate range, and open fire a couple of hundred yards short of it. Then he would work quickly up to his target, exactly as if he held a garden hose, and guided by the dust which flew up as the stream of bullets struck the ground. When he arrived at the bobbing white figures, the lateral movement would begin . . .[5]

The butcher's bill at Atbara was nothing compared to that of the decisive battle of the campaign, at Omdurman, on 2 September. By then, Kitchener had mustered his full force of some 23,000 men, while the Dervishes numbered upwards of 50,000. The superior numbers facing them gave the British officers no cause for concern for they were able to tell each other, in the words of Hilaire Belloc's recently published poem *The Modern Traveller*,

> Whatever happens, we have got
> The Maxim gun, and they have not.

And they were proved absolutely right, for the Dervish losses were put at at least 15,000 killed, and perhaps the same number wounded, while the British and the Egyptians lost a mere handful: reports put the figure at 5 officers and 85 other ranks killed. There is little doubt that the Anglo-Egyptian Maxims had accounted for a very great number of the Dervish dead (the official account credits them with having inflicted three-quarters of all the casualties), though their ammunition expenditure was low, by later standards: the six Maxims of the 1st British Brigade fired some 4,000 rounds each; the four of the 2nd Brigade some 2,500 each.

As one observer reported:

> The Dervishes seemed to rise up out of the ground, making full use of [the available cover]. For a moment, it seemed that they might overwhelm Kitchener's forces [as] in dense array, the Dervishes moved to consume their feast of flesh, but their ranks were torn by murderous machine-gun fire. As soon as the gunners found the range, the enemy fell in heaps, and it was evident that to the Maxims went a large measure of credit in repelling the Dervish onslaught.[6]

The same reporter described the final action of the campaign, at Abu Adil, when the Dervish leader, the Khalifa, who had managed to escape the carnage of Omdurman, was cornered by the Anglo-Egyptian force under General Wingate: 'The

Maxims opened fire from a hill about 800 yards from the Dervish zareba. With their usual courage, the tribesmen left their camp and, making straight for the hill, which was bare of scrub for some 100 yards from the base, desperately tried to carry it. The Maxims beat off the assault, the foremost enemy falling ninety-four paces from the gun position.'[7]

Said Sir Edwin Arnold of Omdurman: 'In most of our wars, it has been the dash, the skill, the bravery of our officers and men which have won the day, but in this case the battle was won by a quiet, scientific gentleman living in Kent.'

Arnold, who was a writer, not a soldier, perhaps lacked the insight to conclude that the days of dash, if not of skill and bravery, were actually gone for ever, though the evidence was laid out before him clearly enough. As a direct result of the part his guns played in Kitchener's triumph in the Sudan, Hiram Maxim was knighted by Queen Victoria in 1901, having previously renounced his American citizenship in favour of British.

Thus far, the Maxim gun had only ever been used against enemies denied the benefit of the machine-gun themselves (a number of manually operated guns – Gardners and Nordenfelts were discovered in the Khalifa's armouries after Omdurman; but the Dervishes had had no idea how to operate them). Soon, however, that imbalance was to be rectified in an African war of independence fought between white men – the Boers and the British.

There is no reason to go into the causes of the Boer War here, save to say that the future of British plans for the whole of South Africa were at stake when the Boers rose up in revolt, but the very different strategic styles (and lifestyles) of the protagonists did have a bearing on the matter. Britain fielded a regular army composed of cavalry, infantry (some of it mounted) and artillery, disciplined, trained and above all, led and ordered, used to a strict choreography hardly changed from Waterloo or even Blenheim; the Boer forces consisted of every able-bodied man and boy they had, virtually all of them mounted, using hunting skills and their knowledge of the terrain to hit the British formations hard and then retire, just as they had done during an earlier encounter in the Transvaal in 1880.

Now there was one major difference: the Boers had Maxim guns, both rifle-calibre machine-guns and one-pounder pom-poms, to use against the British formations. How would the tradition-bound British, who had experienced no really major military set-back in the course of the entire century (though their pride had been hurt on a number of notorious occasions in Afghanistan and elsewhere), cope with having to evolve new tactics 'on the run', so to speak, to deal with a weapon which clearly threatened the very core of their power: the ability of their army to fight and win against an assembled enemy across open terrain? There is no real evidence that the British General Staff even addressed this fundamental question in advance. Given the mind-set of the vast majority of the individuals involved, it is even conceivable that it never occurred to them to do so – after all, even fifteen years later, as the Great War became inevitable, the machine-gun was still largely underestimated.

The Boers of the Transvaal and the Orange Free State had been buying Maxim guns for some years, both 'World Standards' and 'Extra Lights' in rifle calibre and 3.7cm 'pom-poms', and used them to good effect, particularly in the first phase of the war. The British Army battalions were armed with one and occasionally two rifle-calibre Maxims each, while many of the Volunteer units (a legacy from an earlier time, such irregular bodies still made an important contribution) were also Maxim-armed but employed the new

Hotchkiss and Colt air-cooled machine-guns as well, and used them rather more widely. On the advice of Captain Ackland, MNG&AC's military adviser and later General Manager (a man Maxim himself referred to as 'Captain Calamity') the British at first had no one-pounder guns, and soon lamented (and only later made good) the lack of them.

'When war broke out', said Maxim in his autobiography, 'it was found that three or four Boers, concealed in the bush and using smokeless powder, were able to put a whole battery of English field-guns out of action in about ten minutes [with the pom-pom firing common shell]. As a rule, they succeeded in killing all the men and horses before the English could find the range or ascertain from what quarter the explosive projectiles were coming.'

When the British tried to assault prepared Boer defensive positions – particularly at Magersfontein (where Cronje, Jameson's captor, was in command) and Colenso (and later at Paardeberg, though that was, nominally at least, a British victory, notwithstanding the 1,500 dead and wounded it cost, since Cronje was forced to surrender), they at last discovered the truth about modern weapons in defence: that they were unapproachable. The high-velocity repeating rifles with which the Boers were armed were bad enough, but when it came to facing machine-guns and state-of-the-art light artillery from Krupp of Essen . . . The British infantrymen, sent out to attack the defenders at bayonet point, died in their hundreds, cut down at long range by an enemy they could not even see.

'What range do you make it?'

'Eight hundred, at the nearest. That's close-quarters nowadays. You'll never see anything closer than this. Modern rifles make it impossible.'[8]

It was a very accurate, if small-scale, rehearsal for what would happen in Europe fifteen years later. 'A dress-parade for Armageddon' Kipling called it, presciently, in *The Captive*, published in 1903.

It is easy to imagine the rest of the world waiting with bated breath to see if the might of the British Empire would succeed in crushing the upstart Boers, but, of course, that was not the case at all. Even relatively close at hand, in Africa, people went about their daily business blithely unaware, for the most part, that the war was even under way. The Ashanti on the Gold Coast revolted again, and this time it was the machine-gun which subdued them, even if, like the Gatlings Wolseley had taken there three decades earlier, they were still occasionally prone to jamming. A little to the north, the Fulanis of Hausaland in northern Nigeria – now ruled by Frederick Lugard, as Governor-General – proved troublesome in their turn, and were quickly subdued by General Morland and an 800-strong force of native infantry, with five Maxim guns, manned, as always, by white officers.

Like Wolseley, Morland demonstrated the power of his machine-guns, but this time with rather greater effect: in the aftermath of the capture of the Fulani capital, Kano, there was an outbreak of looting; Morland ordered one of the chief offenders executed, and had the sentence carried out by Maxim gun, with an entire belt of 125 rounds. There can have been little of the cadaver to dispose of.

Elsewhere, the Germans in Tanganyika and Namibia were girding themselves up (and stocking themselves up, with Maxim guns) to subdue the native populations of these two colonies, while all over the Dark Continent, white men were pushing at the bounds of their land grants and their protec-torates, their colonies and their private kingdoms, and as often as not, the only thing between them and a violent passage across to the next life was a well-worn but equally well-maintained 'World Standard' gun and a box of belted ammunition, ready for use at all times and watched over like the crown jewels.

Chapter Five

Towards the Great War – developments up to 1914

THE POOR distribution of machine-guns in the British Army in South Africa during the war there is usually attributed to the low regard in which the weapon was held, both by the War Office and in the regiments themselves, but there is another factor to be taken into account, too: there were really not that many Maxim guns in existence when the war began in 1899, and that affected training, as well as combat readiness. It took the Maxim Nordenfelt Company a great deal longer than predicted to fill the British Army's first sizeable order for automatic guns, and it was not completed until 1890. Up until the end of 1892 the British armed services acquired only 169 guns from Maxim, 120 of them in the .45-inch Martini-Henry (MH) calibre, five in the .45-inch Gatling Gardner (GG) chambering (for the Royal Navy, which still had a large number of Nordenfelt and Gardner guns in that calibre) and the rest in .303-inch rifle calibre (RC) chambering. The RC chambering was not effective at that time with standard issue ammunition, for reasons we shall soon discover and it is quite possible that these last were bought for trials of the new propellants then becoming available.

Despite their being somewhat underemployed, the rate

of production achieved at Maxim Nordenfelt's factories at Erith and Crayford was unsatisfactory, even to a War Office which was far from committed to the weapon, and the government began negotiations for a licence to produce the Maxim gun at the Royal Small Arms Factory at Enfield. Production of the 'Gun, Machine, Maxim, 0.45-inch (Mark I)' began in 1891, and continued in a variety of forms for twenty-six years, until 1917. In that time the RSAF turned out 2,568 Maxim guns, for which it paid Maxim Nordenfelt and its successors a royalty of £25 per gun.

As well as improving the flow of finished guns, production at Enfield had another huge advantage – it brought down the cost of the gun dramatically; the lowest unit cost achieved was during the year 1902–03, when .303-inch RC guns were produced for £47/10/4d (£47.52), compared with considerably over £250 from MNG&AC, a huge saving even when the licence fee was added in. None the less, in a memorandum describing the 'Position of Affairs re Automatic Rifle Calibre Guns for the Army', issued on 18 July 1901, with the Boer War at its height, the picture still looked decidedly gloomy: there were just 1,150 Maxims on inventory, including those on active service in South Africa, with 350 more on order and another 75 due to be ordered. In addition, there were 94 Gardner guns and 32 Nordenfelts (all of which had also been converted to .303-inch calibre) still on inventory.

The British Army had adopted the .303-inch Lee-Metford rifle in place of the .45-inch Martini-Henry in 1888, but it was November 1891 before it began issuing smokeless ammunition – and the old black-powder-charged .303 rounds would not operate the Model 1887 Maxims which had been converted to fire the smaller ammunition. As soon as effective .303-inch ammunition became available, RSAF stopped producing GG and MH Maxims in favour of the RC guns, which both permitted the use of lighter working parts and reduced the size of the receiver – the body of the gun itself.

MNG&AC and, from 1 October 1897 its successor, Vickers, Son and Maxim (VSM), went on producing guns chambered for the .45-inch Gatling Gardner round until 1898, while Enfield made its last .45-inch MH guns, for the Indian Army, as late as 1904. RSAF also converted all the British Army's remaining .45-inch guns to .303-inch, reducing the weight of the moving parts, including the barrel; even then, it still took some ingenuity in the shape of a variety of muzzle-end recoil enhancers to persuade the heavier mechanism of the original guns to function with the smaller round.

Meanwhile, the gun's future with the British Army was still, almost incredibly, in question, thanks to the influential prejudice of a large group of senior officers. As late as 1893, a War Office Committee, made up of four officers from the Royal Artillery (which is perhaps significant in itself, considering the bickering between artillery and infantry as to who should control the guns tactically) and one civilian, delivered a report very clearly biased against the Maxim gun and declaring that its 'advantages were not sufficient to warrant further orders being given for guns of the present pattern, in face of the serious drawbacks enumerated'. Happily for the British Army this view was not universal, and neither was it accepted, and the .303-inch RC Maxim Mark I was adopted just two months later.

There were many lessons to be learned from the Boer War, and the War Office set about gathering data from brigade and battalion commanders, including the commanding officers of volunteer units as to the effectiveness – or otherwise – of their machine-guns. Lieutenant-Colonel Thorneycroft, of Thorneycroft's Mounted Infantry, was one respondent. He criticized the stability of the patent Ackland tripod at ranges of over 1,400m (1,500 yards) (the tripod was soon re-designed and replaced), but went on to praise the weapon's effectiveness in very certain terms:

> The moral effect produced on the enemy by machine-gun fire has been great. I have frequently used it to support the advance of my scouts when approaching a ridge, when the firing of the Maxim and Colt's guns have either stopped or very much reduced the effective fire of the Boers and allowed my scouting line to advance with little loss.
>
> Machine-gun fire, on one occasion, entirely cleaned the camp of German [sic] commando; and on all occasions has given valuable assistance in keeping down the enemy's fire, especially their long range sniping.
>
> I would advocate the greater use of machine-guns ... in the scouting lines. To obtain best results these guns [he preferred the lighter Colt to the Maxim for this purpose] should be pushed forward with great boldness, even at times risking the loss of the gun. In view of this, the guns should be used singly, when they are more easily concealed, more quickly brought into action, and more quickly withdrawn.[1]

The respondents were also asked to list the faults they had encountered. The greatest number of the seventeen types of fault reported – and the only one reported in double figures – was the rupture of cartridge cases in the chamber. After that, the faults were attributable to broken firing pins, unevenly filled belts and sundry other problems with cartridges. All officers reporting agreed that the effect of machine-gun fire on the enemy's morale was considerable, and that whenever machine-guns were used, there was a slackening of return fire. About a dozen officers replied that they had not used their Maxims, saying that they believed the guns to be of little military value!

If the British military establishment was reluctant to accept the machine-gun, there was considerably greater enthusiasm for it across the North Sea, in Germany. As early as 1888, Friedrich Alfred Krupp, *der Kanonenkönig* (the 'Gun King'), had met Hiram Maxim and concluded an agreement to manufacture Maxim guns, though in fact it was never exercised in the case of the rifle-calibre guns, and the only Maxims Krupp made were 37mm pom-poms.

Late in 1891 Maxim Nordenfelt began negotiations with a second German concern, Ludwig Loewe & Co, a precision engineering company with a successful line of sewing machines, which ended in the latter securing the right to manufacture 'Maxim Automatic Machine-Guns (to the exclusion ... of muskets and guns to be fired from the shoulder and all shell guns and cannon for solid shot)', in other words, the Model 1887/89 'World Standard' gun as it then was, and any development thereof. Maxim Nordenfelt took care of the possibility of Krupp belatedly deciding to exercise his option to manufacture the same weapons by setting the royalty level unrealistically high, at 50 per cent of the purchase price. The Loewe agreement was more realistic; MNG&AC paid the manufacturing costs and the two companies split the profit, two-thirds to Maxim, one-third to Loewe.

The first Loewe-made Maxims – part of an order for some hundreds of guns – were delivered to the Imperial German Navy in 1894. Apart from their markings, these guns were identical in every way with those being manufactured at Erith and Crayford. On board ship they were mounted on pedestals, but tripods were also supplied for the use of shore parties. Many of these guns were still in service at the end of the First World War. In all, Ludwig Loewe manufactured around 300 rifle-calibre guns before its weapons-manufacturing operation was hived off, in 1896, to become Deutsche Waffen und Munitions Fabrik (DWM).

On the expiry of the initial seven-year agreement in 1898, DWM effectively began trading in competition with VSM, now paying a royalty on each gun sold. It began to take orders from outside Germany – from Austria, Argentina, Switzerland and, most substantially, Russia – as well as from the German Army and Navy, and later added Chile, Bulgaria and others to its growing customer-base. By 1910, although Russia had taken up the manufacture of the Maxim for herself, DWM was still supplying a dozen other governments with their machine-guns.

The German Army was somewhat behind the Navy in seeing the advantages of the machine-gun, and placed its first quantity order only in 1899, whereupon the German gun (though still identical to the British model of 1889) was designated the MG99. Further orders followed in 1901, and the guns produced under them showed the first German deviation from the original. They were fitted with light steel water jackets in place of the original heavy brass, while some other brass parts were also fabricated from steel. The 'new' gun was designated MG01.

Over the next few years, DWM made detailed improvements to the gun, specifically aimed at reducing its weight and improving on its mounting. A new mount altogether, the *Schlittenlafette* or sledge-mount, was developed; it was retro-fitted to all MG99s and MG01s and was standard for all new deliveries (though tripod mounts were also available). It was to prove considerably more stable than the carriages, tripods and tables previously tried, and had the advantage that a gun mounted upon it could be dragged by one man, or comfortably carried, stretcher-fashion, by two, without demounting it. By this time the Government Arsenal at Spandau was working alongside DWM – and soon started manufacturing guns in its own right.

By 1908, the gun had shed a quarter of its weight – from 25.8kg (57 pounds) to 18.1kg (40 pounds) as a result of paring down components and using lighter materials, and in that year was redesignated as the MG08. By then, Maxim's original key patents had expired, and foreign sales were no longer subject to a royalty or licence fee (though they were for any more modern VSM-originated modifications). Perhaps for that reason the German guns were not fitted with the most potent improvement Vickers, Son & Maxim had made to their own guns in the meantime, the 1901-style lock, which simplified field-stripping and allowed the head-space (the clearance between the bolt and the chamber) to be adjusted, to compensate for machining errors in those components. The new VSM lock was a dramatic improvement, and DWM were certainly aware of it, for they offered it themselves the following year in the guns they made for commercial sale, but it was not specified for the MG08 until much later.

Machine-gun tactics, too, were coming in for attention in Germany. As early as 1908, the *Deutscher Felddienst Ordnung* (the equivalent to British *Field Service Regulations*) had very trenchant observations to make on the subject of the employment of machine-guns:

Machine-guns enable commanders to develop the maximum volume of fire at fixed points on the smallest possible front. Machine-guns can be employed over any country

65

that is practical for infantry ... In action they offer no greater target than riflemen fighting under like conditions. Cover which is barely sufficient for a platoon [60 men in the German Army of the day] can protect an entire machine-gun detachment.

The fire effect of machine-guns is influenced principally by correct sighting, possibilities of observation, size and density of the target area and methods of fire. It is further affected by the suddenness with which fire is opened, and by the number of guns firing at the same target.

The high rate of fire concentration of the bullet sheaf and the possibility of bringing several machine-guns into action on a narrow front enable great effect to be produced in a short time even at long ranges. When the front of the target is broken and irregular, the effect is reduced. A wrong sighting elevation or imperfect observation of fire may render the fire completely ineffective.

Dense lines of skirmishers standing [exactly the sort of targets which would be offered to German machine-gunners just over half a decade later] suffer severe losses at ranges of 1,500 metres and under. At lines of skirmishers lying, good effect is to be expected at 1,000 metres and under, provided observation is good.[2]

Not that the British General Staff was unaware of the desirable attributes for machine-gun fire itself, or of the advantages it offered over rifle fire, even if it did not always seem to pay too much attention: 'The beaten zone is perhaps the most important factor in obtaining effective fire', said Captain R. V. K. Applin in a lecture in 1910. 'Machine-gun fire is always collective and concentrated unless deliberately dispersed by the firer, while rifle fire is always dispersed unless specially controlled by fire-discipline under a leader.'[3]

We can accept the start of the twentieth century as being a turning point in the history of the machine-gun. Still less than twenty years old, the automatic gun had already proved itself, though not to the satisfaction of certain traditionalist factions, and had matured into an essential – if not yet a major – part of the inventory of any army worthy of the name (and not a few which were not). By 1900 the world's machine-gun makers could sell every weapon they were able to produce. The Maxim had the field to itself for the first ten years, but soon others caught on, and VSM found themselves in real competition not only with their erstwhile licensees in Germany, but with out-and-out rivals in France and the United States – Hotchkiss and Colt, respectively – neither of whom was to be taken lightly.

The Colt in question was the Model 1895 'Gas Hammer' air-cooled machine-gun, devised by John Browning, one of the most competent gun designers of that or any other period. Unlike the Maxim guns (if we exclude the designs Maxim patented in 1884), it was operated, as its name tries to suggest, by the pressure of the propellent gas in the gun's barrel acting on the breech mechanism. Maxim always insisted that the Browning/Colt design infringed his 1884 patents, which he had renewed wherever possible, and there is little doubt that he was right, despite Colt's trying to obscure the issue with a complicated arrangement of levers designed to make it appear, at least, as if their system was based on a different operating principle. It was not.

Browning's design for Colt appeared somewhat cumbersome; its operating mechanism was partly external, a swinging arm mounted beneath the barrel, the fore end of which was driven down and back through 170 degrees by gas pressure acting on a short piston, forcing a secondary linking arm to open the breech, extract the spent cartridge case and load a new one, cocking the gun at the same time. Its rather eccentric action led to the gun becoming known as the 'potato digger', but while it looked clumsy, it was actually very smooth and progressive. It was fed by a cloth belt similar to that used by the Maxim, each one of which had a capacity of 250 rounds.

The Colt Model 1895 was originally produced in 6mm (0.236-inch) calibre, for the US Navy, and first saw action with the US Marines during the landings at Guantanamo Bay, in Cuba, in 1898. It was subsequently sold to the US Army and to a number of overseas customers – particularly Italy and Spain – in a variety of calibres; as we saw briefly, it was a favourite with Volunteer mounted infantry units fighting with the British Army during the Boer War.

While it was effectively obsolete long before the First World War, a lighter variant manufactured by Marlin-Rockwell in .30–06 calibre and designated the M1918 'Marlin' (in which the ponderous under-lever was replaced by a straight-acting piston) saw service with the US Air Corps and in armoured vehicles. The M1918 was itself a derivative of an interim development, the M1914, supplied by Marlin to the governments of Imperial Russia and Italy, among others (though never in large quantities), which was eventually modified by a Swedish engineer, Carl Swebilius, to become the M1918. Several thousand even found their way to Britain during the 'Lend-Lease' days before the United States entered the Second World War, and were used for anti-aircraft defence on coastal merchant ships.

The Colt gun and a Maxim in similar calibre, together with two Gatlings and a Hotchkiss (it must have been a very early model indeed, for that was the year it first appeared), were tested against each other by the US Navy Board in 1895, and to Maxim's horror, the Colt proved superior to his own tried-and-tested design, chiefly, it must be said, due to the eccentric characteristics of the 6mm cartridge. This had some of the attributes of the modern magnum load, being very heavily charged; consequently chamber pressure was very high, which made it impossible to extract the spent case soon enough to maintain the normal rate of fire.

That did not stop Hiram Maxim branding the Colt Firearms Company as pirates, of course, any more than did Colt's embarrassment at having their bona fides challenged stop them from retaliating, both by insisting that Maxim's own gas-operated patents were developments of work done elsewhere some thirty years previously (they never did substantiate that particular claim) and by waving a red herring in the form of a suggestion that the recoil system of operation was fundamentally flawed, that recoil tended to throw the barrel forward, an influence the breech had to overcome before it could move backwards. Even a very basic understanding of the physics involved shows this to be a falsehood, but Maxim took the bait anyway, and turned to and designed the 'Solid-Action' gun of 1896, his last patented gun design, solely to demonstrate the truth of the matter.

In-fighting aside, the 1895 trials had one important outcome: the Gatling gun was finally shown to be decisively out-classed by the new generation of automatics (even if two years earlier Gatling had fitted an electric motor to one of his guns and persuaded it to fire at an almost incredible rate of 3,000r.p.m.), and when trials recommenced, only the Colt, the Hotchkiss and various different models of Maxim, all of them now in a more appropriate .30-inch calibre, were left. The trials were, in point of fact, quite useless, and were doomed to be so even before they began, because there was no one individual on the selection board powerful enough to bully his fellow members into risking their collective careers by wholeheartedly recommending the purchase of any one gun over its rivals. As a result, five years later the still-undecided US Army found itself with antiquated Gatlings and a very few 6mm Colts, facing Filipino rebels armed with Maxim guns. It was to be late in 1903 before the US Army finally accepted that neither the Colt nor the Hotchkiss – nor a late-comer, the Danish Schouboe/Madsen light automatic rifle – could really come up to the standard set by the Maxim, and ordered 50 Model 1901 'New Pattern' guns in .30-inch calibre from VSM for field testing, at a price, including tripod, tool box and belt-filling machine, of $1,662.61 each – guns which were essentially similar in nature to those they had first tested some sixteen years before. All the long-drawn-out selection process had achieved was to deny the American armed services the use of the most effective infantry weapon in the world for a decade and a half.

Vickers, Son & Maxim built a total of 90 Model 1904 guns, as the slightly modified American version was to be known, and then had to rework them all when a new version of the .30-inch cartridge (the slightly shorter but much longer-lived M1906, usually called the .30–06) was introduced to replace the .30–03. By that time, Colt's had swallowed their pride – or perhaps it was their gall – and had signed a contract to make Maxims under licence, the first order from the US Army being placed with them on 25 October 1905. In all, Colt's were to make 197 Maxim Model 1904 guns for the US military (and a 198th, from unused parts, un-numbered and unproofed, which was eventually presented to the Museum of Connecticut History). Production ceased in 1909, when the much lighter but fragile and complex Benet-Mercie Machine Rifle, Model 1909, replaced the M1904.

The Maxims were never popular because of their weight.

A gun and tripod weighed 65kg (142 pounds), an increase of over ten per cent on similar British and German guns, thanks to the American insistence on over-engineering everything. They were quickly relegated to storage, and many never saw the light of day again until 1914, when they were used for training purposes.

By the time the United States entered the war in 1917, her Army's machine-gun inventory comprised just 1,305 'modern' machine-guns – 665 Hotchkiss/Benet-Mercie Model 1909s; 287 Maxim Model 1904s and 353 Lewis guns, the latter mostly issued to troops guarding the frontier with Mexico – plus a handful of Gatlings and Colt Model 1895s. That, quite frankly, was both scandalous and unbelievable, a cancerous state of affairs which was compounded when the only gun available to issue in significant numbers to the American divisions arriving in France proved to be the quite odious *Fusil Mitrailleur Modèle* 1915, called the Chauchat after the chairman of the committee which oversaw its design, quite the worst machine-gun design of that or any age ever to gain official approval. There was a gleam of light on the horizon, though: orders had been placed with Colt's for the manufacture of 4,125 Vickers Class 'C' guns, the Maxim's eventual successor, though none had yet been delivered, and the externally similar Browning water-cooled recoil-operated gun was soon to be adopted as the M1917.

France has a history of being slightly out of step with the rest of the world – though naturally, no Frenchman would ever accept that it was anything but the other way round – and the development of the machine-gun there was no exception. A total of thirty-four Maxim guns were sent to France in 1888–89 and just seven more over the next four years, and during that time domestic development stagnated.

The large-calibre Hotchkiss manual machine cannon had proved successful, and it was at the Hotchkiss factory at St Denis that such development work as did proceed in France was carried out. There seemed to the French armaments industry to be no way round Maxim's 1883 and 1884 patents (even if they proved not to be so effective in the land of Maxim's birth), but then, in 1893, an Austrian cavalry officer, the Baron Odkolek von Augezd, arrived at St Denis with a prototype of a gas-operated machine-gun he had built which seemed to offer a way to solve the problem. Odkolek was rather naive: Hotchkiss said the gun clearly still needed considerable development work, and that they would take on the project only if he sold his design outright to them. He agreed, thus forgoing what would in the end probably have amounted to a fortune, and promptly disappeared from the scene (apparently, to Monte Carlo; perhaps to lose his small payment to Basil Zaharoff, an habitué of the Casino who once bought the gambling concession there for himself).

The Chief Engineer at Hotchkiss at the time was, like the recently deceased Hotchkiss himself, an American: Laurence Benet. Benet's father then held the post of Chief of Ordnance in the US Army; this relationship has sometimes been put forward as the reason the US Army later adopted the M1909 Benet-Mercie. It was Benet (with Mercie as his assistant) who took on the responsibility for the development needed to bring the gun to production, and unveiled it in 1895. Two years later the French Army adopted the *Mitrailleuse Hotchkiss Modèle* 1897 in 8mm Lebel calibre, and it was also produced for export. The Mle'97 differed little from the experimental Mle'95, except that where the first gun's barrel had been smooth, it had brass fins to help dissipate the heat, a constant problem with these guns. Like the prototype, it used brass (later steel) strips holding either twenty-four or thirty rounds each to feed ammunition to the gun, and this feature in particular was never satisfactory, though it was retained throughout the relatively long life of the gun and its successors, the Mle'00, the *Fusil Mitrailleur Mle'09* (the gun the Americans adopted, where the problem was compounded by reversing the feed unit, so that the strips had to be presented upside-down) and, albeit with some attempt made to modify it, the Mle'14, with which France went to war in 1914 and which was still in service with some units in 1939.

The early Hotchkisses had a reputation for being fragile and overly complex, and thus prone to breaking down, but the later models were very popular with the troops to whom they were assigned, who rated them highly in the sustained-fire role – always the benchmark by which a heavy machine-gun must be judged. For the last model of the gun, the troublesome cartridge strips were cut down to contain three rounds each, and then linked to form a semi-flexible belt; this arrangement solved some of the problems previously encountered – and also permitted the gun to be used aboard aircraft – but it was still not entirely satisfactory. It is difficult to understand why the search for a solution to that particular problem was not given the highest priority.

There were other machine-guns available in France in the first decade of the twentieth century – something of the order of 325 Model 1901 'New Pattern' Maxims were sold to a trading company, the Société Française, in 1904 and 1905 alone – but they were all for consignment to third parties who were not keen to disclose their identities as purchasers to the British. They need scarcely have worried; by then, VSM had long been supplying guns, often in ones and twos, to literally every corner of the globe, with very few questions asked, probably due to the influence of Sir (as he was by then) Basil Zaharoff, never a man to confuse patriotism with profit.

Elsewhere, most of the significant European armaments producers were making an effort of some sort to come up with an alternative to the Maxim. In Austria–Hungary, the giant Skoda company of Pilsen acquired from Grand Duke Karl Salvator and Colonel Georg von Dormus rights granted under a patent of 1888 for a gun operated by a delayed blowback system. The gun, which had an ingenious rate-of-fire regulator in the shape of a sliding weight on an oscillating pendant suspended below the receiver, appeared as the Skoda *Maschinengewehr*, in 8mm calibre, in 1890, and was superseded three years later by the *Modell* 1893, which was even more eccentric in appearance but was, none the less, adopted by the Austro-Hungarian Army and Navy. It was one of these guns – and not, as is usually reported, 'an Austrian Maxim' – which (together with a .303-inch Nordenfelt and a Model 1895 Colt 'potato digger') was the mainstay of the defence of the legation area of Peking during the Boxer Rebellion of 1900.

The Skoda gun went through three more evolutions, acquiring a cooling water jacket and a 30-round gravity-fed box magazine in place of the earlier hopper, in an effort to overcome feed problems, in 1902. This was never much of a success either, and an unconventional belt-feed system was substituted in its reincarnation as the *Modell* 1909. This was in fact a comprehensive redesign. At last the rate-of-fire regulator was abandoned – it had hardly been necessary in a weapon which could not exceed 250 rounds per minute anyway – and largely by brute force, the cyclic rate was increased to around 450 rounds. The Salvator-Domus system last saw the light of day (but never front-line service) as the Skoda *Modell* 1913.

In the meantime, in 1899 Waffenfabrik Roth of Vienna developed a belt-fed gun firing a specially-designed 5mm calibre round using the long-recoil principle from a design executed by Karl Krnka. Unlike most guns of its day, the Roth gun could be fired in either full-automatic or semi-automatic modes, but it never got beyond the experimental stage.

Skoda lost the Austro-Hungarian armed services machine-gun contract to Österreichische Waffenfabrik-Gesellschaft, Steyr, in 1905. The gun in question, designed by Andreas Wilhelm Schwarzlose, who had already had a degree of success with semi-automatic pistols, was certainly more successful than the Skoda, but it, too, was somewhat eccentric in that it employed a simple retarded blowback action with an unlocked breech mechanism, the only one of its kind ever to see widespread service use until the advent of the MP18 machine pistol. Its action relied on the mass of the breech-block, aided by a heavy spring and a jointed toggle arm which worked at a mechanical disadvantage when the breech first started to open. That meant that the barrel had to be short, to ensure that the bullet had left the muzzle by the time the breech was opened, in order to limit the back-pressure to a workable level, and that in turn resulted in low muzzle velocity and relatively short range. Nevertheless, the *Modell* 07/12, the best of the Schwarzlose guns, was popular with the troops who used it (it was sold widely through eastern Europe, in a variety of rifle-calibre chamberings, and first saw service in the Balkan wars of 1912–13), who liked its rugged simplicity. Its chief failing was a susceptibility to stoppages caused by poor quality ammunition, but that did not prevent it from staying in second-line service until the Second World War.

We have already encountered the Danish Madsen briefly, as a late-comer to the US Army machine-gun trials held around the turn of the century. Though it did not succeed there, it had considerable merit, apart from being the first true light machine-gun ever produced. It was to go on to become one of the most successful early examples of its type, being sold to over thirty countries (without ever being officially adopted by any of them) and remaining in production, with very few modifications to the original design, until the late 1950s.

Let Maskingevaer Madsen, to give it its full name (the Madsen in question was the Danish Minister of War at the time of its adoption by the Danish Army; the gun was invented by Schouboe and originally manufactured by the Rexer Arms Company), had a remarkable action, based loosely on the Martini falling-block, with a separate rammer and extractor to replace the non-existent bolt. It worked by recoil, and the movement of the hinged breech-block was controlled by a system of cams and lugs on the block and on the side of the receiver, respectively. Though complex, it worked well. Its most-copied feature was its curved spring-assisted top-mounted box magazine. Often mounted in vehicles – and sometimes in aircraft – the Madsen was really a versatile infantry weapon, weighing just 9kg (20 pounds) without ammunition. It could be adapted to either bipod mounting, in the LMG role, or tripod mounting for sustained fire. The British, who insisted on rechambering it for the rimmed .303-inch service cartridge, found that it jammed frequently as a result; other versions, using rimless ammunition, performed rather more reliably.

Away from St Denis, the French armaments factories at Puteaux and St Etienne both tried independently to improve on the existing Hotchkiss machine-guns during the first decade of the twentieth century, and failed abysmally. The authoritative *Military Small Arms of the 20th Century* calls the Puteaux 'an abject failure', and the St Etienne 'a hopelessly unsuccessful attempt to improve upon it'. There is no justification for describing them further; those readers who wish to learn how not to design a machine-gun will doubtless make a better job of it by starting from scratch. A third French contender, described as 'the worst design of machine-gun ever formulated' – the *Fusil Mitrailleur Mle* 1915, normally called the CSRG, and by the Americans (on whom some 16,000 examples were foisted when they arrived in France in 1917; they could not really refuse, having no machine-guns of their own), the M1918 Chauchat – also falls into the pre-First World War category, having been accepted by the French Army the year before hostilities opened, but we will take a closer look at it in the context of that War.

In Germany, there were three serious competitors to DWM's Maxim guns in the pre-war period: Theodor Bergmann (not to be confused with the Swede, Bergman, in whom Nordenfelt had interested himself), obtained his first patents in 1900, and produced his first working examples two years later, as the MG02. A later model, the MG10, was tested exhaustively by the German Army, but never achieved the success it perhaps deserved, for it was always up against the example of the DWM/Spandau MG08. The MG10 (and the slightly modified MG15) were water-cooled recoil-action guns, chiefly notable for their quick-change barrels (an unusual feature of a water-cooled gun) and for their use of disintegrating-link belts, known as Ruszitska Belts after their inventor, at a time when most contemporaries were using canvas belts. A lightweight air-cooled, drum-fed version, the MG15nA, was issued in 1916.

There is considerable speculation that the basic Bergmann design was actually the work of Louis Schmeisser (though Bergmann himself had an equally high reputation in his day), but in the case of the Dreyse MG10, there was no doubt. Schmeisser patented the design in 1907, and the confusion in the name stems from the fact that the guns' manufacturer, Rheinische Metallwaren und Maschinenfabrik (RMM, now Rheinmetall) had acquired the Dreyse business in 1901 (it was the original Dreyse, Nicholaus, who had invented the needle gun in the 1830s). Like the Bergmann guns, the Dreyses were overshadowed by the DWM MG08, and an 'improved' version, the MG15, intended for the Middle East and Mesopotamia (Iraq), was at best only marginally better than its forerunner. The guns worked by recoil action on a hinged block, though this time it rose instead of falling, as in the Madsen. Original guns were water-cooled and belt fed, but many were rebuilt long after the war to become drum-fed, air-cooled MG13s, a limited-production forerunner to the MG34 of the Second World War.

The last pre-1914 German machine-gun was designed and made by DWM in response to a request by the Government for a lightweight automatic weapon suitable for flexible mounting in aircraft and airships. Karl Heinemann started work on it in 1909 and two years later produced the water-cooled Parabellum-Maschinengewehr, subsequently known as the *Modell* 14, having adapted the Maxim design so that the toggle broke upwards, in a manner similar to that of the famous Luger-designed, DWM-manufactured Parabellum pistols. The Parabellum MGs, now converted to air-cooling, and known as the LMG14, were widely held to be the best flexible-mount aircraft guns of their period, and some knowledgeable commentators have suggested that the German Army would have been better served by adopting it itself, rather than concentrating on converting the MG08 to the role of light machine-gun as the MG08/15. The name Parabellum (Latin for 'For War') was derived from DWM's pre-war telegraphic address in Berlin, and was later adopted as a trade name.

Though Italy had been the first country in the world to adopt the Maxim gun officially, after the La Spezia trials of 1887 – and subsequently bought hundreds more, chiefly the 1901 'New Pattern' gun to American specification, as well as almost a thousand Vickers C guns, when they became available in 1911 – there was also a small domestic machine-gun development programme which led to an Italian-designed and -made gun eventually being adopted.

The first and most ingenious production was the design Giuseppe Perino patented in 1900. It was a hybrid recoil- and gas-operated gun using the rather under-powered 6.5mm rifle cartridge (adopted by Italy along with the Carcano-carbine in 1895) as did all the Italian machine-guns after the turn of the century. Originally it was fed with ammunition by a metal chain contained in a drum magazine, but this system was later superseded by an even more unorthodox arrangement: a stack of five trays holding twelve rounds each. One of the most interesting features of the Perino was its system of assisted cooling: the barrel was enclosed in a fixed cylinder, and fitted with sealing rings reminiscent of those found on the piston of an internal combustion engine. The movement of the barrel in the cylinder forced cooler air across the breech and into the chamber via angled vents. A later arrangement enclosed both barrel and cylinder in a water jacket, and pumped water around the barrel. Perino tried in vain to interest not only his own War Ministry, but the British too, but met with limited success; the main drawback to the gun, which was judged to be robust and well engineered, was its weight: almost 23kg (50 pounds) without water or tripod. By 1913, Perino had reduced the weight by 9kg (20 pounds), but by that time it was too late.

That same year Ansaldo, Armstrong & Co – a conglomerate arms manufacturer and shipbuilder with strong ties to the Armstrong company in England – acquired patents obtained by Giovanni Agnelli for a form of delayed-blowback action and tried to interest the Italian Army in a light machine-gun, with no success. FIAT, on the other hand, finally succeeded in breaking the effective monopoly which Maxim and later Vickers had established with another retarded-blowback design from Bethel Revelli. This one was even more complicated than Agnelli's. As with all retarded-blowback designs, extraction of the spent casing was an uncertain business, and to assist it (and give a measure of protection against rounds breaking up in the chamber) each incoming round was oiled from a reservoir on top of the receiver, which had the secondary effect not only of attracting whatever dirt, dust and grit was available locally to ensure frequent stoppages but to achieve the same effect in cold weather, when the oil thickened to the consistency of grease.

Many later blowback machine-gun actions required the assistance of oiled cartridges because they all suffered from the same problems but this was an unsound and unsatisfactory solution to a basic weakness of the blowback design. In the case of the FIAT-Revelli, the stoppages were probably welcome, for behind the oil reservoir an exposed buffer rod attached to the bolt (reciprocating backwards and forwards with each round fired, thus up to 400 times per minute) acted against a stop only a few centimetres in front of the firing handles, which must have been a trifle disconcerting for the gunner, to say the least! Like the Perino, the Revelli used a wonderfully complicated system of passing ammunition into the breech: a magazine divided vertically into ten compartments, each of which held five rounds. As each stack emptied, a pawl engaged an arm which pushed the magazine one step to the right, bringing the next stack into line.

Amazingly (or perhaps not; the Revelli gun had one insuperable advantage over its competitors: it was designed and made in Italy) the FIAT–Revelli Modello 14 was adopted by the Italian Army in 1914, and was still to be found in first-line service until the Italian capitulation in late 1943, its original water cooling jacket having been discarded in favour of air cooling in a major modernization programme instituted in 1935.

Japan shares with Russia the dubious distinction of having fought the first major war of the twentieth century, and the first in which machine-guns on both sides played a prominent part in significant numbers. Maxim Nordenfelt and later VSM supplied both protagonists – the Japanese bought four 8mm Maxims in 1893, and later nine 'New Pattern' Model 1901s; the Russian Navy bought almost 300 guns of various types between 1897 and 1904, while the Russian Army obtained perhaps as many as 1,000 guns from Loewe/DWM between 1899 and 1904. Later, the Japanese switched their allegiance to the Hotchkiss, and the Mle'00 was the gun which armed most front-line units of the Japanese Army by the time of the outbreak of war with Russia.

Initially, both sides deployed their machine-guns like miniature artillery, laying down indirect fire from rear positions, over the heads of their own infantry; observers (and, just as during the American Civil War, there were many) reported that the Maxims, in particular (they were chambered for a heavier round than the Japanese Hotch-kisses) were actually more effective in this role than the artillery they mimicked. Shades of things to come; the same tactics were to be used on the Western Front during the First World War, but not at first.

More important than the role of supporting attacking infantry, though, was the machine-gun in static defence. In an engagement near Lin Chin Pu, in January, 1905, a German observer reported:

> The Japanese attacked a Russian redoubt defended by two Maxim guns. A Japanese company about 200 strong was thrown forward in skirmishing order [that is, in rough line abreast, with some space between each man]. The Russians held their fire until the range was only three hundred yards and then the two machine-guns were brought into action. In less than two minutes they fired about a thousand rounds, and the Japanese firing line was literally swept away.[4]

At the battle of Mukden, which began on 21 February 1905, when the Japanese attacked Russian positions over a wide front, and proceeded to encircle them, the Russians employed their Maxims in batteries of eight, with one gun undergoing overhaul for each battery in action – the defenders were expending machine-gun ammunition at the height of the battle at a rate of over 200,000 rounds per day. The Japanese encirclement was completed (notwithstanding the fact that the Russians had withdrawn by then) on 10 March by which time the defenders had lost an estimated 90,000 men killed, to the attackers' 50,000; as many as half the casualties have been attributed to machine-gun fire.

As the war in Manchuria played itself out, it became exceedingly clear to participants and observers alike that the machine-gun had come of age with a vengeance. The British observer, Sir Ian Hamilton, writing in his *Staff Officer's Scrapbook* of the Russo–Japanese War, described an incident which took place the following October, after six Japanese Hotchkiss guns had been allowed to occupy high ground overlooking the Russian lines:

> In less than one minute hundreds [of Russians, who were complacently eating their lunch] were killed, and the rest were flying eastwards in wild disorder. Next moment the machine-guns were switched on to the Russian firing line who, with their backs to the river and their attention concentrated on Penchiho, were fighting in trenches about half-way up the slope of the mountain. These, before they could realize what had happened, found themselves being pelted with bullets from the rear. No troops could stand such treatment for long, and in less than no time the two Brigades which had formed the extreme left were in full retreat. Altogether the six machine-guns had accounted for . . . 1,300 Russians.[5]

Despite Hamilton's warnings, the British Army establishment still took little heed of the danger posed by the machine-gun; not so the German, even if the conclusions of one of its observers in Manchuria proved to be faulty:

> Machine-guns are extraordinarily successful. In defence of entrenchments especially, they had a most telling effect on the assailants at the moment of the assault.
> But they were also of service to the attack, being extremely useful in sweeping the crest of the defenders'

parapets. As a few men can advance under cover with these weapons during an engagement, it is possible to bring them up without much loss to a decisive point.

The fire of six machine-guns is equal to that of a battalion (of riflemen) and this is of enormous importance at the decisive moment and place.

Whichever of the two opponents has at his disposal the larger number of machine-guns has thereby at his command such a superiority of fire that he is able to give an effective support to his infantry. He can occupy a considerable front with smaller groups – an economy of man-power. *Infantry is thus more free to manoeuvre and becomes more mobile.* (Italics added)[6]

Both sides used their machine-guns to enfilade dead ground, and thus deny it to the enemy, with considerable success, but the Japanese went one better when they pioneered the use of indirect overhead fire to support infantry assaults. On 13 March 1905 Japanese infantry crossed a river and assaulted enemy defensive positions on the other side with comparative impunity thanks to a covering barrage from machine-guns sited 1,800m (2,000 yards) in the rear, which kept firing until the assault troops were within 40m of the Russian trench line.

If there were shortcomings in their chosen machine-guns (the Japanese Hotchkisses, in particular, were prone to jams caused by the breakage of essential parts), neither side thought them important. As soon as the war was over, the Russians immediately began manufacturing Maxims themselves, at the Tula Arsenal, buying new guns from both DWM and VSM whenever a new development appeared and incorporating it. The most significant of these was the VSM 'New Light' Model of 1906, which was put into Russian production in slightly modified form as the Model 1910 (*Pulemyot Maxima obr* 1910 or PM 1910) in 7.62mm long calibre. It was with this gun that Russia went to war in 1914, and again in 1940. In all, it has been estimated that Russian and Soviet production of Maxim guns probably exceeded 600,000 units in all – production in 1944 alone (the year in which it was effectively, though not completely, superseded, by the SG43) is said to have topped a quarter of a million. Some of those guns were still in use up until the 1960s and later in Viet Cong hands and elsewhere in South-East Asia.

Although the Russian Maxims were indeed robust and reliable throughout their remarkably long lives they did have other disadvantages, as this account from the Spanish Civil War suggests:

One [Russian weapon I became familiar with] was the Russian Maxim machine-gun. These, no matter how old they were, operated with really maximum efficiency. They were a tremendous weapon.

The Maxim machine-guns that the Russians supplied had a heavy armoured metal shield and a water-cooled jacket. The carriage was not a tripod, as it was in the case of British Maxim machine-guns but was a miniature gun carriage which the poor No 2 on the gun had to carry. And as I was No 2 on one of these guns for some time, I know exactly what I'm talking about! It was a very heavy beast indeed. It had an extension to the carriage which was a long U-shaped steel tube, which was fixed on to the wheeled part of the carriage by hinges. The wheeled part of the carriage went over your back and the U-tube was hinged down over your shoulders in front. As you marched along over rough ground, the wheels of the carriage used to bump up and down on your back, which made fast progress on soft ground not very easy. But in action, of course, the gun was mounted on the carriage and if you had to move swiftly you just got hold of the end of the U-tube and pulled the gun along. But there again, if you were moving through muddy ground, huge tyres of mud developed on the wheels and made it extremely difficult to pull. Then you just had to dismount the gun and pick it up and get going as fast as you could.[7]

Japan started making guns very similar to the Hotchkiss (the *Modèle* 1914, in this case, though that was only a very nominal redesign of the *Mle'00*), chambered for the inferior 6.5mm × 30 round, in 1914, under the name of 3 *Nen Shiki Kikanju*, 1914. It was virtually identical to the original save for having seven, instead of five, cooling fins around the barrel and being fitted with a grip safety.

The only other country to produce a machine-gun of its own prior to the Great War was Sweden. The heart of the *Kulspruta Kjellman* – a locking system using two pivoting lugs, forced into recesses in the receiver as the bolt and firing pin were propelled forward – was conceived by a serving officer named Friberg, back in the 1880s, but no further development took place until Rudolf Kjellman incorporated it into a gun he designed in 1907. It has since become widely used – in the German MG42 and its successor, the MG3, for example – but Kjellman's gun was passed over in favour of French Hotchkisses and Austrian Schwarzloses, and was never adopted for the Swedish armed forces nor, as far as can be ascertained, was it ever sold commercially.

In the face of all this potential competition, even with the Maxim gun firmly established as the best machine-gun in the world, VSM could not rest on its laurels, but had to maintain a continuous process of refinement and development to hold on to its share of the market. As we shall see, there were to be many lean years to come. The 'New Pattern' gun appeared in 1901, with the lighter steel water jacket, improved crank lever, lightened feed-block and simplified lock, but commercial sales were slow, and the British Army and Navy were, of course, being supplied by the Royal Small Arms Factory (with out-of-date Model 1893 guns). Only five years later VSM announced a new product in the form of the 'New Light' Model 1906, reducing the weight of the gun and mount still further; the gun now weighed just over 18kg (40 pounds), the new tripod just under 14kg (30 pounds) – a total of 32kg (70 pounds) instead of the 50kg (109 pounds) of the 'Service' Maxim being produced at Enfield.

At this point the engineers at VSM had probably gone as far as they could without a radical rethink in the gun's basic layout. One set of problems still not comprehensively solved by then were connected with the gun's cooling system. The water jacket of the 'New Light' model held about four litres (7.5 pints), which meant that about 600 rounds could be fired, from cold, before the water in the jacket started to boil – only a little over one minute's continuous firing. In practice, because it was most unusual to fire off six hundred rounds non-stop, it was possible to discharge about 2,000 rounds in bursts before the water in the jacket needed replenishing, whereafter it consumed just under one litre (say 1.5 pints) of water for each 500 rounds fired.

As early as 1893, Maxim had devised a means of dealing with the potentially dangerous build-up of steam (causing it to act on a plunger which actuated an escape valve and also caused a forward pressure on the trigger bar, thus warning the gunner that the jacket would soon need replenishing) but escaping steam could give away the gun's position to an observer. That was prevented by drilling and tapping the water jacket to accept a small nipple, to which a length of reinforced tube was attached. The tube was run into an Army-issue 'Mark IV General Service Nose Bag, with Strap', which was kept at least half full of water, and used to replenish the jacket as necessary. A two-gallon (nine-litre) fuel can was later substituted for the nose bag. Later models of Maxim gun made in Russia were equipped with an extra-large filler aperture, to enable crews to cram snow into them quickly.

Liquid other than water – particularly urine – was used as a cooling agent in times of extreme need, with the proviso that being acid in nature, it might act as a corrosive agent, particularly in the heat of battle, as one might put it, and would need to be replaced as soon as possible (though anyone who has ever smelled boiling urine would not need telling).

There is a persistent myth that British 'Tommies' used their machine-guns as expedient kettles, employing the boiling water from the cooling jackets to make their tea, but that should be disregarded. There would inevitably be propellant residue present in the water jacket which, if it did not render the resulting tea actually poisonous, would certainly have made it unpalatable. American firearms expert Jim Thompson, who fired every machine-gun he could get his hands on while researching his book *Machine-Guns: A Pictorial, Tactical and Practical History* says he tried it as an experiment, and found that 'There was so much metallic junk in the "tea" that it stained the cup black on contact.' However, he then goes on to relate how he and his companions cleaned out the water jacket with a lye solution and, after washing it out repeatedly, used it as a type of still, producing palatable liquor. Given that a still has to be maintained at a temperature above the boiling point of alcohol (93 degrees Celsius) and below that of water, it is difficult to see how this can have been, unless he was very careful to keep count of the rounds he was firing; perhaps Mr Thompson is more concerned to enhance the mythology than he is to debunk it entirely.

Excessive heat was only one aspect of the problem, however. During the Boer War, there had been reports of the Maxims' water jackets freezing at night, locking the barrel in position and preventing all but single shots from being fired. In 1904 a series of trials were run to determine how much of a problem this was, and how it could best be addressed. Four guns were prepared, their jackets part-filled with 2.8 litres (five pints) of water, to which varying amounts of glycerine had been added, and frozen for six days and nights at minus 6 degrees Celsius. In the worst case, it was necessary to fire 240 single shots before the gun would cycle itself, but by increasing the concentration of glycerine, increasing the tension on the recoil spring, and fitting the gun with a recoil-enhancer, cycling commenced after between six and a dozen rounds had been fired.

Ultimately, the re-think Vickers engineers embarked on after unveiling the 'New Light' 1906 model almost amounted to a redesign (and permitted VSM to apply for new patents to supplement the originals, many of which were now time-expired, and thus attempt to secure future earnings from licensees). In 1908, a prototype of a much smaller, and at 15kg (32 pounds) considerably lighter, gun was demonstrated. The crucial modification in this was that the lock had been inverted so that the toggle arm broke upwards instead of downwards. Three years later, this gun went into production as the Vickers Class 'C'. It was an immediate commercial success, and eventually did much to revive the fortunes of what was by then but one division of a very large armaments and ship-building company, which was later to branch into aircraft and armoured vehicle manufacture, too. (It is worth noting, perhaps, that the machine-gun 'arm', Vickers, Son and Maxim, had anything but a smooth financial history; it made a modest profit between 1899 and 1902 but returned a loss for the next two years and also in 1908, 1909 and 1912. Its most profitable year was 1906, when it made £233,000.)

A number of countries who had switched their allegiance to DWM now switched back to Vickers for the new design. The British armed services adopted it in 1912 as the 'Gun, Machine, Vickers, .303in, Mark 1', and after a brief flirtation with the French Benet-Mercie, the Americans followed suit, Colt's taking up a licence to manufacture the new gun just as they had its predecessor.

Vickers, Son and Maxim Ltd became simply Vickers Ltd on Sir Hiram Maxim's retirement in 1911, though in truth Maxim had had little to do with the enterprise, save for drawing a director's salary, since 1902. Thus it was that Maxim's name finally disappeared from the gun he invented, almost on a whim, some thirty years before. In Great Britain, the total number of Maxim guns (as distinct from the Vickers C and later models) produced by the three commercial enterprises – The Maxim Gun Company, Maxim Nordenfelt Guns & Ammunition Company and Vickers, Son & Maxim – was less than 6,000, to which can be added the 2,500 made at Enfield by RSAF – hardly a significant number, particularly when one considers the disproportionate effect the gun had whenever it was brought into action.

The day of the Maxim gun was far from over, of course; as we have seen, the Russians were to continue manufacturing them until the end of the Second World War, and another force – the Nationalist Chinese, who did not even begin to produce the gun until 1935 – went on to make almost 40,000 Type 24 Maxim guns, as they styled them (they were actually versions of the DWM Model 1909), in the following two years, for use in their war against Japan.

Chapter Six

The war to end war, Part One

GERMANY DECLARED war on Russia on 1 August 1914 and followed it with a similar declaration on France on 3 August, simultaneously invading neutral Belgium; next day Britain declared war on Germany in support of Belgium. Other cross-declarations followed, until all the parties on one side were at war with all the parties on the other.

What followed was conventional enough, in the historical sense; seven German armies marched west, the northern-most making the great right hook called for in the Schlieffen Plan, while simultaneously the Germans confronted the Russians, who had invaded East Prussia on 2 August, in the east. The picture was to become clouded and muddied as soon as the war started, of course – though just how muddied (and muddy) it would get before the end, none of the more or less willing participants can possibly have known. The reason for that was soon plain, and very simple: they had all ignored the power of the machine-gun. In conjunction with barbed-wire entanglements to slow the advancing troops down, properly deployed machine-guns ensured that any attack en masse, be it by daylight or under cover of smoke or darkness, would be a disastrous affair, virtually doomed to failure before it even began, no matter what its extent. Thus they pinned the opposing combat troops into fixed defensive positions, unable to advance, unwilling to retire, meat for artillery fire from well to the rear, the big guns out of reach of all but occasional retaliation. And thus began the long four years of the worst war the world had ever known.

As early as mid August 1914 it had become all too clear that the tactics the French were relying upon were fatally flawed. The attack *à outrance* – the infantry assault pressed home with the bayonet, which was its ultimate root – stood no chance at all against defenders in hardened positions, protected by entanglements of barbed wire and overseen by machine-guns; that the French High Command should not have foreseen this (after all, they had the Russo–Japanese War as a ready-made template) is first incredible, and second nothing short of criminal; that they should not have tried, at least, to formulate some new way of waging war as soon as they realized their mistake is diabolical, though in their defence one should perhaps say that such a far-reaching change of strategy would soon become unthinkable with large sections of France under German occupation.

All French training was based upon the doctrine of the offensive. Accordingly, they sent wave after wave of men into the attack, based on the totally outdated notion that an infantryman could cover 50m (55 yards) in the fabled twenty seconds it was supposed to take the defenders to ready themselves, steady themselves and fire a rifle volley, paying no heed whatsoever to the reality of the situation, which was that the opposing machine-guns would mow them down like wheat before the reaper's scythe before they had covered even one-third of that distance. As the American historian Barbara Tuchman put it, in her splendid *August, 1914*: 'The bright flame of the doctrine of the offensive died on a field in Lorraine where at the end of the day nothing was visible but corpses strewn in rows and sprawled in awkward attitudes of sudden death as if the place had been swept by a malignant hurricane.'

Such defensive fire as they would meet, went the theory, would be suppressed by shrapnel from the French 75mm field guns, the celebrated *soixante-quinzes*, capable of up to 30 rounds a minute, brought in to fight at close quarters in the direct-fire role. This proved to be a miscalculation, too, though the gunners did have some sporadic success.

It was not until the retreating Germans had been stopped on the Marne, east of Paris, recrossed the Aisne and dug in beyond it, along the Chemin des Dames ridge-line, that trench warfare began in France, and immediately the German machine-guns made their positions unassailable. The French dug in, too, though they had little practice in the technique; during exercises pre-war, the troops were not encouraged to carry entrenching tools or shovels. Digging-in made them 'sticky', and besides, it went against the offensive doctrine. Rapidly enough, however, this prejudice was forgotten, and lines of trenches sprang up on both sides of no man's land – itself an entirely new concept – all the way from the sandy beaches of Nieuport in briefly neutral Belgium to the frontiers of more-determinedly-than-ever-neutral Switzerland, with machine-guns sited at strategic intervals.

There has been considerable confusion as to the number of machine-guns the opposing sides had at the outbreak of the Great War. Estimates of German strength varied from 1,600 to 50,000, but the true figure, according to a survey carried out by the head of the German Army's machine-gun department, a Colonel Erdmann (and used, almost incredibly, as the basis of a postwar demand by Vickers Ltd for licence fees from DWM and the Spandau Arsenal), indicates that it had a total of just over 4,900 machine-guns in August 1914. Most of these were MG08s but with a sprinkling of MG01s. Of these, 3,975 were with the armies bound for France, or defending East Prussia and in reserve; the rest were in defensive fortresses. Victories, though not at first decisive, came frequently and swiftly in the east, and we know for certain that many Russian Maxim guns were captured and sent west at once (presumably with ammunition stocks, since there cannot have been sufficient time then to modify them from 7.62mm × 54 calibre to the German standard, 7.92mm × 57, though that was certainly done later), and brought into action against the British and French, but the number cannot have come even close to doubling the existing establishment.

The French started the war with something approaching half the German total – about 2,500 – virtually all of them Hotchkisses, while the British Expeditionary Force had just 108 machine-guns in total for its six divisions (a total of 72,000 infantrymen), allocated at a rate of two per battalion. At that, the guns were already considered obsolescent, being 1893-pattern Enfield-made Maxims, with brass water jackets; the Vickers C gun, known to the Army as the Mark I, had superseded the Maxim in British service some two years previously but chiefly on paper: only 109 of the new guns had been delivered by August 1914.

It is perhaps worth noting the total output of Enfield's Maxim production line between 1906 and the outbreak of the war: it was 63 guns (and another 22 destined for India). There were not even enough modern guns available to mount a proper course of training, let alone to supply the fighting troops. By way of contrast, by the time the war ended, Vickers had delivered a total of 71,350 guns, and a further 133,000 Lewis guns and 35,000 Hotchkisses had also been procured.

Like the French, the British in the early part of the war still believed wholeheartedly, almost incredibly, and with no thought whatsoever to the evidence of the recent past, in the power and virtue of cold steel. The bayonet, the troops were told, was the weapon with which this war would be won, and they were constantly drilled and exercised in its use, close-order foot-drill with rifle and bayonet occupying much of their time even as late as the summer of 1916, during the Battle of the Somme. Despite the clearest evidence, there were those – and unfortunately (or inevitably), they were in positions of command, able to dictate both strategy and tactics – who could not, or would not, get it through their heads that the machine-gun – 'concentrated essence of infantry', as J. F. C. Fuller was later to call it – now ruled the battlefield, and left no room whatsoever for the combat skills of a bygone age.

Just what well-directed machine-guns could achieve against an ineptly managed attack can be seen in an example from 15 July 1916 (during the Battle of the Somme) as described by Captain (later Lt-Col) G. S. Hutchinson, commanding 100 Machine-Gun Company:

I raised my head as the Highlanders rose to their feet, bayonets gleaming in the morning sun. My eyes swept the valley-long lines of men, officers at their head, in the half-crouching attitude which modern tactics dictate . . . moving forward over a three-mile front.

For a moment the scene remained as if an Aldershot manoeuvre. Two, three, possibly four seconds later an inferno of rifle and machine-gun fire broke from the edge of High Wood, from the tops of its trees and from all along the ridge to the village [of Martinpuich]. The line stag-

96

gered. Men fell forward limply and quietly. The hiss and crack of bullets filled the air and skimmed the long grasses. The Highlanders and Riflemen increased their pace to a jog-trot. Those in reserve clove to the ground more closely.

Looking across the valley to my flank I could see men of the 1st Queens passing up the slope to Martinpuich. Suddenly they wavered and a few of the foremost attempted to cross some obstacles in the grass. They were awkwardly lifting their legs over a long wire entanglement. Some 200 men, their commander at their head, had been brought to a standstill at this point. A scythe seemed to cut their feet from under them, and the line crumpled and fell, stricken by machine-gun fire . . .

My orders were to move forward in close support of the advancing waves of infantry. I called to my Company, and section by section, we prepared to move forward. As we rose to our feet, a hail of machine-gun bullets picked off here an individual man, there two or three, and swept past us.

On my right an officer commanding a machine-gun section had perished and all his men, with the exception of one who came running towards me, the whole of the front of his face shot away. On my left, two other sections had been killed almost to a man, and I could see the tripods of their guns with legs waving in the air and ammunition boxes scattered among the dead.[1]

But the German defenders were not to have the battle entirely their own way. Hutchinson – who won the Military Cross for his actions that day – was not one to give up, even under such stern provocation as this. He continues:

> With my runner I crept forward among the dead and
> wounded and came to one of my guns mounted for action,
> its team lying dead beside it. I seized the rear leg of the
> tripod and dragged the gun some yards back, to where a
> little cover enabled me to load the belt through the feed-
> block. To the south of the wood, Germans could be seen
> silhouetted against the sky-line, moving forward. I fired at
> them and watched them fall, chuckling with joy at the
> technical efficiency of the machine . . .[2]

The other essential infantry combat skill – musketry, as it
was still called – was not neglected, however, and the com-
petence of British regular soldiers with their rifle was legendary. A trained man could get off as many as twenty aimed
shots a minute; the British Army record in 1914 was held by
one Sergeant-Instructor Snoxall at the School of Musketry at
Hythe in Kent, who had got off thirty-eight rounds in one
minute, every one of which finished in the inner ring of a
four-foot target at 300 yards. Even so, it was widely accepted
as early as 1909 that 'the fire-power of a machine-gun is
equal in fire-effect to that of fifty rifles, while it occupies five
feet of frontage instead of over fifty yards'.[3]

Certainly, at Mons, German troops who came under
sustained rifle fire from British veterans were convinced that
they were actually under fire from machine-guns, and
inflated their estimates of the number of automatic weapons
fielded against them as a consequence (though as one 'old
sweat' from the Royal West Kents remarked, 'Even if you
were a Third-Class Shot, you were bound to hit something.').
This could not last; 80 per cent of the old BEF (the 'Old
Contemptibles') were dead by Christmas, 1914, their places
taken by a volunteer army, the best of whom rarely managed
more than six to eight aimed shots per minute. With their

passing the brute firepower of contingents of riflemen (and the discipline which made them so formidable) dwindled until it was a shadow of what had gone before – and there were easy-to-direct, little-skill-required machine-guns to make up the deficit. And that, and not simply that it spat out bullets at such an ungodly rate, was the secret of the machine-gun's success: just as technology had made master-craftsmanship available to all, via the machine-shop, so the machine-gun supplanted the trained body of marksmen, and put a platoon's – or even a company's – worth of firepower in one man's hands, and under one man's command. In the words of Sir Basil Liddell Hart, perhaps the most straight-forward of historians of the Great War, power had passed from the artist to the artisan. (In passing, as it were, one should note that there *were* machine-guns at Mons; just not enough of them. The recipients of the first two Victoria Crosses awarded during the 1914–18 war were Lt M. J. Dease and Pte F. Godley – both of the Royal Fusiliers, and both machine-gunners. Dease died at Mons, and Godley was gravely wounded and taken prisoner.)

From the autumn of its first year, and thanks in great part to the machine-gun, the Great War on the Western Front was a static affair. It is misleading to talk of offensive or defensive positions, except perhaps during times of all-out attack; suffice to say that the two sides were deadlocked. Having essentially similar skills and weaponry, they employed almost identical tactics as a result; lived in similar conditions; experienced the same hopes and fears. It was only when one side made a determined effort – a 'big push', as the British called it – that the day-to-day life of the individual fighting man changed, and even then, on the grander scale, it was soon clear that the essential effort was actually beyond either side, for the time being, anyway. Each held the other away at machine-gun-point across the fields of France and Belgium, hoping to find some external means of breaking the impasse before it broke them.

By mid-1915, the British Army still had only some 1,000 machine-guns with the troops in France, and astoundingly, orders for new guns, both from Vickers and RSAF Enfield, had amounted to fewer than 2,000 since the opening of hostilities (about another 2,000 had been ordered from the USA). Lloyd George, who was more conscious than most politicians (and even most senior Army officers) of the shortfall said, in his memoirs:

> It took our General Staff many months of terrible loss to realize the worth of the machine-gun . . .
>
> How completely the military direction failed to appreciate the important part [the machine-gun] would play in the war is shown by the fact that between August 1914 and June 1915 four contracts only were placed with Messrs Vickers, for a total of 1,792 machine-guns. This would work out at two guns per battalion with none left over for training at home, as provision for Machine-Gun Companies, and no margin for loss or breakage . . . The whole 1,792 guns were to be delivered by June 1915. In fact, however, only 1,022 had been received by that date.[4]

Those who are less critical of the performance of the War Office point out that the 1,792 guns ordered already represented a massive expansion of production capacity and suggest that, as the delivery record alluded to by Lloyd George showed, ordering any more would have been at best an exercise in wishful thinking.

By the end of 1915, the British Army in France numbered some 38 divisions, each of around 18,000 men; the French had over 3 million men under arms, and the Germans a similar number in the theatre. Throughout it, the opposing armies had achieved very little, save for filling innumerable cemeteries, for artillery, wire and the machine-gun, that Devil's trio playing in concert, had pinned men fast in place, like specimen insects in a museum case, and killed them where they lay.

Even the use of poison gas, fearsome though it was, had not broken the deadlock, yet for the British and the French (though each was operating separately from the other, and quite in isolation) there was a gleam of light, perhaps, in the enveloping darkness, in the form of a new sort of motor vehicle, which the British coded-named 'The Tank', hoping to pass it off as a perambulating water-carrier, destined for Mesopotamia. Tested for the first time in the later part of 1915, it was designed to be able to cross the rough, broken ground of no man's land and to be proof against machine-gun fire and hand grenades; now all that remained to be done was make it work in practice.

At almost the same time that the first tank was tested, the British Machine-Gun Corps (MGC) was formed, with its headquarters and training school at Grantham, in Lincoln-shire, the machine-gun sections of the infantry battalions being passed over into the command of the new corps. First priority was to set up a course of instruction, which lasted six weeks, and by the year's end, hundreds of newly-qualified machine-gunners were being turned out each week. By the following summer, the MGC amounted to 85,000 officers and men, and by the end of the war had grown to 6,432 officers and 124,920 other ranks. Training was two-fold: firstly learning how to operate the gun on a day-to-day basis, including how to deal with stoppages, strip it, clean it and perform routine maintenance; and secondly learning how to use it in action. To deal with stoppages, a procedure known as 'Immediate Action' was introduced, and drilled into the gunners until it became quite automatic. It was a simple enough matter, for the position in which the crank handle, on the right-hand side of the receiver, came to rest at the time of the stoppage indicated that the mechanism had stopped in one of four positions, and from that the real cause of the stoppage could be quickly diagnosed and corrected. Tactical training consisted mainly of how to create a zone of fire and interlace and interlock it with those from the other guns in the Company (the MGC's basic unit of organization) in order to give mutual support and thus control an allocated area.

Like the action taken to clear stoppages from the gun (and like virtually every other action in the entire army), tactical schema were taught by rote, literally drilled into the would-be machine-gunner's head by endless repetition. Before the formation of the Machine-Gun Corps, this sort of essential co-operation between guns had been impossible to achieve, and as a result, much of the machine-gun's potential had gone unexploited. The creation of the Corps, and the single act of bringing all the heavy machine-guns in the British Army under unified command within its bailiwick, instead of allowing them to be used individually, by individual battalion commanders (or worse, at the whim of a junior officer in whose zone they happened to be located), maximized that potential, and multiplied the effectiveness of the gun by a considerable factor.

It soon became second nature for the individual guns of a machine-gun company to arrange themselves within their sector of the front so as to control both the enemy front line opposite and the whole of no man's land in between. The ideal combination was six to eight guns working together to control a battalion front, each one set up so as to sweep a comparatively narrow arc – not necessarily directly to its front – which interlocked with that of two or more of the others. There was a variety of different prearranged patterns and combinations of arcs of fire worked out to meet different tactical requirements. The only measure of control the individual gunner had was in sweeping his weapon from side to side within the limits of his ordained arc of fire, and he achieved this by a series of controlled taps to the side of the spade grips with the butt of his hand, each one designed to move the muzzle of the gun just a quarter of a degree to the right or left. Learning exactly how hard to tap the gun occupied much of a gunner's training – that and learning studiously to avoid getting distracted by targets of opportunity. The use of tracer ammunition, one in every five to ten rounds, helped both to concentrate the gunners' minds and gave the unit commanders a very ready indication of where fire was going. Tracer ammunition was good for no more than an indication, though; it was lighter than conventional 'ball' ammunition to start with, and got lighter still as its pyrochemicals burned off, causing a tracer round to adopt a higher trajectory. The overall task was somewhat simplified since at that time the machine-gun was used exclusively as a line-of sight weapon. It was to be 1916 before it was used in the indirect role.

Having both set the stage and introduced the players, as it were, we will now condense the play. We have no space – and no justification – for a history of the Great War, and instead will concentrate on one small part of it, in a geographical area bounded on the south by the Roman road which runs straight as an arrow from Amiens almost to St Quentin, and on the north by another, from Arras to Cambrai. Within that microcosm, and with the aid of the occasional aside, we shall learn almost all there is to know about the employment of the machine-gun during the war it shaped and ruled.

Sir Douglas Haig became C.-in-C. British Expeditionary Force in mid-December 1915, and almost at once began planning for a new attack to take place in Flanders in the midsummer following. Marshal Joffre, the French Commander-in-Chief of the day, desperately needed a new offensive but mistrusted the selection of an old (and much-scarred) battlefield as its site; he out-manoeuvred Haig politically, and by holding out the prospect of French troops joining in too, in significant numbers, managed to get the location moved south, to the junction of the British and French sectors, on the River Somme. Even the best part of a century later, with the benefit of all the data, reports and insight contained in the hundreds of books written on the subject, it is very difficult to believe that Haig thought he was really going to achieve a breakthrough in the Somme sector, where the German line was, by every applicable standard, virtually impregnable, but soon that became irrelevant anyway, for the Germans attacked Verdun and the operation took on a new significance. After the attack on Verdun, any possibility of meaningful French participation in the attack on the Somme vanished. It is both useless and pointless to enquire why Haig did not shift his attention back to the Ypres salient at that point; an attack of the magnitude he was contemplating might well have succeeded there, and would certainly have been just as effective a means of distracting the Germans' attention away from the battle for Verdun.

The main difference between the Somme and the campaigns which had gone before was the degree of 'softening up' by artillery bombardment to which the German defences were to be subjected: five days and nights of it (which actually stretched to seven, when 'Z-Day' was moved back from 29 June) virtually non-stop, until more than 1.5 million shells – almost as many as the entire output of all Britain's armaments factories in the first twelve months of the war – had been fired off, a total of about 21,000 tons of steel and high explosive, into an area some 25,000 yards wide by 2,000 yards deep. Nothing, surely, could survive through such hell? Not man, not machine-gun, not barbed-wire entanglement, not defensive bunker . . .

An Intelligence Officer on the GHQ Staff, James Marshall-Cornwall (who later reached the rank of General, was knighted and much decorated), put the problem into perspective and gave some of the reasons why the barrage did fail:

> The infantry had in front of them a triple line of German defences which went back from the front line for six or eight kilometres – three lines of defence each defended by a chain of concrete pillboxes, which were machine-gun posts, surrounded by acres of barbed-wire entanglements. The whole thing depended on our artillery being able first of all to locate and then smash up the concrete machine-gun posts and then with the field guns to sweep away the barbed-wire entanglements. This was the primary essential.
>
> Well, bombardments started with 1,500 British guns – 450 of them heavies – but, unfortunately, the weather broke. For five days out of the six [sic] of the bombardment there was low cloud and drizzle. Air observation was impossible and artillery observation was very hampered. The fact was that neither did they pin-point the machine-gun posts opposite them, they also failed to cut the wire and the failure of the cutting of the wire was the most disastrous.

Our procedure at the time was to use a shrapnel shell which burst about twenty feet above the ground and the hail of bullets [*sic*] going forward when the shell burst in the air swept away the wire entanglements. But it all depended on the accurate setting of the time fuse which ignited the shrapnel shells and our munitions factories were only just getting into full swing. There were a lot of manufacturing faults in the fuses. They didn't all burn the right length and, I'm afraid, a lot of the half-trained gunners of the New Army divisions didn't set the fuses exactly accurately. The fact was that many of the shells burst too high and the bullets dropped into the ground, or the fuse didn't work and it [the shell] buried itself into the ground.[5]

Incredibly, some ten minutes before H-Hour the guns fell silent, and then, all along the length of the British front line, for 25km (15.6 miles) from Fricourt in the south to Gomme-court in the north, there came the sound of whistles, as officers signalled, and sergeants pushed, the men over the top into no man's land. Line after line of them, bayonets fixed and rifles at the high port, a hundred paces separating each from the one behind, subalterns in front, one of them, at least, kicking a rugby ball ahead of him, as if determined to live up to some half-remembered exhortation of Sir Henry Newbolt's to 'Play up! Play up and play the game'.

Even had it not been for the ten minutes grace the early cessation of the bombardments gave the German defenders, in the time it took the British infantry to cross no man's land, 'bent almost double, as men will when walking into a hailstorm', the German fusiliers, grenadiers and machine-gun crews had ample opportunity to emerge from their bunkers and man their defensive positions. (The bunkers were 10m (30ft) deep, most of them, and proof against even

106

a direct hit; intelligence as to their strength had been ignored by the British GHQ; the damage done to them was minimal – only 6,000 Germans died in the course of the entire day.) In many cases the German defenders were actually laying down fire before the assault troops had heaved themselves over the parapet of their trenches to commence their long, lonely and all-too-often-last walk, almost always uphill, towards the German positions overlooking the shallow valley of the River Ancre from the east. Very few Tommies made it to the other side of no man's land that day, and some units were cut down to a man.

A single well-sited machine-gun wiped out two infantry battalions tasked with assaulting the fortified village of Fricourt, close to the very end of the British sector, where no man's land was a gently up-sloping hill. Just to the north, the British III Corps lost 80 per cent of its effective strength as it advanced abreast of the Bapaume road, between the twin villages of La Boiselle and Ovillers, virtually all of them cut down by sustained machine-gun fire. Seven kilometres (4.3 miles) north, near Thiepval, where the front lines followed the valley of the Ancre, the hillside much steeper, and no man's land only a few hundred metres wide, two companies of Northumberland Fusiliers were reduced to just eleven men by two machine-guns covering the one and only usable gap in the wire. The German redoubts there – the Schwaben and the Leipzig – were to hold out for three full months (though the Schwaben actually fell on the morning of 1 July, to men of the 36th (Ulster) Division, who were forced later to retire, when they discovered themselves outflanked).

Further north still, at the head of the so-called Y Ravine, hard by Beaumont Hamel, men of the 1st Royal Newfoundland Regiment attacked across open ground, in fact from the British *second* line; over 700 men fell in minutes, most before

107

they had even reached no man's land. The site is a memorial park today, the Newfoundlanders' graves close by; it has been left just as it was after the fighting was over, and one may walk over the ground those infantrymen had to cover, and perhaps try to imagine how it was then, criss-crossed by barbed wire and blanketed by machine-gun fire a metre off the ground.

On 1 July 1916, the first day of the Battle of the Somme, 19,240 British and Colonial infantrymen died and 38,230 more were wounded. The dead-to-wounded ratio, almost exactly one to two, was very high; throughout the war as a whole it averaged a little under one to four. It has been said that 50 per cent of all other ranks and 75 per cent of junior officers (lieutenants and captains, many of whom advanced at the head of their men with no weapon but a stout walking stick) became casualties, but that does not square with the figures – approximately 200,000 troops were launched into the assault, some certainly failed to leave their start-lines and about 30 per cent of the rest were killed or wounded. It is true that the casualties among junior officers were significantly higher than the norm, and that is explained by the simple fact that they tended to lead from the front – and be the last men back; as we have had cause to observe before, they may have been stubborn, but they were stubborn through and through.

Not all offensive operations were characterized by bloody stalemate, however. We left Captain Hutchinson 'chuckling with joy' as he mowed down lines of German soldiers in a vengeful coda to the disastrous attack on High Wood on 15 July; in the same place less than six weeks later, on 23 August, the tables were turned during a machine-gun bombardment which was to go down in history:

Ten [Vickers C] guns were grouped in Savoy Trench, from which a magnificent view was obtained of the German line at a range of about 2,000 yards. These guns were disposed for barrage. On August 23 and the following night the whole Company was, in addition to the two Companies of infantry lent for the purpose, employed in carrying water and ammunition to this point. Many factors in barrage work which are now common knowledge [this account was published in 1919, in the *History and Memoir* of the 33rd Battalion] had not then been learned or considered. It is amusing today to note that in the orders for the 100th Machine-Gun Company's barrage of ten guns, Captain Hutchinson ordered that rapid fire be maintained continuously for twelve hours, to cover the attack and consolidation. It is to the credit of the gunners and the Vickers gun itself that this was done! During the attack on the 24th, 250 rounds short of one million were fired by ten guns; at least four petrol tins of water besides all the water bottles of the Company and the urine tins from the neighbourhood were emptied into the guns for cooling purposes; and a continuous party was employed carrying ammunition. A prize of five francs to the members of the gun team firing the greatest number of rounds was offered and was secured by the gun team of Sergeant P. Dean, DCM, with a record of just over 120,000 rounds.[6]

None the less, the attack was not actually a success; it was 15 September before High Wood was taken.

The total cost in human suffering of the 1916 Somme Offensive, after four and half months had passed, after seven 'phases' of attack had gone in, and in some cases hardly gained a square yard of ground, was 419,654 British casualties, plus perhaps 200,000 more Frenchmen in the southern part of the sector. Of 73,412 of the British dead there never was any trace found; all that remains of them are faded memories and every single one of their names, engraved in the huge, Lutyens-designed Memorial to the Missing which stands at Thiepval. Most of the rest – 109,430 of them – were laid to rest, at last, in the British War Cemeteries which litter the area, and which mark still the front lines of the fighting. Just how many German casualties there were is not known. The (British) *Official History* of the Great War suggests roughly 680,000 in total; there are 82,616 German graves within the confines of the Somme battlefield. It is impossible to know, too, just how many souls the Grim Reaper took there.

Barely twenty-one years old in its finished form, Maxim's gun came of age with a vengeance. As Sir Basil Liddell Hart said of its inventor in his *History of the First World War*:

His name is more deeply engraved on the real history of the World War than that of any other man. Emperors, statesmen and generals had the power to make war, but not to end it. Having created it, they found themselves helpless puppets in the grip of Hiram Maxim, who, by his machine-gun, had paralysed the power of attack. All efforts to break the defensive grip of the machine-gun were vain; they could only raise tombstones and triumphal arches.

With that, it would be heartening to be able to report that the hopeless man-versus-machine-gun battles were now over, and Hiram Maxim's dead grip (he died on 24 February 1916) was broken at last – after all, perhaps one million men had already given their lives to substantiate the case. Tanks had appeared for the first time at the Somme; while they had not been entirely successful, they had displayed considerable promise, particularly in as much as they were relatively immune to machine-gun fire – but they did not yet offer a solution. The generals had done their worst, just about, but they had not yet done their last ... And we have not yet heard the last of the Somme.

Chapter Seven

New tools to finish the job

WHILE THE 'War to end Wars' dragged through its third winter and the adversaries licked their wounds after the mauling they had given each other at Verdun and the Somme, war production on both sides had reached a very high level, and many new weapons, some relatively simple and others very complex, had begun to appear on the battlefield. The new weapons were starting to have a discernible effect by the end of 1916; two in particular were destined both to change the way in which wars were fought and take a strong hold on public imagination: the fighter aircraft and the armoured fighting vehicle. Neither would have existed without the machine-gun, the fighter aircraft because the automatic gun was central to its role, the tank because it existed solely to counter the machine-gun.

The machine-gun dominated the First World War. Artillery fire actually accounted for considerably more casualties, but that is not quite the point; it was the machine-gun, ably abetted by the barbed-wire entanglement, which made attack so difficult with the means then available, and presented the artillery with its sitting targets. The machine-gun was at the peak of its power in 1916–17. After that, with improvements in artillery techniques and the invention and deployment of the armoured fighting vehicle, it ceased to rule the battlefield so conclusively, even though it certainly had not yet reached the peak of its technological development.

As far as the infantry was concerned, it had finally become clear to even the most thick-headed and tradition-bound commanders that the machine-gun was the dominant weapon of the day. Now the infantry battalions not only wanted as many long-range heavy machine-guns as they could get, but also a lighter weapon, too, one that could be taken into the attack more easily than the cumbersome water-cooled Vickers or the even heavier air-cooled Hotchkiss.

At the outbreak of war, the British took up an offer from an American, Isaac Newton Lewis, to supply a gas-operated, magazine-fed machine gun he had developed from an original design by Dr Samuel McClean (another physician, though, unlike Gatling, McClean did practise, in his native Iowa, for a dozen years or more before turning his attention to weapons of war). Lewis's own government had shown no interest in adopting the weapon, probably due to personal animosity between Lewis (a retired US Army officer) and General William Crozier of the US Army Ordnance Board. Before 1914 Lewis had established a factory at Liège in Belgium and by August 1914, production had also begun at the Birmingham Small Arms factory in Britain (thanks in part to an order placed by the Royal Flying Corps) and the air-cooled, gas-operated Lewis gun was duly adopted by the British Army as the Gun, Machine, Lewis, .303in., Mark One. It was an instant success, and by mid-1916, some 40,000 Lewis guns were already in action with Allied forces.

So pleased were the British with the Lewis gun that BSA's output did not satisfy their demand, and additional manufacturing capacity was eventually established at the Utica, New

York, plant of the Savage Arms Company. The Lewis gun was equally at home in the trenches, in aircraft, in armoured vehicles and on board ship, and like the Vickers, it was to continue in service for decades to come. Even at the outset in 1915, the Lewis gun cost considerably less than a Mark I Vickers gun to manufacture. The contract between BSA and the British Government of 6 September 1915, priced them at $750.75 each, about £150. Lewis received more than half of this sum in royalty fees (no wonder he could – very publicly and supposedly patriotically – renounce any similar fee he might have expected from the US Government). By the time the first contract with Savage was signed, in May 1917, the price was down to $239.89.

Much of the official popularity the Lewis gun enjoyed was due to the cost savings it permitted, if only because that meant that more guns could be manufactured, but the men who went into action with it sometimes found its potential somewhat limited, largely because it fell between two stools. It was certainly not designed for sustained fire, and one authoritative work describes 'the astounding variety of malfunctions and stoppages which could result from its complicated action'. And even though it was self-contained, at a little under 14kg (30 pounds) with a 47-round magazine, it was still quite a weight to lug around the battlefield. None the less, it was the first truly effective 'light' machine-gun, and inspired many imitations, some of which were marked improvements, and some of which decidedly were not, as we shall see. It was very popular with German troops, who valued captured examples highly. The German Army even went so far as to issue a handbook for the gun.

The British also addressed the shortage of lightweight machine-guns by RSAF Enfield's obtaining a licence to manufacture the Hotchkiss *Modèle* 1909, which it produced as the Gun, Machine, Hotchkiss, .303in, Mark One, from March 1916.

The Lewis and Vickers guns had also been accepted by the US Army, and were supplemented, in 1917, by a gun very much like the Vickers in appearance but rather different in the manner of its operation, designed by John Browning and adopted as the M1917. It can be readily distinguished from the Vickers guns in action – its ammunition belt feeds from the gunner's left. The Browning action, which was to be used in all the guns he designed from then on, was a short-recoil system, the barrel and bolt recoiling backwards together over a short distance in response to the first round being fired. The bolt was then unlocked and the barrel's travel halted while an accelerator took over, and threw the bolt back further, advancing the ammunition belt at the same time, and extracting the next round from it. The recoil spring then threw the bolt and round forward to rejoin (and relock with) the barrel, the firing pin was released and the cycle began again (contrast this simple system with the complexity of the later German MG34, described below). Browning developed the system as early as 1910, but it was to be 1917 before the US Government took it up, in a variety of forms, first in .30-inch M1906 calibre, and later in .50-inch calibre. The original water-cooled gun was later superseded by an air-cooled model.

Meanwhile, in France, an execrable weapon in the shape of the infamous *Fusil Mitrailleur Modèle* 1915 was being foisted off on the poor *poilus*. This gun is sometimes known as the CSRG (from the initials of Chauchat, Suterre, Ribeyrolle and Gladiator, the four men who made up the committee which approved its design) but is more commonly given the name Chauchat. Poorly manufactured, of inferior materials, to an abominable design, the Chauchat failed in every role in which it was tried. Its long-recoil action was totally unsuited to a lightweight weapon and it was awkward (and painful) to fire and notoriously inaccurate as a result, but thanks to Crozier's obstinacy, it was with this third-rate weapon, rather than the very much superior Lewis gun, that American infantrymen entered the war. The French supplied around 16,000 Chauchats in 8mm Lebel calibre to the first American troops who landed in Europe in 1917, and then sold them a further 19,000 the following year, rechambered for the heavier .30–06 round, which further strained an already deficient mechanism. As one (American) authority on machine-guns put it:

> The best that can be said for the Chauchat is that it was available in great numbers and may have taught our troops much about machine-gun tactics. One of the main things they needed to know was to have plenty of them available since the odds were that a good percentage would not function . . .
>
> This is one of the few guns whose de-activation [a constant bone of contention with American collectors] does not seem to trouble most enthusiasts at all. In fact, these guns should probably be welded on principle.[1]

By late 1916 the German Army had begun to equip itself with a lightened version of the MG08 fitted with a conventional rifle-type stock and pistol grip/trigger, its sledge mount exchanged for a simple bipod, renamed the MG08/15. It was still water-cooled, however, and it was not until two years later that the very much more convenient air-cooled MG08/18 appeared, by which time it was too late; it would probably have been more effective to have concentrated on the other DWM product then available, the Parabellum

MG14. Though in theory the number of LMGs in the German infantry regiments never exceeded the number of heavy machine-guns (the 1918 establishment was for each front-line division to have 108 LMGs – three per company – and 144 heavy weapons, likewise distributed three per company, with an extra 36 for the machine-gun marksmen) some 130,000 MG08/15s were produced in all, by a total of seven different manufacturers, while DWM and the Spandau Arsenal produced, between them, a total of about 72,000 MG08s. Even though the MG08/15 weighed more than the Lewis gun (20kg/44 pounds with water but without ammunition), it, too, was considered to be a one-man weapon, and was used as such; it was to have a direct effect on German infantry tactics during their 1918 offensives.

The only other rifle-calibre machine-gun to be developed in Germany during the First World War was the curious twin-barrelled Gast, developed by Vorwerk. A recoil-operated gun, the Gast fired each barrel alternately, a pivoting connecting lever transforming the rearwards motion of the recoil of one mechanism into a charging motion in the other. It was fed by paired spring-driven drum magazines, each holding 180 rounds of 7.9mm ammunition, and achieved a very respectable 1,200 rounds per minute cyclical rate. At almost 20kg (44 pounds) without ammunition, it was judged too heavy for infantry use, but suitable for aircraft. Perhaps 1,500 Gast guns were manufactured in all, and it went on test in early 1918, but was never adopted officially.

By the winter of 1916 the battlefields of Europe had become decidedly three-dimensional, with the skies overhead patrolled by reconnaissance and fighter aircraft. The machine-gun had accordingly inherited a new role: trying to shoot them down. Only a simple modification was necessary to turn the terrestrial heavy machine-gun into an anti-aircraft gun: a mount which allowed it to point and shoot at an elevation of up to 90 degrees. The most simple of these – and one of the most effective, certainly for a single-gun installation – resembled the head atop a photographic tripod, and was mounted as an accessory to the normal terrestrial tripod or the sledge mount. It allowed rapid traverse and change of elevation, but called for deft footwork on the part of the ammunition belt handler. A clumsier solution was sometimes adopted in the trenches, mounting the tripods or sledges on inclined tables, sometimes fixed into the trench walls, sometimes with their own supporting framework. The only other necessary accessories were a large multi-ring rear sight (to assist the gunner to calculate the deflection necessary to hit a moving target) and a pedestal foresight. Thus modified, heavy machine-guns proved remarkably successful in shooting down the relatively slow-moving, low-flying aircraft of the day – the 'Red Baron', Manfred von Richthofen, was brought down and killed by ground fire (probably from a Vickers gun manned by Sgt Cedric Popkin and Pte Rupert Weston of the 24th Machine-Gun Company, 4th Australian Division) over the Somme battlefield in April 1918, and Edward Mannock, the greatest of the British 'aces' was killed by ground fire, too, in July that same year.

The Germans had high hopes of an upscaled version of the MG08, firing 12.7mm *T-Patrone* ammunition developed by Polte at Magdeburg for use in a bolt-action anti-tank gun, the Mauser Model 1918. The T.u.F. (*Tank und Flieger*) machine-gun came too late to see service, and though 4,000 were ordered from a consortium of over fifty small engineering companies led by Maschinenfabrik Augsburg-Nürnberg (M.A.N.), for delivery in late 1918, it appears that very few were ever assembled. One example, together with less than a hundred rounds of ammunition, found its way into American hands in 1921, and the cartridge contributed to the later development of the ammunition for the .50-inch Browning M1921 and M2 machine-guns, possessing better ballistic characteristics than the original round developed in the United States.

Of the two wholly new weapons systems, one – the fighter aircraft – relied entirely on the machine-gun; without it, it would not and could not have existed. The first attempts at mounting machine-guns on aircraft concerned a Lewis gun, one of the originals in .30–06 chambering, manufactured by Buffalo Automatic Arms as a demonstrator. The tests began at College Park, Maryland, on 7 June 1912, and the gun was hand-held, by Captain Charles Chandler. The trials were generally favourable, but it was clear that a solution would have to be found to the problem of pointing aircraft-mounted machine-guns in the right direction. It was simple enough aboard a two-seater aircraft, where the observer could be equipped with a flexibly mounted gun, but almost by definition, two-seaters tended to be slow and ponderous. In a single-seater the pilot had quite enough to do to handle the machine itself, without the added complexity of aiming a gun. The solution was to mount the armament parallel to the aircraft's longitudinal axis so that the pilot could aim it by pointing the entire aircraft. Given the need to keep the guns within reach of the pilot – jams, and the consequent necessity to reset the gun by hand, were a frequent occurrence, even though the more careful pilots regularly checked each round loaded into magazine or belt for irregularities – there was just one thing standing in the way of that: the propeller.

The French, who pioneered axially-mounted machine-guns, were not to be deterred by such a minor difficulty. As early as 1914 Raymond Saulnier had devised a means of synchronizing the action of the gun with the revolution of the propeller, but ran into trouble due to irregular ammunition quality affecting the gun's real rate of fire. He fitted substantial wedge-shaped steel plates to the propeller blades in the hope of deflecting the odd round which might fire late, but was still dissatisfied, and lost interest in pursuing the project further.

In March 1915 Roland Garros – already an eminent pilot, and frustrated by his singular lack of success in air-to-air combat – disconnected the synchronizing gear from the Morane–Saulnier L monoplane which Saulnier had been using as a test-bed, prayed and fired the gun, relying on the steel plates alone to deflect bullets off the propeller blades. (Presumably, the aircraft was safe on the ground at the time – there are limits even to Gallic sang-froid, after all.) It must have given passers-by the odd bad moment, thanks to the inevitable ricochets off the shield-plates, but it worked and in the three weeks which followed Garros shot down no less than five German aircraft, presumably capitalizing on the element of surprise his daring 'invention' accorded him.

Garros himself was forced down behind German lines on 10 April 1915, and though he set fire to his aircraft, German engineers were able to examine the deflector gear. One can perhaps imagine their horrified reaction to a design solution which relied entirely on chance. They would have none of that, and approached Anton Fokker, a Dutch engineer who produced some of the best fighter aircraft of the War, with the problem of interrupting the machine-gun's operation to prevent it from firing while one or other of the propeller blades was in line with the barrel. Within a few days he came up with a mechanical linkage based on an earlier patent granted to a Swiss engineer, Franz Schneider, which relied on a series of rods connecting a cam on the propeller shaft with the trigger mechanism, blocking (or disengaging) it when the propeller blade was about to come within the line of fire and then allowing it to operate freely again. Fokker demonstrated the system with a Parabellum MG14 mounted on a Fokker M.5K monoplane on 23 May 1915, but the Parabellum – which could achieve a very high rate of fire indeed, perhaps as much as 800 rounds per minute – was replaced almost immediately by a Maxim MG08 working at a steadier and actually more efficient 400 r.p.m. Parabellum machine-guns continued to be employed in flexible mounts, however.

The chief additional modification made by all sides to the guns to be taken aloft was to remove the cooling-water jackets as soon as it became clear that the airflow alone was sufficient to prevent them from overheating (and in some instances, would cause the cooling water to freeze). The Lewis gun, in a slightly modified form (a spade grip was provided instead of a rifle-type buttstock), was more popular among British aircrew, and the Germans soon produced a properly engineered air-cooled version of the MG08/15, the Luftgekühlt ('air-cooled', sometimes rendered as Leicht– 'light') Maschinengewehr 08/15 or LMG08/15. Fokker's interrupter mechanism gave the Germans many months' superiority in the air.

The Allies produced a similar system at last, in the spring of 1916 (in all, there were no less than nine quite discernibly different British interrupter/synchronizer gears tested, and two French), and soon superseded it with a more reliable hydraulic design, produced by an expatriate Romanian engineer named Constantinesco.

The problems of synchronizing the operation of the gun with the revolution of the propeller caused a number of German minds to turn away from the concept of the automatic machine-gun and look again, instead, at the basic structure of Richard Jordan Gatling's gun. Ironically, the very reasons Maxim had advanced for the superiority of the automatic machine-gun over the manual machine-gun were now reversed! Supply the motive power to the gun from the aircraft's engine, they argued, and perfect synchronization would inevitably follow as a by-product, with no possibility of a 'slow' round upsetting the timing. No less than six different versions of an externally powered gun were produced during the First World War in Germany (one of them by Anton Fokker himself, another by the industrial giant Siemens), but none was ever accepted (and sadly, no example of any now remains). It was to be another forty years before the wheel came full circle, and the principle Gatling had originally devised came back into favour, and by then, of course, propeller-driven combat aircraft were things of the past.

There were plans to mount the 12.7mm T.u.F heavy machine-gun in aircraft – and at least one report of trials being carried out – but it certainly never saw service. Relatively large-calibre machine-guns did sometimes put in an appearance – the 20mm Becker machine cannon (which eventually became the splendid 20mm Oerlikon) was fitted in Gotha bombers and in some airships; FIAT–Revelli guns in 1.0-inch (25.4mm) calibre were installed in selected Caproni bombers of the Italian Air Force, and the 37mm Maxim pom-pom (albeit with a reduced charge) was tested in British aircraft, but the latter, especially, proved unwieldy, even in the ground attack role for which it was intended, its recoil soon threatening to shake the flimsy aircraft of the day to bits.

Initially, air superiority was only important in as much as the possessor of it was able to get a better view of what was going on where it really mattered: down below. The aircraft

Above: The French *Mitrailleuse* was one of the early 19th century attempts to create a multi-fire weapon. The *Mitrailleuse* was not a machine-gun in the proper sense, but rather a volley gun which discharged all its 37 barrels in a single shot. It was used to some effect during the Franco-Prussian War of 1870-71.

Below: A late model Gatling in service with US marines on the South Pacific Island of Samoa in 1899. By this time, the hand-cranked Gatling had been made obsolete by the fully-automatic action of the Maxim, which had already been successfully introduced into the US Navy in 1896, as well as the armies of Britain (in 1891) and Germany (in 1895.)

Main picture: Though it was first used in very small numbers during the last years of the American Civil War, the destructive potential of the multi-barrelled Gatling gun was not fully exploited until the late 1870s, when it became one of the principal weapons of Western Imperial expansion.

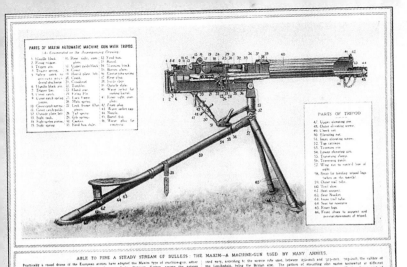

The Maxim machine-gun has rightly become synonymous with the mass slaughter of the First World War. First developed by the American engineer Hiram Maxim in 1884, the weapon first found favour with the Imperial German Army.

PARTS OF MAXIM AUTOMATIC MACHINE GUN WITH TRIPOD

As Enumerated on the Accompanying Drawing.

1. Handle block.
2. Fixing trigger.
3. Trigger pin.
4. Trigger spring.
5. Safety catch.
6. Handle block pin.
7. Trigger bar.
8. Sear catch.
9. Sear catch swivel.
10. Cover catch swivel.
11. Cover catch.
12. Chamber plate.
13. Sight tank.
14. Safety-action piston.
15. Sear spring.
16. Rear sight, com. plate.
17. Barrel.
18. Upper guide block.
19. Cover.
20. Hand plate.
21. Crank.
22. Crankshaft.
23. Tumbler.
24. Hand axis.
25. Firing Pin.
26. Lock Frame.
27. Main spring.
28. Link frame.
29. Gib spring.
30. Canister.
31. Feed box slide.
42. Feed box.
33. Barrel.
34. Traverse block.
35. Bottom plate.
36. Central tube spring.
37. River plate.
38. Inside door.
39. Outside slide.
40. Water socket for cooling barrel.
41. Front sight, com. plate.
42. Front plug.
43. Water socket cap.
44. Nipple.
45. Barrel link.
46. Water plug for cooling.

PARTS OF TRIPOD

47. Upper elevating pin.
48. Outer elevating screw.
49. Check nut.
50. Elevating nut.
51. Inner elevating screw.
52. Top cutinges.
53. Traverse rim.
54. Lower elevating pin.
55. Traversing clamp.
56. Traversing catch.
57. Wing nut to raise base of sight.
58. Strap for binding tripod legs (when on the march).
59. Outer trail tube.
60. Trail shoe.
61. Seat socket.
62. Seat bracket.
63. Inner trail tube.
64. Seat for operator.
65. Front legs.
66. Front shoe to support and prevent movement of tripod.

ABLE TO FIRE A STEADY STREAM OF BULLETS : THE MAXIM—A MACHINE-GUN USED BY MANY ARMIES.

Practically a round dozen of the European armies have adopted the Maxim type of machine-gun, either exclusively or partially : Great Britain, France, Germany, Serbia, Belgium, Turkey, among the nations taking part in the war ; Roumania and Bulgaria, Greece, Spain, and Switzerland. Across the Atlantic the Army of the United States has also largely adopted the Maxim. The calibres of the ammunition used vary, according to the service rifle used, between 256-inch and 315-inch, 303-inch, the calibre of the Lee-Enfield, being the British size. The pattern of mounting also varies somewhat in different armies, the tripod-carriage being mostly used. A trestle-gun section of two Maxims forms part of the establishment of every British cavalry and infantry regiment.

The British Vickers M191 Mark I in action around the Somme in 1916. The Vickers was organized int battery groups of four guns per battalion, and each gun was served by team of up to six men.

During the Great War, the Germans never satisfactorily developed a light machine-gun of their own. One attempt they did make was the MG 08/15. However, at 17 kg (39 lb) the weapon was still far too heavy to be carried into battle by advancing infantry.

The Lewis Gun was first introduced into the Belgian Army in 1913, and won favour with the British Army after the first year of the First World War. Weighing only 11 kg (25 lb), and being able to lay down up to 500 rounds a minute from its 47 round magazines, the air-cooled Lewis was light enough to provide close fire-support to attacking infantry, the first time a machine-gun had been able to do this.

Above: Produced by Royal Small Arms at Enfield, the Bren Gun first entered service with the British Army in 1938. It was a direct development of the Czech ZB vz 26 machine-gun, and throughout the Second World War proved itself to be one of the finest light machine-guns ever to see service.

Below: Like the Bren gun, the British Besa machine-gun also originated in the late 1930s from a Czech-designed weapon (in this case the ZB zv 53). Since the Besa was manufactured specifically for use in armoured vehicles, it was decided to retain the gun's original 7.92 mm calibre, rather than change it to the standard British .303.

First introduced in 1936, the MG34 was both the world's first general purpose machine-gun, and the first light machine-gun to be belt fed. The weapon, though extremely well engineered, nevertheless tended to jam in bad conditions, and like its successor, the MG42, its air-cooled barrel required replacing on a regular basis to avoid overheating.

Above: Seen here in action in Russia in 1943, the year of its introduction, the German MG42 was a development of the highly successful MG34. Designed to be both faster and cheaper to produce, the MG42 nevertheless shared the excellent performance characteristics of the earlier weapon, and made a name for itself with its rugged reliability.

Below: First proposed in 1942 as a replacement for the Red Army's ageing Maxims, the SG43 was a medium machine-gun. The weapon, seen here on 'Sokolov' wheeled mounting, was introduced into service before 1945, but never really superceded the Maxim until after the war, when it became the Soviet's standard medium machine-gun.

had little real relevance to the way the infantry operated, and thus, could do nothing to break the stranglehold the machine-gun had on the battlefield. For that, something completely new was required: the armoured fighting vehicle. essentially a means to make the impregnable machine-gun post mobile.

The credit for having first thought of equipping caterpillar-tracked agricultural tractors (in service since 1910 as prime movers for the artillery) with armour and weapons for the purpose of suppressing enemy machine-gun positions generally goes to a serving British officer, Lieutenant-Colonel Ernest Swinton, who had been responsible for producing a history of the Russo-Japanese War for the British Government and was thus exposed to considerable material evidence of the danger the machine-gun posed to unprotected troops. (In fact, plans for a vehicle not unlike the first actually built were submitted by an Australian engineer named L. E. de Mole as early as 1912. His submission was ignored.) Swinton's proposal was initially rejected also, but was later revived by Winston Churchill when, as First Lord of the Admiralty, he formed the Royal Navy's Landships Committee (there were Naval Brigades serving on the battlefields, hence the Navy's somewhat unusual involvement). We can gloss over the many dead ends (such as Thomas Hetherington's land battleship, thirty metres long and armed with three twin-gun turrets) would-be developers zealously explored, and come to the Number One Lincoln Machine, on which work started on 11 August 1915, and which began its first tentative trials just over a month later.

The Landships Committee's original specification led to a prototype known as 'Little Willie' but even while development work was going ahead, the War Office realized that something bigger was needed. William Triton and Walter

Wilson, the project leaders, soon came up with a new plan, and 'Big Willie', as the new 28-ton vehicle was almost inevitably called (though it had alternative names, too: 'Mother' and 'HMLS Caterpillar' being just two of them), began trials in January 1916. It was slow and clumsy, but it could cross trenches 2.7m (8ft) wide, and the politicians and soldiers were impressed enough to give an immediate go-ahead.

In February the Ministry of Munitions ordered 100 'Tanks, Mark One', half of them to be built as 'male' variants, with two six-pounder (57mm) guns in side sponsons and four Hotchkiss (later Lewis) machine-guns fore and aft, the other half to be 'females', with Mark I Vickers guns in place of the field-pieces (later there were to be 'hermaphrodites', too, with one male sponson and one female). Machine-guns thus became from the start, and have remained, an essential part of the armament of the weapon system that had been designed specifically to counteract them. British developments led to the much-improved Mark IV and Mark V types in service by the end of the war as well as to faster Whippet medium tanks.

French armoured vehicle development ran alongside the work in Britain, with Colonel J.E. Estienne in the role Swinton played, though the two projects hardly touched. Two heavier designs were produced, the chars d'assaut Schneider and Saint-Chamond. Neither was an unqualified success but like the British types they were usually armed with a combination of a 75mm field gun and several machine-guns. There was also a lighter, faster, alternative in the shape of the revolutionary Renault FT–17 ready to go into production by 1918. This ultra-light two-man tank was the first to be fitted with a revolving turret, in which an 8mm Hotchkiss machine-gun or a 37mm cannon could be mounted. It was first employed in the Forêt de Retz in May 1918, and took part in all the French tank actions which followed.

German strategists were by no means convinced of the efficacy of the tank, unlike their counterparts twenty years later. Eventually, they did employ a heavy tank, the A7V, a 33-ton monster which required a crew of eighteen, powered by two 400-horsepower engines, protected by armour plate 30mm thick and armed with a 57mm cannon and six Maxim guns. On 24 April 1918, at Villers Bretonneux, a group of German tanks, A7Vs and captured British Mark IVs, came upon a contingent of British tanks, and the first combat between armoured vehicles ensued, the Germans being driven off after damaging two female Mark IVs. Only some twenty A7Vs were ever produced, and work on the development of a 100-plus ton supertank known as the K-Wagen, and on the Model LK light tank was halted at the armistice.

Chapter Eight

The war to end war, Part Two

THE WINTER of 1916–17, just like the previous two, put a stop to most military activity on the Western Front, and on the Allied side, much of what little there was took the form of high-level conferences at which Haig and the French Commander-in-Chief, Nivelle, tried to agree on a plan for the next year's offensive operations. Meanwhile in Berlin, von Hindenburg and his deputy, the very able Erich Ludendorff, appointed to the German Supreme Command after considerable success on the Eastern Front, were making preparations for an exercise in consolidation in the west designed to enable Germany to launch a final decisive offensive in the east. The serious German losses at Verdun and the Somme in 1916 led them to decide that to carry out this policy they should retire to new specially prepared defensive positions along a large part of the Western Front. In February 1917 the Germans therefore retreated eastwards to the newly-finished, massively constructed Hindenburg/ Siegfried Line, straightening and shortening their front (and their lines of communication) considerably in the process and destroying everything in their wake.

Not least among the casualties was Nivelle's plan for an

offensive in the area centred on Noyons. The French attack was to have been but one arm of a massive two-pronged offensive, the other side of which was a British attack at Arras. Coincidentally, it was at Arras that the old front line joined with the new, and Allenby, who commanded the British and Empire forces in that sector, was ordered to go ahead anyway, in April 1917, in the hope of outflanking the new fortifications and rolling them up from the side and rear. The hope was forlorn, though the attack did make some headway, including capturing the notorious Vimy Ridge.

The assault was led by Canadian troops, with the newly formed Canadian Machine-Gun Corps in support. It was here that Allied troops first used machine-guns extensively in the indirect-fire role in the attack, firing over the heads of advancing infantrymen from a range of 1,800m (2,000 yards), making use of the natural trajectory of the rifle-calibre round. At that range, the natural vibration of the gun and the slight variation in the characteristics of the propellant combined to produce a distinctive 'beaten zone' of fire, an elongated ellipse, some 50–60m (55–65 yards) long and some 15m (50ft) wide, into which 75 per cent of all rounds fired would fall. The trajectory was quite extreme, and the bullets arriving in the beaten zone were descending quite sharply. This meant in effect that even deep trenches offered little real protection from such a barrage. There was little danger of hitting one's own troops with the supporting fire, except perhaps in the very final stages of the assault. In order to achieve the necessary accuracy, machine-guns used for long-range indirect fire were fitted with the sort of complex sights used by the artillery. Stereoscopic range-finders, also as used by the artillery, became necessary items of equipment, too. (To achieve the maximum range of about 3,500m [3,800 yards], the gun was elevated to 32 degrees from the horizontal; the incoming rounds would arrive at a much steeper angle than that.)

Nivelle's French offensive commenced on 16 April and rapidly turned into a fiasco, but one with 120,000 French casualties and very dangerous overtones. The French troops had had quite enough of being thrown against barbed wire and machine-guns, and began to show their contempt by a form of limited mutiny, if there can ever be such a thing. Their basic message, clearly vocalized, was: 'We are not so stupid as to march against undamaged machine-guns', and though they were prepared to defend their positions, they refused to obey orders to go forward. By the second week of May, the revolt, which started in colonial regiments, had infected no less than sixteen army corps, and there was good reason to fear the imminent collapse of the French Army as a fighting force. The power of the machine-gun had transcended its immediate impact on the battlefield, and become a thing of terror, unfaceable because it was unbeatable; unbeatable because it was unfaceable. Fear of the machine-gun had almost broken a whole Army.

The rest of 1917 on the Western Front saw the long and bloody brawl in Flanders resume in the Third Battle of Ypres or Passchendaele as it is often known which, for all its muddy horror and terrible casualties for both sides, added little new to the story of the machine-gun with which we are concerned here. The tank finally got its chance to show what it could do at the Battle of Cambrai in November. The early gains made in that battle proved that the tank could indeed overcome the defensive machine-gun, but that the gains were so quickly retaken by the Germans proved equally clearly that the tank had not yet reached anything close to a perfected state.

Save for Cambrai, and the American decision to declare

war on Germany in April 1917, the only bright spot on the British horizon that year was far away in Palestine. Allenby, transferred to take command in the Middle East in June, broke the Turks at Gaza, and rapidly drove them back north through the Holy Land, taking Jerusalem in time to celebrate Christmas there. The war in Palestine was a contrast to that on the Western Front in many ways, of course. One interesting feature of it, and a precursor of things to come, was the success, in the dry, open conditions of the desert, of the far-ranging machine-gun-armed armoured scout car – the earliest were converted Rolls-Royce Silver Ghosts, but they were soon joined by Lanchesters and Wolseleys – which had proved a singular failure in Europe earlier in the war. Later models of armoured car were to prove effective behind the German front line when they penetrated (towed across the battlefield by tanks) after the Somme counter-offensive in August 1918.

Ludendorff's tactical withdrawal behind the Hindenburg Line had its desired effect by the spring of 1918; morale was high, his *matériel* situation was improved and best of all, his numbers were swollen by troops brought from the east following the end of the war there with the beginning of the Russian Revolution. On 21 March he struck on a broad front from just to the north of Arras to La Fère on the River Oise, in an offensive aimed at cutting off the British from the French to the south, and eventually driving them into the Channel. Faced with terrain which, by virtue of its open character and the ease with which it could be excavated, had given Haig's attacking army so much trouble twenty months before, Ludendorff elected to fight a very different sort of battle, using different tactics and different tools.

The tools, it will come as little surprise to learn, were provided by Maxim, by way of the Spandau Armoury, and by a man whose name was to become synonymous with a new variant on the automatic weapon: Louis Schmeisser's son, Hugo. The tactics, which are often incorrectly ascribed to General Oskar von Hutier, had been developed by the German General Staff from lessons learned at Verdun in 1916, though Hutier was the first army commander to put them into practice, at the battle for Riga at the end of 1917, and did so again as the commander of Ludendorff's southernmost army on the Somme in March 1918.

The essence of the plan was strategic surprise, overwhelming firepower and rapidity of movement, and while the surprise was by no means completely achieved, it was an important contributory factor because the time available for the British to react was so short. Another, and perhaps a more important advantage, could not have been foreseen: the thick fog which hung over the battlefield as dawn broke. A hurricane artillery barrage, as it was later described, opened up at 04.30, concentrated on the opposing artillery for two hours, and then, supplemented by mortars, turned on the trenches, destroying both telephone and radio links. Thanks to the fog, the British found themselves fighting in isolation when, at 09.40 or thereabouts, the German infantry advanced under a creeping barrage, their lead elements made up of relatively small squads of *stosstruppen*, 'shock troopers', armed with sub-machine-guns (or machine pistols) and hand grenades, and supported by light machine-guns, bypassing and isolating strong points and leaving them to be dealt with by follow-up teams of regular infantrymen.

The light machine-gun which played such an important role in these proto-Blitzkriegs was almost without exception the MG08/15, developed three years earlier by the Spandau Armoury from the MG08. At 22kg (48 pounds) with a full water jacket and a 100-round drum of ammunition, it was hardly light, but it was within the capabilities of one man to carry it at the run, and even use it from the hip (with the sling provided for the purpose) or more usually from the prone position with the built-in bipod. It was also readily adaptable to the static role, fixed either on one of a number of simple 'expedient' mountings or on a conventional sledge mount or tripod.

On the other hand the sub-machine-gun, or machine pistol, as the Germans called it, was a completely new weapon – in fact, a completely new *type* of weapon, quite unlike anything which had gone before. It had been developed over the previous two years by Hugo Schmeisser, who had stepped into his father's shoes and gone to work for Theodor Bergmann. Sometimes called the Bergmann *Muskete*, the *Maschinenpistole* 18/I (MP18/I) was adopted by the German Army in the opening weeks of 1918, and was an immediate success with the troops to whom it was issued. It fired the 9mm Parabellum pistol round from a simple open-bolt blowback action, to achieve a cyclical rate of 400 rounds per minute. It was truly revolutionary, and a landmark in the history of the automatic weapon, being the first sub-machine-gun conceived as such. Though it weighed less than 5kg (11 pounds), it gave the individual infantryman vastly enhanced firepower, and it mattered not at all that it was of limited value outside a range of 50-100m (or yards), and in terms of real accuracy was no great shakes at even a fifth of those distances, because it was intended for close-range work, particularly within confined spaces such as trenches and dugouts. In the years to come, machine pistols or sub-machine-guns – the terms are quite interchangeable – were to become the assault-infantryman's weapon of choice.

Just how successful the tactics were can be gauged from the advances the German Army made. By 5 April, they had occupied the right bank of the River Ancre to a point downstream of Albert, and come within artillery range of Amiens. As soon as the gains on the Somme were consolidated, Ludendorff mounted a second offensive on the Lys, and followed that with a third, south across the Aisne, in late May, his troops reaching the Marne on the 30th. That advance brought American troops into battle in significant numbers for the first time in Europe. The Second Battle of the Marne proved to be the high-water mark of the German offensive of 1918, just as the previous battle on that same river had marked the limit of the 1914 advance.

Stopped on the Marne and then gradually but relentlessly driven back in the west, with unrest at home growing, the Germans tried vainly to hold on to the gains they had made, and slowly but surely found their grip weakening. All along the length of the Hindenburg Line the Allies pushed forward. British and British Empire forces struck a range of powerful blows, especially near Amiens on 8 August, the day Germany lost the war, according to Ludendorff's later account. In mid-September, French and American troops attacked the St Mihiel salient south of Verdun, and in a short, sharp battle reminiscent of Ludendorff's spring offensive, 'straightened the line' decisively. On 11 November 1918 the guns in the west finally fell silent. The Great War, the war to end wars, was over. The machine-gun had been a ruling factor through so much of it, first in defence, and later in the attack too – but towards the end it began to look as if an effective counter had been found in the shape of the armoured fighting vehicle. Now it remained to be seen if its power had finally been broken, or if it would still dominate warfare in the future.

When the Great War ended, most of the industrialized world settled down to trying to reassemble the elements of its life, the major exception being Russia, which was still smashing itself to pieces in the struggle to become the Soviet Union. All in all, the 1914–18 war killed at the very least 9 million people, the vast majority of them on the battlefield itself, and wounded a further 12.5 million: some 22 million casualties. Even at a conservative estimate, 25 per cent of these casualties were due to machine-gun fire, giving a total of 5.5 million. No one now can say for sure how accurate this is, but official War Office figures for British combatants killed and wounded show that 58.5 per cent of casualties were caused by shells and mortar bombs; 38.9 per cent by bullets. We can safely say that well over half of that last would have been machine-gun bullets, which gives a certain credibility to the conservative estimate made above.

By the time of the Armistice the machine-gun's formative period was over, and it existed – either in tried-and-tested, battle-proven form, or as an experimental model – in every type we now recognize. From then on the process became one of development and refinement, though for all that – or maybe just because of that – the period which followed was to be most productive in terms of new models and types of automatic weapon, to the point where cataloguing them all, while at the same time continuing to try to set the machine-gun in its social and military context, will be impossible. For a more complete listing of individual weapons than we can present here, the reader is directed to one of the publications which has that as its prime purpose, such as Ian V. Hogg and John Weeks's *Military Small Arms of the 20th Century*. More up-to-date information is available from an annual, such as *Jane's Infantry Weapons*. From this point on, we will describe in detail only those machine-guns which either incorporated a new methodology, or which combined existing components in a way so far untried, and content ourselves with referring to copyists and technological plagiarists in brief, pausing perhaps to mention other weapons which achieved some sort of celebrity even if their technology did not actually merit it.

Chapter Nine

The development of the sub-machine-gun

IT WAS the old standards – the Maxim and its German counterparts and derivatives; the Maxim-based Vickers; the only-slightly-different Browning, newly arrived on the scene; the air-cooled, gas-operated Hotchkiss and Lewis guns and all their many derivatives – which continued to dominate military thinking regarding the infantry battlefield during the interwar years, together with a new general-purpose gun concept being formulated in Germany. As we have seen, also, tactics during the last part of the Great War came to encompass the need to clear defended positions by means of close-quarters combat, and that spawned a new type of automatic weapon, called variously the sub-machine-gun (SMG), machine carbine or machine pistol.

The proto-machine pistol Hugo Schmeisser produced for Theodor Bergmann in 1917 was one of those very rare cases of an inventor getting it right (or at least, right *enough*) first time, though it must be said that he had lots of indicators to send him down the correct path. Once the decision had been made to use pistol ammunition – and we do not know if that was actually Schmeisser's own choice, or whether it formed part of a specification furnished to him – it was clear that he

135

could use the simple-but-effective unlocked breech/direct blowback system of actuation. This was already found in the many self-loading pistols, some of them designed and made by Bergmann himself, which had appeared after Mauser-Werke showed such an arrangement to be practical with the Feederle-designed *Selbstladepistol* C96.

As we have previously seen, the blowback system has the advantage of simplicity – the number of moving parts is minimized, which makes manufacture cheaper and reduces the chances of a mechanical breakdown; the action itself is easy to understand, and therefore to strip, clean and reassemble, and the gun is much lighter to carry. Its primary disadvantage is poor ejection of spent cartridge cases, but this is not critical in the case of the relatively low-powered pistol rounds. It can be made to fire very rapidly indeed if the weight of the only moving part which matters – the bolt – is kept low: a cyclic rate of over 1,000 rounds per minute is quite easy to attain; though a high cyclical rate is not, in fact, necessarily a desirable feature, for two reasons. Firstly, even a short burst (in terms of the time the finger keeps the trigger depressed) will probably empty the magazine, and secondly, the faster the gun fires, the more the muzzle will tend to rise and veer off to the side (which side depends on the direction of the rifling).

Even when its cyclical rate is reduced to something more manageable – 400 r.p.m. for example – the average SMG is still not a particularly accurate weapon, even when fired from the shoulder. The barrel is generally short, to make the weapon more 'handy', and that does not promote accuracy, and the way in which the speed of the action is customarily controlled – by increasing the weight of the bolt (and therefore its inertia) – tends to throw the gun off line, too, even while firing the first round. The majority of such guns fire from an open bolt. When the action is cocked, the bolt is drawn back against the spring and held there by the trigger mechanism. When the trigger is actuated, the bolt is thrown forward violently by the spring, over a distance of perhaps 5cm (2in), in the course of which it strips off the first cartridge from the magazine before slamming to a stop against the rear of the barrel/chamber assembly. The integral firing pin hits the percussion cap in the base of the cartridge, thus initiating the firing sequence, before the bolt has come completely to rest and the resulting recoil differential (the first part of the recoil force from the firing of the new round goes toward arresting the forward travel of the bolt assembly) reduces the overall effect. Some sub-machine-guns use this principle to good stabilizing effect. The considerable mass of the bolt rapidly accelerating and even more rapidly decelerating tends, however, to shift the point of aim, even when the gun is used in semi-automatic (single shot) mode (though not all early sub-machine-guns by any means were equipped to fire in both semi-automatic and full automatic modes; the MP18, for example, was not).

Even with its built-in shortcomings, the MP18 was an effective weapon, and was to enjoy a long life, particularly after its one major fault was corrected. As originally produced it used a 32-round 'snail' magazine (a helical feed drum, in this case with a clockwork advance) developed by Tatarek and von Benko for the long-barrelled 'Artillery' version of the Luger P08 pistol. This was never wholly satisfactory, and a simple box magazine of 20- or 32-round capacity was substituted. In the interest of economy of manufacturing effort, the MP18 also used a rather shorter-than-necessary 190mm (7.9-inch) screw-in barrel also developed for the Artillery Luger, shrouded by a perforated guard.

The MP18 was finally superseded, nominally at least, in

1928, but then only by a very close derivative, the Haenel-manufactured MP28/II, which differed mainly in being capable of firing single shots and being available in a wide variety of calibres, from 7.63mm Mauser to .45-inch ACP. The later British Lanchester, hastily put into production in 1941 for issue to the Royal Navy, was a direct copy of the MP28.

There has always been a degree of controversy over the primacy of the Bergmann MP18, because when Schmeisser was at work on his original designs there was already a blowback-action machine-gun firing a 9mm pistol cartridge (in this case the *Modello* 10 Glisenti) in existence. Under the circumstances, it is perhaps unlikely that Schmeisser was aware of what was going on in Italy, and in any event, as first presented the Italian gun was clearly intended to be used in the light-machine-gun role, however unsuitable it might have been by virtue of its chosen cartridge.

Designed by Revelli for the Officina Villar Perosa in 1915, the *Mitragliatrice Leggera Villar Perosa* M15 was actually two guns in one, twin barrels and actions being mounted side by side, each one with a vertical box magazine, sharing a single trigger. The guns were fitted with paired spade grips, and had no buttstock. They were notable chiefly for their extremely high cyclical rate: said to be 1,200 r.p.m. from each barrel. However, since the magazines held but 25 rounds each, the rate actually achievable was considerably less. Many different mountings were available, including bipods and tripods, pintle mounts for vehicles and even a bicycle mounting, but the gun was never a success in its original form – as a light support weapon – due to the inadequacies of the ammunition for which it was chambered.

Most examples were later converted, either by OVP or by Beretta, into more conventional sub-machine-guns with solid wooden buttstocks, each one original making two new weapons, of course. The *Moschetto Automatico* OVP and the Beretta *Modello* 1918 were both equipped for single-shot or automatic operation by the simple if confusing expedient of having two triggers in tandem, one for each mode. The successor models Beretta manufactured retained this feature, even as late as 1949. Beretta also produced a self-loading carbine based on the Villar Perosa, rechambered for the more powerful 9mm Parabellum round, and later standardized on this cartridge for their sub-machine-guns too, before switching to the more-powerful-still *Modello* 38A round.

The *Modello* 1918 was a very direct ancestor indeed of the other two machine pistols Beretta produced before the Second World War. The *Modello* 18/30 (as its designation suggests, it was an update of the earlier gun) was rechambered – and re-sprung – for the more powerful 9mm Parabellum round, and with the position of its magazine switched from above to below the receiver; and the *Modello* 38A, an excellent design, manufactured to a high standard (until wartime economy measures were introduced, whereupon some of its machined parts were swopped for stampings). The gun was again rechambered, this time for the even more powerful *cartucia pallottola Modello* 38A, which gave a muzzle velocity of around 420 metres per second (1,380 feet per second), against the 320 m.p.s. (1,050 f.p.s.) the original Glisenti round achieved and the 380 m.p.s. (1,250 f.p.s.) of the Parabellum.

Even the economy measures practised on the *Modello* 38A were not enough to satisfy wartime production requirements, and the gun was subsequently extensively revamped to make it easier and cheaper to manufacture. We will consider the results – the MAB 38/42 and its later variants – in due course.

Arms production in Germany dropped to virtually zero after the Versailles Treaty finally ended the First World War; weapon stocks were either transferred to the victorious Allies, broken up (or, in some cases, sold off) or transferred from the Army to the police of the new Weimar Republic. It would be over a decade before armament manufacturers became openly active again, and in the meantime they chose to function clandestinely, using factories located outside Germany – in Holland, Denmark and Switzerland, for example, but also in the Soviet Union – or disguising their new products as weapons intended for the civilian authorities.

Bergmann had the MP34 and MP35 made in small quantities in Denmark, by Schultz and Larsen, before transferring production back to the Reich, to the Walther and the Junker and Ruh factories, respectively. The MP35 became the automatic weapon of choice of the Waffen-SS, but was still only produced in moderate quantities – perhaps 40,000 altogether. The MP34 and MP35 were peculiar in that their 24- or 32-round box magazines fed from the right, and in having a 'double acting' trigger. Taking up the first pressure produced single shots; pulling it hard back switched the gun over to automatic fire.

Bergmann had produced the first reliable machine pistol, but it was a rival, Erfurter Maschinenfabrik B. Geipel – commonly known as Erma-Werke – which produced the best known German sub-machine-guns, the MP38 and MP40. Erma's early experience was gained from about 1930 onwards, with the MPE, a simple blowback machine pistol using a telescopic bolt and recoil spring, chambered for the 9mm Parabellum cartridge. The gun was developed from a Vollmer design of ten years earlier, and had already been made in experimental quantities before coming to the attention of the German Army. It was made under licence in Spain, as well as at Erfurt, and saw extensive use in the 1930s during the Chaco Wars between Paraguay and Bolivia, and in the Spanish Civil War.

In appearance, the MPE – the first machine pistol to be produced from seamless, drawn steel tubing, wherever possible – looked not unlike an MP18, -28 or -35 (save for a rather clumsy vertical wooden fore-grip); it was fitted with conventional wooden furniture, a perforated barrel sleeve and a horizontal box magazine. Though their actions were almost identical, it could not have been more different in outward appearance from its successor, the all-metal, folding-butt MP38, with its exposed barrel and vertical underset magazine. The latter was an unpopular feature with front-line troops, who preferred the lower profile which could be achieved with a side-mounted magazine; the vertical magazine was adopted because the gun was originally intended for tank crews and security personnel, and only later were it and its successor issued to line infantry units.

Widely and quite erroneously known as the Schmeisser, for Hugo had nothing whatsoever to do with its development (though a company in which he later figured, Haenel-Schmeisser, did manufacture a small number of MP38s, together with many MP40s), the MP38 was made to an official German armed forces' specification. It served, in effect, as the prototype for the MP40, the first mass-produced automatic weapon. Despite the absence of traditional wooden furniture and a considerably lower unit cost than the MPE, the MP38 was still a high-quality item, with many parts individually machined out of the solid – so much so that when it came time to turn it out in huge quantities, with the outbreak of war in 1939, it had to be completely respecified, substituting welded steel pressings for machined parts, both to reduce the cost per unit and to speed up manufacture, becoming the absolutely-no-frills MP40 in the process. The cost-reduction exercise in no way undermined the effective quality of the gun, surprisingly, and both MP38s and MP40s were consistently reliable.

Another excellent German machine pistol was never produced in its country of origin at all, except that Austria formed part of the Third Reich from the time of the Anschluss to the end of the Second World War. It was produced first in Switzerland – by Waffenfabrik Solothurn, a subsidiary of Rheinmetalll – and later by Steyr, to a 1920s design, and reflects what will be by now the familiar traditionalist preference of that period for heavy forgings, components machined out of the solid and comprehensive wooden furniture. The S1-100 or Steyr-Solothurn, as it was generally known, was clearly derivative of the MP18/I and MP28/II, and enjoyed considerable popularity from 1930, when it was first put into production, until 1945 and later, despite its considerable weight and rather old-fashioned unwieldiness. It was variously chambered for 7.63mm Mauser and 7.65mm Parabellum, as well as for three popular 9mm cartridges: the low-powered Steyr, the Parabellum and the up-rated Mauser Export, which had both a heavier charge and a heavier round. Like the Czech ZK/383, it was also offered as a light machine-gun, with a longer, heavier barrel and bipod (and even tripod) mountings. Like most Swiss weapons of the period, it was beautifully engineered – a quality which was rapidly disappearing elsewhere, as the war clouds gathered over Europe once more, and every nation began arming itself as fast as ever it could.

*

This discussion of developments in German machine pistol design and manufacture inevitably leads us somewhat out of our time context, and it is necessary to retrace our steps, back towards the years immediately following the First World War, in order to broaden our view. Impressive though the firepower of the sub-machine-gun/machine pistol had proved itself to be, it had few early adherents. Save for Revelli, Schmeisser and Vollmer, few arms makers in Europe showed much interest in the concept, with the exception of Aimo Lahti in Finland, who experimented with a simple blowback design as early as 1922 while working at the state-owned Tikkakoski armaments factory. He produced a gun very similar in appearance, save for an exaggerated buffer housing at the rear of the receiver, and a suspended magazine, to Schmeisser's, and like the MP18, the Suomi M/26 and its successor, the M/31, which were later also manufactured under licence in Denmark, Sweden and Switzerland, were 'old-fashioned' guns, their operating parts machined out of the solid or forged, with wooden furniture. Thanks to their relatively long barrels, and the 7.63mm Mauser ammunition for which they were chambered, they were surprisingly accurate, and were certainly popular with the men who used them. Early models had box magazines varying in capacity from 20 to 50 rounds, but Lahti eventually also produced 71-round drum magazines reminiscent of (and more than likely inspired by) those fitted to the most famous sub-machine-gun of them all, the Thompson.

The high capacity of the drum (though not the operating principle Lahti used) was a feature the Russians copied, in turn, for the Degtyarev-designed PPD34 and -40 as well as for the mass-produced PPSh41 which Georgii Shpagin drew up and got into production at creditable speed in the aftermath of the German invasion of the Soviet Union in June 1941. Tokarev and Korovin had started experimenting with sub-machine-guns in the Soviet Union as early as 1926, though there is no trace today of any of the guns they produced – probably by hand – and thus the *Pistolet-Pulemyot Degtyareva obr* 1934/G was not the first Soviet-designed SMG, though it was the first to go into serial production. Once again, the PPD34 clearly owes much to both the MP18 and Lahti's designs. The gun was representative of the period, being solidly made and utterly conventional, and was superseded by the PPD40, which was also made to peacetime standards and was quickly abandoned when war came, to be replaced by one of the crudest machine-guns of all, the PPSh41. Both Degtyarev and Tokarev were involved in the design of heavier weapons too: Degtyarev designed what was probably the most widely used series of light machine-guns ever produced, the DP/DPM/RP/RPD, while Tokarev produced a design for an air-cooled lightweight Maxim.

Meanwhile, across the Atlantic in New York, a man whose name was to become synonymous with the hand-held machine-gun, Colonel John Tagliaferro Thompson, had long been at work. Thompson had served in the US Army and with the Ordnance Department, and had acquired some commercial experience with the Remington Arms Corporation, when he began work on a design for an automatic rifle to rival that of John Browning. Due largely to the influence of an associate, Thomas Eickhoff, the gun metamorphosed during the design stage, and finally emerged as a sub-machine-gun chambered for the heavy .45-inch ACP/M1911 round. The prestigious *Scientific American* magazine, in those days a rather more practically-minded mass-market publication than it was later to become, called the gun 'the most efficient man-killer of any firearm yet produced'. Thompson

called it the 'trench broom', and set up a company named
the Auto-Ordnance Corporation to market it. Once again,
there is no real reason to think that Thompson and Eickhoff
were inspired by Schmeisser, Revelli or anyone else, but that
instead they conceived the idea of a short and light close-
combat weapon with a high rate of fire for themselves, quite
independently. In fact, by the time the design had been
refined sufficiently to go into production – and by the time
Thompson had found an arms manufacturer willing to make
it – the war was long over.

Both the US Marine Corps and the US Army carried out
tests during 1920 and 1921, but ordered very few M1921A
guns, as the first production model was called, as a result.
Thompson, with all his money invested in it, looked elsewhere for a potential market for the 15,000 mechanisms
Colt's had manufactured for Auto-Ordnance at $45 each. The
early twenties were comparatively peaceful years in the
United States, with the entire country settled and prosperous.
The only serious disruptions came from the ranks of more-
or-less organized labour, particularly but not exclusively in
the mining industry, though there was considerable racial
tension, too. As a result, the police forces which Thompson
targeted next were hardly more enthusiastic over his gun
than the armed services had been, though he did succeed in
selling small quantities to some city forces – New York,
Boston and San Francisco – as well as to some State Police
forces. Like Gatling many years before him he offered a
hybrid cartridge containing so-called bird shot, designed to
wound, rather than kill, hoping by that means to encourage
law enforcement agencies to adopt it for the control of
unruly crowds. Demonstrating it to police officers and journalists in May 1922, he suggested that the combination
would allow disorder to be handled in the most humane way

possible, but did not create much of an impression; his potential customers preferred a lethal load over a non-lethal one any day. One aspect of the gun the audience did like was its capacity – it was available with 20- or 30-round box magazines, but Thompson also offered drum magazines holding 50 or 100 rounds.

Spurned by the military and law enforcement agencies, Thompson could only look to the private sector. At that time, it was perfectly legal for a private individual to own a machine-gun in the United States (and had been in the United Kingdom, too, until about 1920) and so Thompson placed advertisements in appropriate magazines, offering 'The Most Effective Portable Fire Arm In Existence – The ideal weapon for the protection of large estates, ranches, plantations, etc. . . .'

Exaggerating somewhat, for his order book was a slim volume, he went on: 'In addition to its increasingly wide use for protection purposes by banks, industrial plants, railroads, mines, ranches, plantations, etc., it has been adopted by leading Police and Constabulary Forces throughout the world and is unsurpassed for military purposes.'

The path the public at large beat to Thompson's door at 302 Broadway in New York City was so faint as to be hardly discernible, and it began to look as if his venture would fail, but eventually, help in small measure arrived from a most unwelcome source: the world of organized crime – much to Thompson's personal chagrin, one must add. (Perhaps he realized all along that the gun would be attractive to undesirables; certainly, the Auto-Ordnance Corporation's advertising did state, quite clearly, that 'Thompson guns are for use by those on the side of law and order and the Auto-Ordnance Corporation agents and dealers are authorized to make sales

Browning, not .45-inch ACP slugs from a Thompson that cut down the notorious Bonnie Parker and Clyde Barrow in ambush on a country road outside Ruston, Louisiana, on 23 May 1934.

Alphonse Capone, the most famous of all the kings of organized crime, was an early convert to the tommy gun; he ordered three M1921 guns from Auto-Ordnance on 10 February 1926, after Frank McErlane's mob had three times machine-gunned aspects of his bootlegging operation. Before the year was out he had begun to put them to use. He was provoked, he maintained, by a rival, Hymie Weiss, who organized a motorcade to drive past Capone's headquarters in the Chicago suburb of Cicero, riddling the front of the building with over a thousand rounds from their Thompsons. No one was hurt, but Capone's injured pride had to be assuaged, and three weeks later he despatched two men with machine-guns to shoot his rival down as he crossed the street.

It was two and a half years more before Capone's *chef d'œuvre*, the execution of seven men associated with another rival, George 'Bugs' Moran, on St Valentine's Day 1929. Two men hired by Capone – 'Machine-Gun' Jack McGurn and Fred Burke, dressed in police uniforms and armed with Thompson guns – surprised the Moran gang members, lined them up against a wall and shot them repeatedly. One victim, Frank Gusenberg, had no less than fourteen .45-inch bullets in him when police arrived, but was still, almost incredibly, alive. 'Who shot you, Frank?' a curious detective asked. 'Nobody shot me,' replied the taciturn Gusenberg. Seventy cartridge cases were recovered from the scene, and a pioneer in the art of firearms identification was able to state that fifty had come from one gun and twenty from another, suggesting that one was fitted with a 50-round drum magazine, the

Browning, not .45-inch ACP slugs from a Thompson that cut down the notorious Bonnie Parker and Clyde Barrow in ambush on a country road outside Ruston, Louisiana, on 23 May 1934.

Alphonse Capone, the most famous of all the kings of organized crime, was an early convert to the tommy gun; he ordered three M1921 guns from Auto-Ordnance on 10 February 1926, after Frank McErlane's mob had three times machine-gunned aspects of his bootlegging operation. Before the year was out he had begun to put them to use. He was provoked, he maintained, by a rival, Hymie Weiss, who organized a motorcade to drive past Capone's headquarters in the Chicago suburb of Cicero, riddling the front of the building with over a thousand rounds from their Thompsons. No one was hurt, but Capone's injured pride had to be assuaged, and three weeks later he despatched two men with machine-guns to shoot his rival down as he crossed the street.

It was two and a half years more before Capone's *chef d'œuvre*, the execution of seven men associated with another rival, George 'Bugs' Moran, on St Valentine's Day 1929. Two men hired by Capone – 'Machine-Gun' Jack McGurn and Fred Burke, dressed in police uniforms and armed with Thompson guns – surprised the Moran gang members, lined them up against a wall and shot them repeatedly. One victim, Frank Gusenberg, had no less than fourteen .45-inch bullets in him when police arrived, but was still, almost incredibly, alive. 'Who shot you, Frank?' a curious detective asked. 'Nobody shot me,' replied the taciturn Gusenberg. Seventy cartridge cases were recovered from the scene, and a pioneer in the art of firearms identification was able to state that fifty had come from one gun and twenty from another, suggesting that one was fitted with a 50-round drum magazine, the other with a 20-round box. Two guns answering the description were later recovered from a hideout Burke was known to have used, and test-firings proved that they were the murder weapons, but no arrests were ever made.

Almost all the big names in American violent crime in the late twenties and thirties were associated with the Thompson gun; Ma Barker, John Dillinger, 'Pretty Boy' Floyd, 'Machine-Gun' Kelly (whose prowess, Ellis tells us, was entirely manufactured), 'Baby Face' Nelson (whose was not) and Bonnie and Clyde all used them with more or less aplomb, and in the process created a cult of anti-heroism which the American film industry was very quick to take up. Gangster movies, starring the likes of Bogart, Cagney, Raft and Robinson, became central to the cinema, and the genre rapidly established the myth of the tommy gun along with that of its wielders, all the more forcibly because most, having lived by the gun, obligingly died by it, too, both on screen and off.

Other notable Thompson users were the Irish Republican Army, who were early customers, just as they had been among the first to acquire Vickers C guns as soon as they came on the market. The appearance of the Thompson was celebrated in song:

We're off to Dublin in the green, in the green
Where helmets glisten in the sun
Where the bayonets flash
And the rifles crash
To the echo of a Thompson gun.

Demand from such sources was not enough to keep Thompson in any sort of style, but he managed somehow to keep Auto-Ordnance in business. The 15,000 mechanisms he had received from Colt in 1921 underwent numerous small modifications as they were mated with wooden furniture supplied by Remington to Thompson's rather elaborate, futuristic and certainly extravagant design, with sculpted vertical fore and rear pistol grips and quickly detachable buttstock. The most important among the modifications was the addition of a muzzle compensator – a device fitted at the barrel end, which had cross-wise slots machined into its upper surface. Designed by Colonel Cutts of the US Marine Corps, and named after him, the compensator permitted a small quantity of propellent gas to bleed out just before the round exited the muzzle, pushing it down and thus helping to control progressive muzzle climb when firing in automatic mode.

By 1928 Thompson had started to economise on the finish of the guns he was shipping – in particular he deleted the annular cooling fins of gradually diminishing sizes which graced the barrel of the original guns – and now the US military, still an occasional purchaser, redesignated them M1928A1. The gun's workings stayed the same as the original, though – a blowback action cunningly retarded by an implementation of the fact that two dissimilar metals passing over each other create enhanced friction. In the case of the early Thompson guns, this was provided by an H-shaped bronze wedge – the so-called Blish lock – acting vertically on dovetails cut in the steel receiver body, keeping the cyclical rate down to a manageable 600 rounds per minute. At the same time Thompson began supplying guns with a simplified rifle-style horizontal fore grip; he called these the M1928A1 Navy model, and even succeeded in selling some to the US Marine Corps, who used them in action in Nicaragua between 1928 and 1931 against guerrillas led by Augusto Sandino. In the jungle conditions of Central America, where firefights often took place at very close range, the Thompsons proved deadly.

The M1928A1s were superseded by the M1 and M1A1 Thompsons, at the beginning of the Second World War, and the new models all had the simplified furniture. They had simplified actions, too, for by that time the Blish lock had disappeared, and the retardation of the blowback mechanism went with it. The original floating firing pin had also gone, to be replaced by a simple striker machined into the front face of the bolt. All these changes came about in the interest of reducing manufacturing costs, and the result was that in 1944 a complete M1A1 Thompson cost the US Government just $44.85, including basic spare parts, cleaning kit and magazine, instead of the $209 it had been paying for M1928A1s in 1939.

The turnaround in Thompson's fortunes came in 1939, when Britain found itself at war with Germany again, and with derisory stocks of modern weaponry. Procurement officers looked around for weapons of all sorts, and among others they fastened on the Thompson gun. Thanks to Thompson's over-exuberance of almost twenty years before, the Auto-Ordnance Corporation still had some of the original Colt-manufactured mechanisms in stock, and so there were demonstration guns on hand, but nowhere near enough to satisfy British demand. Thompson approached both Colt and the Savage Arms Corp. (Savage had also manufactured sample models of the original gun, in 9mm Parabellum calibre) with a view to resurrecting the production line. Considerable modifications were made, turning the gun from the high-quality precision-made firearm it had originally been into a mass-produceable item fit to equip a conscript army. Eventually it was to be Savage which manufactured the gun in its hundreds of thousands, for the United States armed services as well as the British, not quitting until the end of the war in 1945. Auto-Ordnance continued to make the gun in the M1928 format until 1986, when US firearm laws finally prohibited the manufacture and sale of fully-automatic weapons, even to registered collectors; it then cost $475. Semi-automatic (single-shot) versions of the Thompson gun, both in M1 and M1928 format (i.e. with the straight forepiece and the carved vertical fore grip, respectively) continued in production, retailing at a little under $800.

Despite not selling too well for almost two decades, the Thompson set performance standards in the US gun market, and what few imitators it had wisely stuck to the same .45-inch ACP round – two of them, the Hyde Model 35 and the United Defense Model 42, even went so far as to copy the distinctive Thompson fore grip, though they left out the fancy carved finger-flutes. The Model 35 was tested by both the US Army and the British armed forces but was rejected by both, citing defects in the firing mechanism and magazine feed-path. The UD M42, designed by Carl Swibelius (who had been responsible for the redesign of the Colt 'potato digger' for Marlin), was made only in small quantities – perhaps 15,000 all told – in both 9mm Parabellum and .45-inch ACP. There are stories of it being the preferred weapon of the clandestine Office of Strategic Services, and of it turning up in the hands of partisan groups, particularly those fighting the Japanese.

Slightly more successful were the over-complicated Reising sub-machine-guns, which fired from a closed bolt. Despite a poor reputation for reliability, the Reising is held by experts to have been a better gun than the Thompson in some ways. Like the Thompson, the first version, the Model 50, was available in both civil and military versions, and featured a muzzle-compensator to keep the barrel down. The later Model 55, which retained the same complex action, came with a folding wire butt and a wooden pistol-grip in an attempt to cut down on the manufacturing costs.

It was to be 1941 before an American manufacturer went down the road pioneered by the MP38, and developed an all-metal mass-produceable sub-machine-gun, the M3 and M3A1 'Grease Guns', both of them produced by a division of the General Motors Corporation. We will consider those guns, and their even cheaper British equivalent, the Sten, in a later chapter, along with other weapons of the Second World War.

In all, what the history of the early development of the sub-machine-gun tells us about military attitudes of the time is almost as interesting for what it omits as for what it contains. Nowhere, for example, do we find arms manufacturers in Britain, France or Japan mentioned as pioneers of the genre, or even as exploiting the designs others had laboured to produce – an omission all three were to have to rush to repair when war returned.

Save for the examples cited from Finland, Germany, Italy, the Soviet Union and the United States, only four other true sub-machine-guns were produced before the outbreak of war in September 1939. One was made in Czechoslovakia, which had only come into being formally with the dissolution of the Austro-Hungarian Empire, one in France and the other two came from Spain, one from the established Echeverria company and the other from a Nationalist collective assembled for the purpose.

Echeverria first produced an unsuccessful fully automatic pistol but eventually arrived at a design for a more conventional sub-machine-gun (at least in appearance), the Star S135. In fact, the S135 relied heavily on designs for self-loading rifles, rather than on the simple blowback SMG design which had already established itself so firmly, and was therefore unnecessarily complicated. As a result, the S135 was expensive to produce, and Echeverria later dropped it in favour of a copy of the German MP40, called the Z45, which was most notable for its being the first SMG to have a fluted chamber (a feature first used in the heavy machine-guns of the First World War), introduced to ease spent-case ejection in the higher-pressure environment created by the 9mm *Largo* round.

In the meantime, however, spurred on by the demand for weapons created by the continuing civil war, a Spanish collective workshop, Industrio de Guerra do Cataluña also began to produce a sub-machine-gun, the Labora, chambered, like the S135, for the 9mm *Largo* round. On first inspection, the gun seems to have a certain affinity with the Thompson of a decade earlier, but that is really an illusion based on certain stylistic details and the very high quality of finish the two shared. Experts who have examined the Labora have often commented on the surprisingly high standard of finish displayed by a weapon which one might reasonably expect to be extremely crude; the reason for that, it appears, is that the collective had plenty of skilled craftsmen but little in the way of mass-production capability. Hence, the guns were virtually handmade, and it is very difficult to persuade a skilled gunsmith to do less than his best work, no matter what the incentive. None the less, a Labora was no sooner finished than it was in battle. It was no more than an emergency expedient, and very few examples survived the end of the war.

The French type was the MAS *Modèle* 38, chambered for the French 7.65mm long round, which is both lighter and slower than the better-known 7.65mm Parabellum. The MAS was introduced in 1938 and was immediately accepted as a result of its high degree of controllability; though it is fitted with a full-length wooden butt-stock, it is quite manageable when fired with one hand. Manufactured in very limited quantities until as late as 1949, it was used by both French and German armed forces during the Second World War. It is still to he found in service with French counter-terrorist units into the 1990s, who sometimes prefer it to the heavier, more powerful 9mm MAT49.

The Czech *Kulometna Pistole* ZK/383 and its variants were originally designed in the early thirties by the Koucky brothers, and put into production at Brno by Ceskoslovenska zbrojovka in 1935 or '36. At that time, the company was producing one of the best series of light machine-guns then available (as we shall soon see) and on the surface, at least, there appears to have been a degree of cross-over – or perhaps it is better described as confusion – between them and the SMG as specified, for though it was chambered for the 9mm Parabellum round it appeared at first with both a bipod and a quick-change barrel, features of the LMG not commonly found in machine pistols. It also came with a removable weight in the bolt – taking it out upped the cyclical rate of fire from 500 to 700 rounds per minute. Like most European designs of the day it used the 9mm Parabellum round, and gained a certain measure of approval, particularly in South America, where examples were still to be found in everyday service until well into the 1970s.

Chapter Ten

The birth of the light machine-gun

TOWARDS THE END of its formative period, the machine-gun started to appear in a lighter, rather less robust form, able to provide direct covering fire out to 600–800m (roughly half a mile) where necessary, but not designed to sustain it for hours on end. Typically, it was a self-contained weapon, magazine- rather than belt-fed and light enough for a single infantryman to carry into battle in place of his rifle. Originally there was some confusion as to the worth of these new light machine-guns because they were measured against the standards of the heavy guns of the day; by the 1980s their continuing worth was to be drawn into question again, this time following a blurring of their role (along with that of the conventional sub-machine-gun) with that of a new generation of assault weapons.

We have seen how the Danish Madsen light machine-gun – an excellent weapon for its time – was offered in competition alongside the Maxim, the M1895 Colt and the Hotchkiss *Mle'*97, to which it was in no way comparable, and how it failed miserably as a result. That failure set the LMG concept back some years in the West, but the Madsen was adopted by the Russians, to arm their cavalry squadrons, and many of the excellent guns fell into German hands. It was Madsen LMGs which the first storm-troopers used at Verdun and on the Somme in 1916. We have seen, too, how other sometimes not entirely suitable 'light' machine-guns found favour during the Great War: the Hotchkiss *Mle'*09 (which has some claim to being the first gun widely used in the LMG role); the lightened and modified belt-fed MG08/15 which the Germans used to equip the storm-troopers from the end of 1916, and the Lewis gun, which was rapidly accepted despite its shortcomings in the sustained-fire role, were the best of them. There were failures, too, of course – quite enough has been said already about the dreadful Chauchat – but right at the end of the war an American design, from the doyen of American armourers, John Browning, showed the real potential for a weapon as handy as a rifle but with considerably greater firepower.

The gas-actuated Browning automatic rifle, universally known by its initials as the BAR, did not satisfy its designer – he thought it fell between two stools, as it were. It was really too heavy at over 8kg (18 pounds), including a full magazine, to be used as a rifle, certainly when fired from the shoulder, and was not capable of any great accuracy even in single-shot mode, due to its heavy reciprocating action. In auto-matic mode it was too light, and hence inaccurate again, and its 20-round magazine meant it had to be frequently reloaded. For all that, it actually lived up to its design requirements very well indeed, because the concept it ful-filled called for a weapon capable of rapid fire from the hip while the infantryman assaulted an enemy position at walk-ing pace. Some versions, the M1918A1 and -A2, were fitted with bipods; all were originally chambered for the .30-inch M1906 round. The BAR was adopted by many countries throughout the world, and stayed in continuous front-line service with the US Army and Marine Corps from its inception in 1917 until the end of the Korean War in 1953, when it (and the then-standard M1 Garand rifle) were both replaced by the M14 self-loading rifle, which itself had a limited capacity for automatic fire.

The Belgian Fabrique Nationale d'Armes de Guerre (FN), which had a long and happy association with John Browning dating back to its acquisition of a licence to manufacture his first semi-automatic pistol in 1900, took up the BAR later (as did Carl Gustav in Sweden), and supplied it to the Belgian Army in 1930 as the *Fusil Mitrailleur Mle'30* in 7.65mm calibre. They also supplied Chile, China and Poland. FN even updated the design after the Second World War, with a quick-change barrel and modified internal components. The BAR's major drawback resulted from Browning's original specification for an upwards-feeding magazine, which could not be easily elongated to take more than twenty rounds.

There had been a number of attempts to produce a true light machine-gun before Browning got to grips with the problem. The earliest came from a rather unusual source, Mexico, though the gun was put into production by Schweizerische Industrie-Gesellschaft (SIG) in Switzerland. The *Fusil Porforio Diaz Systema Mondragon Modelo* 1908, as the gun was rather grandiosely called, was in reality a gas-actuated self-loading rifle with a selective fire capability. A version modified by SIG, with a 20-round detachable box magazine and a spindly bipod, was taken up by Germany in small numbers in 1915, and fitted with the unreliable 'snail' magazine. It did not last long in service.

Russia produced a self-loading rifle with pretensions to the LMG role halfway through the 1914–18 war – the *Avtomaticheskaya Vintovka Sistemy Fyodorova obr* 1916G, usually called the AVF, which had a surprisingly modern look to it. It was recoil-operated (which was and still is unusual for an SLR), chambered, also surprisingly, for the Japanese 6.5mm round, and managed a cyclical rate of about 600 rounds per minute. Its development was halted temporarily by the revolution of 1917, but it went back into production briefly in 1919. It was ultimately a failure, but probably due more to its being in the wrong place at the wrong time rather than to any inherent weaknesses of its own, at least in the assault rifle role for which it had originally been designed.

The self-loading assault rifles which followed the AVF into Soviet service were also designed for occasional and temporary use as light machine-guns, a tradition which was continued via the AK 'Kalashnikov' and its successors. One step up from the AVF was the pan-fed light machine-gun developed in 1926 by Degtyarev, the 7.62mm *Ruchnoy Pulemyot Degtyareva pakhotnyi*, usually called the DP in the West. It was adopted in 1928, and stayed in service in its original form until well into the 1950s, when many examples found their way into the hands of Soviet clients of one sort or another. It went through no less than three reincarnations, the last as recently as 1953, during which most of its obvious shortcomings were repaired. It was extremely simple, reliable and robust, suffering only from the ammunition feed problems (considerably ameliorated by the design of the magazine) always associated with the long Soviet round (itself ultimately superseded in 1943 by the 7.62mm × 39 M43 round), and from a tendency for the recoil spring, which was housed beneath the barrel in the piston tube, to lose its tempering when it overheated. A variant, the *Degtyareva tankovyi*, was produced for use in armoured vehicles.

Between the two world wars an important test ground for

the weapons of the larger nations was the Spanish Civil War of the late 1930s. The Soviet Union supplied a variety of weapons to the Republican forces, just as Germany and Italy did to the rebel Nationalists. Machine-guns again took a grievous toll, as the following selections from the diary of one soldier serving with the Republicans' multinational International Brigade show:

11 February 1937. Noon. The time is passing swiftly. We are in the middle of a fight. The Fascist machine-guns are firing their explosive bullets [*sic*] on us, and they make a sharp crackle as they explode around us. . . . We are trying to take a small hill by assault. The Fascists have the advantage in numbers and in arms. Their machine-gun fire is devastating our ranks. Nearly a whole Company has been wiped out. I learn that our machine-guns are out of action. . . .

. . . A rain of steel is falling along the whole of the front occupied by our Brigade. Our advance has stopped. The Fascist machine-guns still have us within range and our own are out of action. We have rifles. . . .

12 February 1937. With the British Battalion, towards dusk. [Two British volunteers] were racing against time to get the machine-guns into action. In the gathering dusk they dragged their guns, one belt in each, to the ridge that had been Battalion HQ. Conical Hill was empty, so was White House Hill; our men were falling back through the olives at the left. The Moors sweeping over and around Conical Hill, their light machine-guns raking the olives, came forward in a charge that would have gained them a footing on our ridge.

Our guns roared out. For three minutes they blazed in

unison. A full Battalion of Moors was caught in the open, from an unexpected angle. Their charge ended there, in veritable mounds of corpses. That half of them got back to cover was due simply to the fact that there had been time for us to fill only one belt per gun.[1]

The same conflict also supplied a revealing commentary on how well an untrained or poorly trained man could cope with a typical Soviet weapon design:

[a tremendous weapon] also was the Russian light machine-gun, the Diktorov [sic]. Well, it was called a light machine-gun, but when I came into the British Army and met the Bren machine-gun, it was several times lighter than the Diktorov. Nevertheless, the Diktorov had a marvellously simple lock and was a very reliable weapon under fire. It was a pan-fed machine-gun. Nothing simpler than the lock could have been devised, except for the final action of the Sten gun, where there was just no lock at all. The Diktorov could be used as an accurate single-shot weapon, as well as for rapid firing, and at maximum distances as much as a rifle or the Maxim machine-gun.[2]

During the First World War the variety of weapons available to the individual infantryman was considerable, and many were fabricated on the spot; tomahawks and nailed clubs were popular among raiding parties, for example, and grenades were often made up from whatever materials were at hand. Naturally enough, it was quite a different matter to produce a machine-gun, but none the less, expedient weapons were manufactured, though not in quite such profusion as during the 1939–45 war.

One such was the Canadian Huot LMG. It used the barrel

and straight-pull bolt action of the Ross rifle, which had been withdrawn from Canadian service in 1916 and replaced by the Short-Magazine Lee Enfield. An Ordnance Branch officer named Huot got to work on a way to modify the stored Ross rifles into light machine-guns by the addition of a simple gas actuation system and a drum magazine. Modification cost just $50, at a time when a Lewis gun was costing over $700! It proved quite effective, within its obvious limitations, short barrel life being not least among them, but the war ended before it could be made in any quantity.

Another wartime expedient – though this time a new design – was the French Darne, manufactured in Spain by Unceta from early in 1918 (and perhaps later, in Czechoslovakia). Gas-operated and chambered for the 8mm Lebel round, it does not meet quite all our criteria for an LMG, being belt-fed. Described as 'one of the cheapest and crudest guns ever marketed', it, too, proved to be effective to a degree and even continued in production, modified to the airborne role, after the war. It was tested for possible adoption by the Royal Air Force in the late 1920s; its inclusion in the selection process was said to have been a major factor in the adoption of the rifle-calibre Browning M2 airborne machine-gun in its place.

The biggest producer of machine-guns in the private sector in France, Hotchkiss, were hardly more successful at producing a true LMG than Darne, who had only ever manufactured sporting guns before the war, and became embroiled in machine-gun production through obtaining a contract to make Lewis guns for the French Army. Hotchkiss failed again with a revised design unveiled in 1922, even though it was offered in a box magazine-fed version as well as one using the by-now fairly notorious strip magazine. The only country where it was at all popular was Greece, where it saw service in 6.5mm calibre.

Slightly later in France the gas-actuated 7.5mm *Fusil Mitrailleur Mle'24/29*, manufactured at the Government armouries at Chatellerault and St Etienne, was a distinct improvement on its predecessor, the long-recoil action *Mle'15* Chauchat, but that was not difficult. It was a modification of the basic BAR design, this time with a top-mounted box magazine, and was later further modified into the *Mle'31*, intended for mounting in fixed defensive positions and on board armoured vehicles. The *Mle'31*, too, was magazine-fed, but this time from a unique 150-round-capacity side-mounted drum. Like most of the Italian sub-machine-guns of the day, the Chatellerault had a double trigger system to select single-shot or automatic fire.

The unpopular Hotchkiss LMG was extensively tested in Czechoslovakia in 1924, some hundreds of guns being supplied in 7.92mm calibre for the purpose (some reports say they were actually manufactured there), but was ultimately rejected. In its place the Czech-made *Lehky Kulomet* ZB vz26 – a progressive development of the first Czech-designed guns to be made in a new factory established at Brno two years earlier for Ceskoslovenska zbrojovka – was adopted. The vz26, designed, as were most Czech guns of the period, by Vaclav Holek, was to be the prototype of a family of light machine-guns which many would place among the best ever made, thanks not only to a very sound design but also to the quality of the engineering which went into them.

Four years later an improved variant, the ZB vz30, was introduced, and licences to manufacture it were acquired by China, Iran, Spain and the United Kingdom, where it became known as the Bren gun (from the initial letters of *Brno*, where it was designed, and *Enfield*, where the British versions were made). The main modification for British use involved re-designing the magazine to accommodate the, somewhat anachronistic, rimmed .303-inch cartridge (other versions had been chambered for 7.92mm, 7.5mm and 7mm). The sights were re-calibrated in yards, the barrel was shortened and the gas port brought a little nearer the breech in consequence. Its cyclic rate was nominally 550 rounds per minute, though the 30-round box magazine (which in British service, anyway, was normally loaded with only 28 rounds, to save the magazine spring somewhat) guaranteed that it would achieve nothing like that, even tripod-mounted in the sustained-fire role it was sometimes called upon to play. The gun was always known as ammunition-kindly, the only diminution of performance when cartridges of questionable quality were used being a clear reduction of the cyclic rate of fire. It was also known for its phenomenal accuracy: with a good barrel, a competent Bren gunner could put an entire magazine into the bull of a practice target at up to 600 yards range.

For the British, the Bren was nothing short of a gift. During the Great War, they had relied on the sometimes-temperamental Hotchkiss and the over-engineered Lewis gun, both of them far too heavy for the role at the best part of 15kg (33 pounds) with ammunition, together with a rag-bag of light guns in odd calibres, some of them captured, some of them bought for purposes of evaluation. There was just one home-grown contender, the Beardmore-Farquhar, which first saw the light of day in 1917 as a putative replacement for the Lewis gun in the hands of air-gunners. Its action – a gas-actuated piston compressed a spring, which in turn acted on the bolt, holding it closed until the residual pressure in the chamber had dropped to a safe level – proved to be unusually smooth in operation, leading to a reduced rate of stoppages and less risk of jamming. It was also considerably lighter than its rivals, and was soon under evaluation by the Army as well as the Air Force. It was too late, though; the war was over before any decision to adopt it could be made. In the new climate of peace funding proved elusive, and good as it was, the gun finally disappeared from contention in 1924.

In 1925, however, an established British armaments manufacturer with adequate funds to see a new gun through the long-drawn-out development process decided to enter the lists. Vickers-Armstrong, as the company then was, bought the rights to a gas-operated, box magazine-fed gun designed by Frenchman Adolphe Berthier and began manufacturing it and marketing it worldwide. They had little initial success (though in 1930 some guns were sold to Bolivia, which had already gone to war with Paraguay once, and was preparing to do so again) until 1933, when the Vickers-Berthier was accepted by the Indian Army (which procured its weapons separately from the British services) as the Gun, Machine, .303in Vickers-Berthier, Indian, Mark 3, to be manufactured locally, at Ishapore. It continued in service – though supplemented by Brens, as and when they became available – until after the end of the Second World War.

In fact, the Vickers-Berthier was a very competent and attractive design, and had it not been for the presence of the ZB vz26 in competition to it, would certainly have been the LMG with which Britain went to war in 1939. It was very similar to the gun which became the Bren, both in appearance and in its operating principles. A derivative, the Vickers Gas Operated machine-gun, called the VGO or the Vickers K – fitted with a pan magazine (i.e. a non-rotating drum) which contained 96 rounds – was adopted by the RAF in 1939, but was almost immediately made obsolete by a new generation of aircraft. It found a ready 'market' almost immediately, though, since it gave a high rate of fire – about 1,000 rounds per minute, as against the 500 or so r.p.m. of the Lewis or the Bren – and so was popular as a flex-mounted aircraft gun. It also found favour during the war with the fledgling SAS and other light-vehicle-mounted reconnaissance troops and special forces, too, both as a support/assault weapon and in the anti-aircraft role.

The Bren gun was officially adopted, as the Gun, Machine, Bren, .303in, Mark 1, in August 1938, production having started at RSAF the previous year. It was eventually produced in five slightly different versions in .303-inch calibre. (Later it would appear in 7.62mm NATO chambering, when NATO adopted that cartridge in the late 1950s, and the Spanish version, the FAO, was converted to belt-feed, too. The .303 and 7.62 versions are easy to differentiate: the .303 magazine is curved; the 7.62mm version is straight.) Many guns were produced in Canada, too, some of them in the original 7.92mm calibre, for shipment to China.

British Bren production was concentrated in just one factory, at Enfield Lock, north of London, and some disquiet was expressed about its vulnerability to air raids. Birmingham Small Arms, the prime producer of the Lewis gun, was asked to prepare a design for an alternative war-expedient model Bren, capable of being turned out by even meanly equipped machine shops, and came up with a simple pressed-steel gun originally known as the Besal and later as the Faulkner, after its designer, to avoid confusion with the 7.92mm/15mm Besa tank machine-gun. The Besal/Faulkner possessed one interesting unique feature – to cock the action the gunner had simply to pull back hard on the pistol-grip – but all the other parts were simplified copies of those found in the Bren itself. In fact, Bren gun production at the Royal Small Arms Factory was never seriously impaired by enemy action, and only a very few Faulkner guns were ever produced, but it stands as a good example of the way in which a sound design can be down-engineered and still be workable.

Just as guns Hiram Maxim designed were used on opposing sides during the Great War, so were the Vaclav Holek-designed LMGs employed during the Second World War, for the Brno factory continued to produce ZB vz30s right through the war, and they saw second-line service with the Wehrmacht as the *Maschinengewehr* 30(t). Germany herself did not produce a true light machine-gun during the interwar period, having devised the general-purpose machine-gun concept and begun to realize it so brilliantly, a development which we will consider later.

Around 1930 existing examples of the old Rheinmetall-manufactured Dreyse MG10 were stripped of their water-jackets and fitted with a stock and bipod and converted to the LMG role by Simson & Co of Suhl, the only German machine-gun works authorized under the Treaty of Versailles. Almost all the MG13s were eventually sold off to Portugal, where they became the *Metralhadora* M38.

By 1930 the Control Commission enforcing the Versailles Treaty was virtually moribund and Rheinmetall went back into the armaments business openly. In 1932 they began production of the MG15, which was intended as a light machine-gun for aircraft installation, and indeed became the first weapon to be adopted by Hitler's Luftwaffe, having been in German warplane prototypes when that air force itself came into being in 1935. Some of the features of the MG15 later found their way into the MG34 and towards the end of the Second World War when stocks of machine-guns were low, many remaining MG15s, obsolete in the air-to-air role by reason of the small capacity of their 75-round saddle-drum magazines, were converted either for anti-aircraft duties, mounted on a tall tripod, or for infantry use, by the addition of a simple stock and bipod. The MG15 was soon joined by the more successful belt-fed MG17, which, while it was also found in the anti-aircraft role, had an action specifically designed to interact with the synchronizing device fitted to aero-engines.

Before the Anschluss in 1938 Austria maintained her own weapons procurement programme, though not unnaturally looked to Germany for inspiration. As well as the S1-100 machine pistol, Steyr-Solothurn produced a light machine-gun known as the M30, which was adopted by the Austrian Army in 8mm calibre, chambered for the decidedly pointed 'S' bullet. After the amalgamation with Germany, Austrian units were re-equipped with German weapons, and guns such as the M30 were re-distributed to reserve units. The M30 had one unique attribute: a rocking trigger; pressure on the top half produced single shots, while pressure on the lower half produced automatic fire. That was just one aspect of its design which found its way into the German MG34, of which, in many senses, it and the MG15 were precursors.

Germany's Axis ally, Italy, having been on the winning side in 1918, and therefore being unconstrained by the provisions of the Versailles Treaty, had rather a different agenda from the Reich itself; to start with, she had imperial ambitions in areas where the character of the terrain dictated that much of whatever fighting there was could only be handled by dismounted infantry, and that in itself dictated her need for an effective light machine-gun. There were two contenders for the job: the *Mitragliatrice Leggera Sistema Scotti, Modello* 28 and the *Fucile Mitragliatori Breda, Modello* 30.

Alfredo Scotti was a freelance designer with a studio in Brescia who had earlier patented a machine-gun action which was a form of locked blowback: gas bled off from the barrel acted on a piston, which unlocked the bolt; residual pressure in the chamber then forced it back in the normal way. A 7.7mm version perhaps more suitable for vehicles and aircraft than for unmounted infantry was offered in both belt- and drum-fed versions, but was not adopted, though a larger 20mm version was later used by the Italian Air Force.

More successful in that it was adopted by the Italian Army – though it was far less logical, and therefore more complicated, in design terms – was the 6.5mm Breda, a design developed over the best part of a decade and finally adopted in 1935. A simple blowback-action gun, it was fitted with a horizontal, non-exchangeable 20-round box magazine which hinged forward for loading by means of rifle chargers. While this meant that the magazine was probably a better fit, with consequently less danger of misfeeding a round, it also made the gun very slow to reload and more vulnerable to both accidental and battle damage. The barrel was easily changed, but was left without provision for the gunner to handle it when it was hot – a surprising omission which has plagued many an otherwise sound design of gun.

Elsewhere in Europe, arms manufacturers in Finland, Sweden and Switzerland all produced more-or-less successful designs for light machine-guns in the late 1920s and '30s Lahti produced the *Automaattikivaari Lahtisoloranta Malli* 26, a light but strong recoil-operated weapon chambered for the long Soviet 7.62mm cartridge which he tried to sell as both an infantry weapon and for use by aircraft observers, but with little success outside his own country. The Finnish Army also took up a Swedish design of poor overall quality, known originally as the *Kulspruta* LH33 and later, after rights to it were acquired by a German car component company called Knorr-Bremse AG, the *Maschinengewehr Knorr-Bremse Modell* 35 (MG35). The Waffen-SS also acquired some of these guns, but hastily passed them on to its second division: the foreign 'legions'.

In addition to the Solothurn M30, two other Swiss companies produced LMGs, the design Furrer produced for Waffenfabrik Bern in 1925 being, in the words of Hogg and Weeks 'exceptionally well conceived, beautifully made and far too expensive to be considered as a mass-production weapon'. It was basically similar to the Parabellum design, but employed differential recoil to produce a decidedly smooth action. SIG was somewhat more successful with the KE7 of 1936, unusual in that it was recoil-operated, though as an automatic weapon it suffered from many of the same drawbacks which characterized the BAR, for it was even lighter than Browning's rather better design.

One may recall that it was SIG which had taken on the manufacture of the Mexican Mondragon self-loading rifle in the years before 1914; when a second talented gun designer, Rafael Mendoza, emerged in Mexico in the 1930s, there was sufficient industrial expertise available locally so that he did not need to look elsewhere for production facilities for his *Fusil Ametrallador Mendoza Modelo B–1933*, but had it taken up by the Fabrica de Armas Nacionales instead. Mendoza's design was original in its overall layout but parts of it were clearly inspired by aspects of the *Mle'09* Hotchkiss (the gas cylinder) and the Lewis gun (the bolt). The resulting gun was light and handy, as well as inexpensive, and was probably as good as any other in its class in the world at the time. It was taken up straight away by the Mexican Army and continued in front-line service until after 1945, when it was revamped and changed over from 7mm Mauser calibre to the American standard .30–06.

The first light machine-gun the Japanese adopted, in 1922, owed considerably more to the Hotchkiss than did Mendoza's design, but the same was true of all the Japanese light and heavy guns up until 1937, when they turned over to copying the Czechs as well. The 11 *Nen Shiki Kikanju*, which was still to be found in service at the end of the Second World War, had one most unusual feature: its ammunition feed system was a return to a form of hopper, which accepted the charger clips furnished for the Arisaka rifle, the principle being that any rifleman could feed the gun without the need to charge magazines or belts – but not from his own ammunition stocks, for the standard 6.5mm round was too powerful for the gun, and a reduced load had to be used instead, to prevent the cartridge cases rupturing.

The follow-up version, the 96 *Shiki Kikanju* of 1936, dispensed with the hopper in favour of a 30-round box magazine, but was otherwise little altered from – or little better than – its precursor, save that the barrel was rather easier to change. The 97 *Shiki Shasai Kikanju* of 1937 was an almost identical copy of the ZB vz26, firing the semi-rimless 7.7mm round, though with less attention paid to the manufacturing process. Curiously, it was introduced as a tank gun, rather than as an infantry weapon – a role to which it was certainly unsuited, by virtue of the need to change barrels frequently and because the magazine was located on the receiver top. The infantry weapon which followed two years later, the 99 *Shiki Kikanju*, was also clearly derived from the Czech gun, but was considerably more successful than its predecessor. It fired the more powerful rimless cartridge, which ejected far more cleanly from the breech, and much closer attention was paid to manufacturing tolerances, result-ing in a light machine-gun which was as good as those in use in Europe at the start of the Second World War. Like all the Japanese guns of the pre-war period, it was capable of automatic fire only.

Chapter Eleven

Heavy-machine-gun developments between the wars

THE MAJORITY OF heavy machine-guns in service at the end of the Great War were eminently successful weapons, perfectly suited to the task allotted to them. However, despite having been in service for more than a decade, in most cases, they all still had design faults of greater or lesser magnitude and importance; some were subject to improvement by modification, and the rest were tolerated, being too fundamental to correct so easily, and by and large the men working them knew them intimately, and thus managed to circumvent potential problems automatically. As a result the position of the heavy machine-gun as the pre-eminent infantry weapon changed very little over the next twenty years. Certainly, the British, the French and the Russians went into the Second World War with many of the same guns they had been using at the end of the previous encounter and – except in the case of the Soviet Union – saw little need to divert precious resources in an attempt to improve upon a tried and trusted commodity.

Indeed, the Gun, Machine, Vickers, .303in, Mark 1 which the British Army adopted as its primary fire-support weapon in November 1912, was still in service in 1965 (and with the

173

South African Defence Force as late as 1990), the only serious modification made to it having been the adoption of the Mark 8Z round, with its boat-tailed bullet, in place of the Mark 7, increasing the gun's maximum range to 4,500 yards as a result.

The Soviet Union manufactured far, far more PM1910 Maxim guns than Imperial Russia ever did, and kept them in service until the end of the Second World War, alongside the newly-developed SG43 air-cooled weapon. Total 'Russian' production of the venerable gun is estimated to have been of the order of 600,000 units.

China did not even begin manufacturing Maxims until 1935, producing perhaps 40,000 units under German supervision between then and 1937, when the production facilities were overrun by the invading Japanese. The Chinese guns were all identical to the DWM 1909 Commercial Pattern guns, and were thus virtually the same as the Vickers Cs. They used the German 1916-pattern tripod, and never fitted optical or indirect sighting systems, though all had provision for the fitting of anti-aircraft sights. They were well finished – not quite up to the standard of the original DWM guns, or the guns the Swiss made as their MG11, but considerably better than the Russian and Soviet guns.

Air-cooled Maxim variants were produced in both China and the Soviet Union, and in the latter, modified lightweight air-cooled versions were also tested, without much success, by both Ivan Kolesnikov and Feydor Tokarev. Intended for use in the LMG role, like the German MG08/15 and /18, neither was adopted.

Germany had, arguably, made the best use of the heavy machine-gun during the 1914–18 war, certainly during the early years of the trench war stalemate, but under the terms of the Treaty of Versailles she was virtually forbidden such armaments and was specifically forbidden to develop new sustained-fire weapons. The German Army was limited to 100,000 men in total, with 792 heavy machine-guns (almost all of them MG08s) and 1,134 light models, though these quotas were subsequently upgraded to 861 and 1,475 guns respectively. All other German automatic weapons were supposed to pass into Allied hands for reallocation, disposal or scrapping, but there was a substantial gap between principle and practice, for the total handed over did not exceed 30,000, a considerable shortfall, even allowing for the number of guns captured previously.

The US Army, for instance, found itself in possession of over 10,000 captured MG08s and MG08/15s by the Armistice, and added to them its allocation of 20 per cent of all weapons handed in, bringing the total to 16,000. There had been a short-lived conversion programme for captured German guns in the autumn of 1918 (though it was more likely that American troops simply used them as they were, with captured ammunition stocks), and some thought was given to restarting it in 1919, and so all the acquired stock of weapons was shipped back to the USA. Finally, however, a decision was made to deactivate the guns instead (normally by removing the locks and breaking off the ammunition belt feed pawl), and distribute them to any American Legion or Veterans of Foreign Wars post which asked – author Dolf Goldsmith relates how a neighbour, a senior (female) functionary in the Red Cross, received one as an unsolicited gift as a rather bizarre form of war memorial. Many more were scrapped, and some thousands were dumped at sea, off the New Jersey coast, as late as 1940.

Many guns had, of course, been destroyed in the course of the war and the best estimate is that perhaps 100,000 more guns of every description were acquired by Allied nations in one way or another. Some more undoubtedly found their way into a variety of unlikely places all over the globe, but that still leaves a good proportion of the total of well over 200,000 MG08 models alone built between 1914 and 1918, and it is safe to suggest that most of them stayed in Germany. Certainly, even though no complete new Maxim-style guns were made in Germany after 1918 (though components, including barrels, were), significant numbers – far in excess of those permitted by the Treaty – turned up during the Second World War in rear-echelon positions, particularly as part of anti-aircraft defences, for they were no less effective against low-flying aircraft at the age of thirty-something than when first made.

It took some time for Germany to recover first from defeat and then from the economic ruin which followed, but by the early 1930s, the revitalization of her army was scarcely a secret any longer, and by 1936 Hitler had reoccupied the demilitarized Rhineland and was rearming steadily. Factories in many countries – in Scandinavia, the Soviet Union, Holland and Switzerland among others – had been operating as a cover for German rearmament for some years, just as had some strategic domestic manufacturing plants. Submarine, tank and aircraft development, as well as that of relatively minor items such as machine-guns and machine pistols, all soon made up for lost time as a result. We may take aircraft production as a case in point: the progenitor of the Ju87 Stuka, for example, made its first flight in 1928 in Sweden, and the Messerschmitt Bf108, a clear precursor to the Bf109 fighter, was designed to compete in the 4th Challenge de Tourisme Internationale, an air race in 1934. If the resurgent Germany could get away with building what were obviously intended to be warplanes, there was little chance of her small-arms research being curtailed, particularly by a group of rather disparate ex-allies who all had troubles – and divergent agendas – of their own.

One aspect of German tactical doctrine did not change through the period of enforced idleness in weapons development. As far as the Army was concerned, the machine-gun still ruled the infantry battlefield, and that conviction was reflected in its procurement policy. In 1932 a development programme got under way, aimed at producing not just a new heavy machine-gun to replace the MG08 but a completely new class of automatic weapon, both more flexible in action and more adaptable to the needs of mechanized warfare – the *Einheitsmaschinengewehr* or universal machine-gun.

At that time, both Rheinmetall and Mauser-Werke were involved in developing air-cooled light machine-guns, and though neither project went far enough to satisfy the Army, both included promising new elements. The Rheinmetall project gun was the already mentioned Steyr-Solothurn M30. It was a production model of the so-called Soda machine-gun, developed at Rheinmetall's Sommerda factory by Louis Stange and then passed to Solothurn in Switzerland and Steyr in Austria for production. The Swiss company was a wholly-owned subsidiary of Rheinmetall, and there is some reason to suspect that the Austrian might have been, too, at the time (it almost certainly was later), though documentary proof of that has never been found. In any event, we do know that Waffenfabrik Solothurn AG, the Swiss subsidiary, was set up in 1929 solely to operate as a front for German research and development efforts.

Mauser at Oberndorf am Necker was simultaneously working up a design by Ernst Altenberger for a light machine-gun of similar capabilities to the M30, known as the LMG32. This was the first time Mauser had been involved in the development of a machine-gun and Altenberger's design had certain very interesting basic features. With a ruthlessness which many other procurement authorities singularly failed to display around that period, the German Army ordered Rheinmetall's Louis Stange to manage the project at the company's Düsseldorf factory, under the overall direction of Major (Dipl. Ing.) Ritter von Weber, but making use of the bolt-locking procedure and barrel-changing method developed at Oberndorf. This has given rise to considerable confusion, and some authorities persist in stating that the MG34 which eventually resulted was a Mauser design. It was not; it was a Rheinmetall-developed composite which used some Mauser features for which Mauser-Werke AG later received a royalty payment from Rheinmetall-Borsig, as the former became in 1936.

The essence of the entire project was a systematic approach to the problems of providing a single gun capable of acting as either a light or a heavy machine-gun (that is, as an individual weapon in the assault mode, or as a crew-served, sustained-fire weapon in the support mode) without compromising either, and to that end the accessories and even the ammunition feed method were modularized.

Experience with the MG08/15 had proved that an LMG in the assault role could not be belt-fed, and so the *Doppeltrommel* 15 75-round saddle-drum developed for the MG15 was employed, feeding rounds from different sides alternately to preserve balanced weight distribution. The *Patronentrommel* 34 as it was known in the context of the MG34, stayed in service until perhaps 1940; it was not a simple device, and the gunner needed a selection of tools to load and unload it. It also required the belt-feed cover and cartridge-feed block to be temporarily removed from the gun.

More straightforward was the 50-round belt contained in

a single drum, the *Gurttrommel* 34, mounted on the left-hand side of the receiver and positioned against the feed block by a simple hook and latch. It was feasible to fire the 12kg (26.5-pound) gun from the hip, with the help of a sling, but more common to employ the built-in bipod, which could be located either close to the muzzle or further to the rear, close to the receiver – the former was preferred, since it was more stable and hence more accurate. A lightweight tripod, the *Dreifuss* 34, was also available in the LMG role, but for sustained fire the *Lafette* 34 tripod, which supported the gun in a sprung cradle, was essential. The *Lafette* 34 was considered a masterpiece of design, combining low integral weight – just 21kg (46 pounds) – with the highest degree of stability, adjustability and flexibility. Only standard belt-feed could be used with the tripod, but that was hardly a drawback in the sustained-fire role. Belts were of 50-round capacity (so as to fit the belt-drum) but could be linked together.

For use in a vehicle the butt-stock could be readily detached, and a ball-mount which fitted over the barrel protector and located with a pintle could be installed. Single and double pedestal mounts for anti-aircraft fire were available, and in the latter case it was a relatively simple matter to change one gun over to feed from the right-hand side and install a central ammunition-belt box. Optical sights for both direct and indirect fire were available; they were mounted on the *Lafette* tripod, not on the gun itself, and were good out to 3,000m (3,300 yards) in direct-fire mode and 500 metres more in indirect mode, one of the few instances of the MG34 being fractionally less capable than its predecessors – though of course it fired the same round. Permanent metal sights consisted of a blade foresight and a notched rear sight, adjustable up to 2,000 metres (2,200 yards).

The gun's designers fixed on a fairly conservative 250

rounds as being the desirable interval between barrel changes; they could afford to keep the period low because the procedure was simple and straightforward, if a little unusual at first sight. With the bolt cocked and the safety lever to 'safe', the receiver latch below the rear sight was depressed and the entire receiver rotated clockwise around an offset axial pin, through almost 180 degrees. Then, as the rear of the gun was lowered, the entire barrel simply slid out backwards, to be caught – at least in training – by a crew member wearing an asbestos glove. A cold barrel was inserted, located at the muzzle within a sleeve which was part of the recoil booster/flash hider which formed a permanent part of the barrel sleeve, and the receiver was returned to the operating position. When the gun was mounted on the heavy tripod, the procedure was essentially the same, save that the barrel jacket was rotated anti-clockwise instead, and the exposed barrel hooked out with anything handy (an ammunition belt tab served) as the gun could not then be angled. Each gun was supplied with two spare barrels, the hot one being cooled after use by any expedient means. It was quite acceptable to plunge it into cold water.

The action of the MG34 was the most complex and complicated ever seen in a machine-gun, up until that time or since, and that, combined with the very fine manufacturing tolerances permitted, were its chief failings. In a sense, it was like an artillery piece in miniature, employing a locking system first used seventy years previously.

It was operated by a short-recoil action, the barrel moving backwards approximately 2cm (0.75in.), unlocking the bolt head within the first 1.5cm before being stopped by the barrel buffer. A short locking collar was attached to the barrel, cut away through two opposed 90-degree arcs; the two quarter-circles left had interrupted threads cut into them. The collar had a pair of lugs on its outside; these travelled in slots in the receiver and prevented the barrel itself rotating. A pair of cams extended to the rear from the locking collar and had two functions: they locked and unlocked the bolt head, and also contributed to the rearward acceleration of the bolt assembly. The bolt assembly was in two parts: head and body. The body reciprocated within the receiver, guided by a pair of simple lateral lugs. On its lower surface was a third lug which engaged with the trigger mechanism (or not, as the case may be) and on its upper a pair of studs which drove the belt-feed mechanism. The rear of the bolt provided the surface against which the pressure of the mainspring acted. The body had a drilling from front to back to accommodate the tubular rear portion of the head, leaving the head capable of some independent rotation around its axis, which coincided with that of the barrel. The shoulder of the bolt head had interrupted threads machined to mesh with those in the locking collar, the engagement being secured by rotating the bolt head through a quarter turn. This was brought about by two pairs of rollers mounted on two extended studs on the head itself, which acted against paired cams on the rear of the barrel collar, the inner pair locking the bolt head and the outer pair reversing that process during recoil. The rollers did not lock or unlock the bolt head themselves; they merely acted on the bolt head to turn it through 90 degrees and thus free it from, or engage it with, the interrupted threads in the locking collar. The face of the bolt head was machined to receive the cartridge case, and contained the simple mechanisms of both the extractor and the ejector. The extension tube to the rear of the bolt head contained the firing pin and its associated spring. The assembly was cocked during the unlocking of the bolt head, and held by a pivoting lever on the right side of the bolt

181

head. When the locking process was complete, the tail of that lever contacted an inclined surface on the bolt body, releasing the firing pin. Acceleration of the bolt assembly, after unlocking was complete and the barrel was on its way forward again, was achieved by means of interaction between the bolt head rollers and a system of cams, both on the barrel collar and in the receiver. And all that happened fifteen times every second!

The early MG34s utilized the same rocking trigger found on the Solothurn M30, pressing on the lower automatic trigger half resulting in a cyclic rate of about 900 rounds per minute. The actual rate varied considerably between one gun and the next, and the spring-loaded Patronentrommel drum produced a distinctly faster rate of fire than a belt. Specially modified versions produced cyclic rates of up to 1,650 r.p.m. but at the price of unacceptable wear on moving parts. A short-lived lightweight variant, the MG34/41 was adapted to fire at 1,200 r.p.m., and was tested in action on the Eastern Front, but was not adopted, for by that time the MG42 project was nearing completion.

The MG34 was far from perfect, but it was undeniably successful. From its basic principle sprang a succession of even more proficient general-purpose designs, starting with the MG42 and leading to the postwar MG3. We will look at those weapons in some detail in due course, but first we have to step back to the final years of the Great War, and west-wards across the Atlantic, to consider the later work of the American master-gunsmith, John Moses Browning, and the pre-eminent part he played in the development of the heavy machine-gun as we know it today, in .50-inch (12.7mm) calibre, casting a passing glance at the evolution of his rifle-calibre M1917 water-cooled gun into the air-cooled M1919 in the process.

Browning was a professional gunsmith, from a family of gunsmiths, and is said to have made his own first firearm from scrap materials at the age of thirteen. By the time of his death in 1926 he had been responsible for two of the best semi-automatic pistols – the .45-inch Colt M1911 and the posthumously produced 9mm Parabellum *Modèle à Grande Puissance*, also called the Hi-Power – an excellent semi-automatic shotgun, the BAR and the two inter-related 'families' of heavy machine-guns as well as a wide variety of other weapons.

By the end of the First World War Browning's M1917 had been manufactured in significant quantities, though few had actually gone into action (the first of them on 26 September 1918), such was the speed of events at the time. Remington, Colt and Westinghouse, the three companies contracted to produce them, made no less than 56,608 M1917 Brownings in .30–06 calibre. They were, in general, both over-engineered and over-specified – they had bronze water-jackets, for example, long after all the similar Maxim designs had dropped them in favour of steel – but at the same time there was concern over some of their features: the base-plate of the receiver was prone to failure, for instance, and was routinely reinforced by the addition of a steel stirrup strap. However, limited combat experience with the gun proved sufficient to highlight this and other faults, all of which were subsequently corrected (though not completely until 1936) with the substitution of the steel-jacketed M1917A1, another 55,000 of which were produced, mostly at the Rock Island Arsenal but also by Browning's long-time European partners, Fabrique National (FN) in Belgium. Production continued until after the Second World War.

The basic design of the M1917 was soon adapted for air-cooling, becoming the M1918, M1919 and M37 in the process. The M1918 was little more than a design exercise, but the M1919 was to appear in eight variants in all, many of them being intended solely for use in armoured or soft-skinned vehicles and in aircraft. The -A4 and -A6 variants were also produced as infantry weapons, suitable for tripod or bipod mounting, the latter with a shoulder stock and carrying handle, and became the US Army's standard medium machine-gun throughout the Second World War. All the air-cooled, rifle-calibre Brownings weighed around 14kg (30 pounds) and operated at a cyclic rate of 500 rounds per minute. Terry Gander, in a survey of machine-guns, states that 729,423 Brownings were produced between 1940 and 1945. Late-model guns were to be found well into the present decade, converted to 7.62mm NATO calibre, in service with most NATO forces, and many more, often in their original calibre, were with the armed forces of third-world countries.

Even as the original M1917 Brownings were starting to appear on the battlefields of France in 1918, American soldiers there had begun to agitate for a gun firing a substantially heavier round, their inspiration being the 11mm Hotchkiss 'Balloon Gun', used with some success to shoot down enemy observation balloons with incendiary bullets. Eventually the .50-inch/12.7mm calibre was specified, even while engineers in Germany were trying to get a machine-gun (the T.u.F.) utilizing the similar *T-Patrone* round into production. Put simply the .50-inch round was roughly four times as heavy as standard rifle-calibre ammunition but was fired at similar velocity and hence was four times as destructive when striking its target.

Over the years the gun has gained numerous testimonies as to its striking power. One from the Vietnam era can perhaps serve to sum them all up: 'A .50 calibre machine-gun is nothing to be fucked with. Movies have done a disservice to that weapon. What they fail to convey is that a .50 calibre machine-gun is big and bad enough that if you look around a city block, you will see almost no structure standing that you can hide behind safely if somebody is firing one of those things at you. It just goes through everything.'[1]

In fact, the First World War was long over before the necessary modifications to Browning's design could be put into production, and the heavier gun finally appeared as the US Machine-Gun, Caliber .50in, M1921. It was subsequently modified, in the light of field experience, and redesignated first M1921A1. These guns were water-cooled, the later variants having provision for a constant supply of water circulating (by means of a pump in some examples) between the ordinary jacket and a much larger header tank.

Meanwhile, Colt and the Rock Island Arsenal were experimenting with air-cooled .30-inch calibre guns using the Browning system, specially modified for installation in aircraft, and soon produced what was to become, when the entire US Army designation system changed in 1927, the US Machine-Gun, Caliber .30inch, M2. The US Army's range of Browning heavy machine-guns was expanded, perhaps as early as 1928, to include a new .50-inch air-cooled gun for aircraft mounting. This was also, rather misleadingly, designated the M2. It soon appeared in a variety of terrestrial forms, but without the super-cooling effect of an aircraft's slip-stream, it proved unreliable due to its barrel overheating after no more than seventy-five rounds had been fired. It was soon joined in service by the M2HB 'Heavy Barrel' gun, as a result; the only material difference between the two versions was exactly that which the name implies, though the M2HB's rate of fire was somewhat lower than that of the original gun.

The 'fifty-cal' Browning M2 went on to become the most

widely used and widely praised heavy machine-gun in the world, and to enjoy a life which spanned the next seven decades and still continues, in fixed, flexible and field mounts, aboard ships, aircraft of all sorts and the widest possible range of vehicles, from main battle tanks to small scout cars and pick-up trucks, as well as with infantry units. Almost two million had been produced by the end of the Second World War, and though production has slackened off since, it is still being manufactured in two locations in the USA and in Belgium at the present time. During the war there were various attempts by American arms manufacturers to improve on the Browning system, but none were successful; perhaps they should have paid more attention to the original acceptance trial, back in February 1917, when John Browning put 20,000 rounds through a pre-production M1917 gun without a single stoppage, at an average cyclical rate of 600 rounds per minute.

The Soviet Union was a late-comer to the development of the heavier machine-gun (in fact, the .50-inch calibre guns usurped the title of heavy machine-gun as soon as they became accepted; the older HMGs were accordingly 'downgraded' to the status of medium machine-guns), and did not introduce a 12.7mm gun into its inventory until 1938: the *Stankovyi Pulemyot Degtyarev Shpagin Krupnokalibernyi* (DShK) *obr* 1938. As its name implies, the design of the new gun was attributed to Degtyarev, who contributed the gas operation and locking system from his DP-series LMGs, and G. S. Shpagin, who devised a novel means of extracting incoming rounds from the belt by means of a rotary feed cylinder. Strictly speaking, Shpagin's name should have been removed from the designation of the modernized postwar version of the gun, the DShKM 1938/46, since the major improvement was the replacement of his feed system with a simple recip-

Above: US Marines on Iwo Jima in 1944 man a captured Japanese machine-gun of the Hotchkiss type. The Japanese took the French-made Hotchkiss Model 1900 as the model for their own machine-gun development, re-designing it to chamber their standard 6.5 mm rifle round.

Below: Like the M2 .50 calibre heavy machine gun, the American Browning .30 calibre light machine-gun began development at the end of the First World War, and made its reputation with the Allied forces during the Second World War. At 14 kg (32 lb) and with a cyclic rate of 500 rounds per minute, this air-cooled machine-gun proved itself to be extremely adaptable in the infantry support role.

The Bren continued in production as a .303 calibre weapon until the 1950s when the British Army adopted the standard NATO 7.62mm rifle round. The Bren was then adapted to the new round, and with one or two other minor improvements, such as a new flash eliminator, was redesignated the L4A1.

Left: Introduced into the British Army in the early 1960s to replace both the Bren and the Vickers machine-guns, the belt-fed GPMG fires the standard NATO 7.62 mm round at a cyclic rate of 850 rounds per minute. It was developed in the postwar period, in light of the acknowledged success of the German MG42.

Main picture: The DShK was the main heavy machine-gun of the Soviet armed forces throughout the 1940s and 50s. Used primarily as an anti-aircraft weapon, it fired a big 12.7mm round from a standard 50-round belt, and in performance was not dissimilar to the American M2 .50 calibre Browning.

For years after its introduction in 1960, the American version of the general purpose machine-gun, the M60, though it featured a number of technical innovations, such as a heat-resistant alloy lining to the barrel, suffered from dreadful problems of reliability and accuracy.

Designed directly from the Wehrmacht's MG42, the Bundeswehr's general purpose machine-gun, the MG3, shares all the major characteristics of the earlier weapon, except that it chambers the NATO 7.62mm round.

The postwar development of the machine-gun has tended towards lighter weapons chambering smaller ammunition. The American M2 .50 calibre heavy machine-gun, with its service record of nearly 80 years, proves that there is still a place for a big gun firing a heavy round.

Above and main picture: The M134 Minigun may resemble the manually operated Gatling of the 1870s, but the multi-barrelled configuration is where the similarity ends. Developed originally during the Vietnam War from the big M61 Vulcan gun, the electrically driven Minigun has a cyclic rate of 6000 rounds per minute.

The RPK is the light machine-gun currently in use with Russian and CIS armed forces. The 104 cm (41 in) long weapon is essentially a standard AK assault rifle with an extended barrel. As this is fixed, and cannot be replaced when the weapon is in action, sustained fire for any length of time is not possible.

Right: Manufactured by the Belgian company FN, the Minimi is one of the best machine-guns in production today and has been adopted by the US Army as a squad support weapon to replace the M60. A short weapon, only 104 cm (41 inches) long, the Minimi chambers the standard American M16 5.56 mm cartridge.

Below: The British Army's Light Support Weapon (LSW) follows the same design concept as the Russian RPK – namely that of a light machine-gun which is in effect a standard assault rifle but featuring a longer, heavier barrel.

rocating action. The gun's performance was comparable in most ways with that of the .50-inch Browning M2, though it fired a slightly lighter round at slightly lower velocity. Although production seems to have ceased in the 1980s it, too, is still to be found in service in the armies of all the countries of the former Soviet Union, and all the ex-Soviet-client states.

Four other nations produced heavy machine-guns between the wars: Britain, where Vickers briefly produced an enlarged version of their Mark 4 and Mark 5 guns firing the .50-inch round developed for the Browning M2, and Rolls-Royce later initiated but did not complete a project to develop a .50-inch machine-gun (throughout the war Britain relied on the Browning M2 for all its heavy machine-gun needs); France, which produced the Hotchkiss *Mle'30*, little more than an enlargement of the by-now well-tried Hotchkiss design; Japan, which pirated it as the 93 *Shiki Kikanju*; and Italy.

In 1931 Italy produced the *Mitragliatrice Breda RM Modello 31* in 13.2mm calibre (the same as that used by the Hotchkiss), primarily as a secondary armament for tanks, though it could be tripod-mounted for use by the infantry. Interest in it was short-lived, and within six years production of it had given way to the *Mitragliatrice Breda calibro 8mm Modello 37*, which was to become the standard Italian machine-gun of the Second World War. The considerably-bigger-than-normal (for Italy, where the 6.5mm round was still in general infantry use) 8mm round had both a heavy projectile and a high velocity, which made it accurate to considerable distances – certainly, it was capable of very effective fire up to 2,000m (2,200 yards), and its maximum range was well over twice that. The gun's strangest feature was its unorthodox feed system. Ammunition was presented to the gun in 20-

round trays, the empty casings being returned to the tray after firing and extraction. This has given rise to some confusion (and not a little derision) since it was assumed that the unfortunate gunner would then have to remove the hot brass from the tray before re-loading it. This was not the case at all; the rather specialized cases were to be reloaded wherever possible, and this system did everything in its power to keep them from distortion and accidental damage before they were returned to the armoury. It was an especial boon and a distinct advantage in the confined space of an armoured vehicle, where loose spent cases rolling around the floor can be a particular hazard. Thanks to its better-than-average performance, the gun was very much in demand; the British captured significant numbers in North Africa, and put them all back into service, the Long Range Desert Group receiving more than their fair share. A subsequent *Modello* 38 came with a heavier barrel and the option of a top-mounted box magazine or a conventional belt-feeding system.

At roughly the same time, the old water-cooled FIAT-Revelli gun of 1914 vintage was given a radical face-lift: air-cooling replaced the original water-jacket, the cartridge oiler was discarded and replaced with a fluted chamber to aid extraction, and the curious magazine replaced by a conventional belt. Despite all that, it was still far from ideal, unfortunately for those infantry units condemned to operate it. The best thing about the revamped gun was its rechambering, to accept the excellent 8mm *cartuccia pallottola Modello* 35 round.

Some way to the north-east, in Brno, the by-now expert Ceskoslovenska zbrojovka began production of a new heavier, more robust air-cooled, belt-fed gun, the ZB vz37, the action of which was not unlike that of the vz26/Bren save that the forward (return) stroke of the piston lifted the rear of the breech-block and engaged it with lugs on the barrel, thus barrel and block recoiled together before separating (the Bren's barrel was immobile). The gun also differed from the Bren in that it employed a differential recoil system – the round was chambered at the limit of the back stroke and fired before the barrel was fully returned; thus, much of the recoil force was absorbed in arresting the forward motion of the barrel and breech-block. Some versions were capable of two rates of fire: either 500 or 800 r.p.m. The Czechs (and the Germans, who put it into second-line service as the MG37(t)) used it as an infantry weapon, mounted on a tripod, but the British, who also bought the design (and this time wisely kept it in 7.92mm calibre, thus obviating the need for an expensive redesign of the feed mechanism), used it as secondary armament for armoured vehicles under the name Besa. It was renowned for its accuracy, and stayed in British service until the mid-1950s. A 15mm version introduced in British service in 1940 was neither so popular nor so long-lived.

In fact, while the new generations of heavy machine-gun were certainly destined for infantry use on the battlefield, they were really more applicable to vehicle mounting, and they also contributed in great part to the coming of age of the fighter aircraft. From their very tentative beginnings in France in 1916, tanks reached relative maturity rapidly, particularly in Germany, where, along with tactical airpower, they became a central component of the new Blitzkrieg or 'lightning war' concept. The tank, being the most fearsome and feared artefact on the battlefield, finds all men's hands turned against it; it is prone to long-range attack from artillery and has to be very wary of infantrymen armed with anti-tank projectiles and grenades. Even engineers, who are rarely called upon to fight, are sent into action against armour; attack aircraft find tanks almost as irresistible as trains, and to other tanks they are the highest priority target on the battlefield. Other tanks are the proper target of the main gun, but to deal with most of the rest, the armoured fighting vehicle is equipped with a secondary armament of machine-guns. Modern AFV designers, like their counterparts in the twenties and thirties, tend to favour the sort of automatic weapons found in aircraft, since they do not have to pay the penalty which comes with the added weight of firepower. Thus the requirement for effective secondary armament in the second-generation tanks and armoured cars was for bigger-calibre guns firing heavier projectiles out to greater distances, both to be effective against other vehicles (and aircraft) and to suppress infantry at long range, before they could bring their own anti-armour weapons into play.

Of course, there was little reason to start from scratch when looking for appropriate machine-guns; by the early thirties all the major military powers had a range of choices of light, medium and heavy guns, either locally developed or available for purchase from abroad, with the singular exception of Germany, which never did develop a terrestrial heavy machine-gun, preferring to employ a variety of types of cannon instead, the 20mm KwK30 anti-tank gun being a firm favourite. Even when existing guns did not exactly fit the part, it was simpler, cheaper and more effective all round to modify them, even quite radically, than to commission a new design. Aircraft manufacturers, too, seldom looked far afield for their armament, either for offensive or defensive purposes: the air forces of both Britain and America used Browning guns in huge numbers, both in rifle calibres and in the heavier .50-inch version.

One exception was the German Air Force, which commissioned new, more effective guns to replace the MG15 and MG17, to be developed independently of the programme which resulted in the MG34. There were many unsuccessful designs promulgated, but perhaps the most important of those accepted was the 13mm MG131, developed by Rheinmetall, which appeared in 1938. This was a radical departure from accepted procedure, being designed to fire ammunition electrically, and not by percussion cap, a novel and successful way to tackle the much greater problems involved in synchronizing the new faster-firing guns with much faster-revolving propellers. The standard aircraft cannon of the time were 15mm and 20mm MG151s, but later developments included a new family of 30mm cannon and the installation of adapted 3.7cm, 5cm and even 7.5cm guns for special purposes. Allied aircraft were sometimes similarly equipped, the most notable being the de Havilland Mosquitoes armed as submarine hunters, with forward-firing anti-tank guns fitted inside their bomb bays. While these guns – they were all designed as anti-aircraft or anti-tank guns – were automatic in operation, they are not generally considered as machine-guns, and so fall outside the scope of this work; the new generation of super-firing aircraft guns will be considered later, when we look at the machine-guns of the latter part of the war which was about to engulf the world.

Chapter Twelve

Blitzkrieg: The mechanization of war

FRIDAY 1 SEPTEMBER 1939 had hardly dawned before it became clear just what the dominant characteristic of war in the mechanized age was to be; German troops poured over the border into Poland at six points, tanks and close-support aircraft to the fore, ripping through poorly manned defensive positions and tearing at the underbelly of the Polish nation. From the very first, the watchwords were speed and sudden, stunning, overwhelming force. The entire rationale of the lightning war, the blitzkrieg, was to smash the enemy into submission before he had time to rally his forces – before, ideally, he even knew what was happening to him. While superb planning and tactical surprise were of the essence, the machine-gun was central to this entire bellicose scenario, for without its firepower there could have been no lightning war, just as without it, the First World War would not have become a static conflict of attrition. Thus, almost ironically, did a single weapon virtually create two quite different styles of warfare within but a single generation.

In 1940, Hitler's forces drove the lesson home with a series of sledgehammer blows: Norway and Denmark; Holland and Belgium and then France all fell to the blitzkrieg, and it seemed for a time that Europe was destined to be not just dominated but directly ruled by Berlin. It was another year before, almost astoundingly, Hitler double-crossed Stalin, his partner-in-crime during the Polish invasion, and initiated Operation Barbarossa, the biggest and most far-reaching blitzkrieg of them all. For that year, Britain and her Empire had stood alone, but now there was a huge force ranged alongside her in the east, capable, as Napoleon Bonaparte had discovered, of soaking up an invading army like a sponge, and wringing it out again, drop by bloody drop.

Compared with the First World War even, let alone those of the previous century, the war of 1939–45 was immensely more complicated. It was also more widespread, of course, and took in every sort of terrain on Earth. And of all the hundreds of battlegrounds over which the war was fought, only the undersea was exempt from the power of the machine-gun.

By 1939 the machine-gun had ceased to be a piece of more-or-less specialized machinery, and had become an ordinary part of everyday soldiering. There were material shortages within the British and French ranks, certainly – and in the German too, even though their offensive agenda had been written long before – but unlike the deficiencies which had blighted the two sometimes-reluctant allies in 1914, they were not due to any philosophical shortcoming, but rather to a weak grasp of a harsh reality.

The success of the blitzkrieg tactics came as no surprise to Hitler and his High Command, for they had seen in Spain, over the previous three years of sponsored civil war, just how devastatingly effective their new weapons and strategy could be. If there were any lasting doubts, they were dispelled in Poland: the entire nation west of the River Bug (save for a few isolated pockets of resistance) was conquered in just eighteen days at the cost of about 15,000 German troops, dead or missing. The key to that success was what we later came to call the air–land battle – fast-moving mechanized forces on the ground attacking the enemy where he was weakest, supported by artillery (and, more importantly, by specially designed aircraft in the close-support role) to neutralize strong points, pinching off and isolating pockets of resistance to be left and mopped up later. And if that scenario seems familiar, it is because we have seen it before, on the Western Front in the spring of 1918 in the so-called 'Hutier Tactics', with their reliance, at least in part, on the firepower of the man-portable automatic weapon, which formed the raw basis of all German offensive planning during the second world conflict.

The German Army of 1939 could not be considered a mechanized force – save for a very few motorized divisions, the infantry travelled by train where it could, and where it could not, it marched, just as it had always done, with horses and mules to pull carts and carry equipment. The infantry's need for a sustained-fire weapon that soldiers could carry without its weight crippling them had been one of the parameters in the specification for the MG34. None the less, the war was essentially a mechanized war, in a way the previous conflict had not been. The new generation of war machines – the aircraft, tanks and towed artillery, not to mention motorized transport – guaranteed that there would be no general return to the siege tactics which the machine-gun had imposed on the opposing armies of 1914–18. That is not to say that the machine-gun did not rule the battlefield still – it did, but in a new mobile role which had only been hinted at in the closing scenes of the first war.

The sub-machine-guns and light machine-guns which

were developed during the interwar period were produced to reflect revisions in tactical thinking, particularly those regarding fluidity and rapidity of movement, but they also engendered changes. They gave the individual infantryman a firepower advantage over his predecessor which has been variously measured at five, ten or even fifty to one, but in fact it is difficult to calculate the real level of advantage because it varies so much, both with circumstances and with the skill and courage of the individuals involved. Light automatic weapons made the four- or five-man fire team, to use the expression the US Army adopted, a viable proposition in the real sense of the word; previously, the firepower of such a small group of men had not been enough to allow them successfully to prosecute an assault on a defensive position; with automatic weapons in support a determined group could hope – at least – to approach close enough to launch a decisive grenade attack and follow it up with a devastating hail of sub-machine-gun fire: a method which became the norm during the Second World War.

Clearly, for the infantry, the heavy machine-gun – or even the physically heavy, rifle-calibre medium machine-gun as it was now called – had very little place in such a scenario, where the emphasis was on leap-frogging fire and movement, though the advantage it offered in terms of firepower was still undeniable. As a result, the heavier automatic weapons migrated – quite smoothly – to a vehicle-borne role. Very few of the millions of heavy machine-guns produced in the Second World War were carried about by infantrymen; virtually all of them were to be found on vehicles or in aircraft. One exception was the Soviet 'Dushka', the DShK, which was mounted on wheels and could be towed behind a vehicle or a mule – or by a team of men – before being set up for operation; adequate for defence, though there was always the risk of losing the gun if a hasty defence was not actually adequate, it was entirely impractical in the attack, except against heavily defended targets which were unlikely to succumb quickly or easily.

It took some time for the realization that the heavy machine-gun *per se* had ceased to be an infantry weapon to sink in, but when it did, that was the cue for the biggest automatic guns to get bigger and more powerful still. That trend was immediately evident both in the air and on the ground during and after 1918. It is only more recently that the .50-inch/12.7mm machine-gun has ceased to be the obvious secondary armament for an armoured fighting vehicle. British tanks were armed with 15mm Besa heavy machine-guns from about 1941, and the German Army adopted a modified version of the 20mm anti-tank gun as its secondary tank armament, though it was less effective (and certainly less cost-effective) in the anti-infantry role which was still the tank's real *raison d'être*. (In this sense, we can view the tank's main gun as – quite paradoxically – defensive armament, and its smaller machine-guns as offensive weapons.)

As well as changing the face of infantry tactics on the battlefield proper, the enhanced portable firepower provided by the new lighter machine-guns was also partly instrumental in introducing a new form of semi-clandestine warfare, involving groups of highly trained, highly motivated men known euphemistically as 'special forces'. At their inception in the British Army in 1940, the fledgling special forces groups had an uncomfortable (to outsiders) 'private army' image which persisted for years, and was helped in no way by the men's own often rather cavalier attitude to the regular army's dress code, chain of command, logistical system and equipment inventory. The fact that camaraderie and respect for ability largely replaced blind respect for rank within the special forces, and manifested itself as a scornful attitude to outsiders, only provided more ammunition for the detractors; the special forces groups were ultimately saved by just one thing: their sometimes devastating effectiveness.

We have no space to divert ourselves with even a skeleton history of special forces operations here, but we may use some of their exploits as exemplars of (sometimes rather unorthodox) small-unit tactics employing automatic weapons, including the conception of the machine-gun-armed light reconnaissance vehicle, as evolved by the Long Range Desert Group (LRDG) in North Africa in 1940–42 and developed by David Stirling's 'L Detachment' of the then-fictitious Special Air Services Brigade into an attack vehicle proper. The story of the creation of a real Special Air Service Regiment to fill out what had been a phantom designed to deceive Axis intelligence officers has been told many times, but it is worth relating an incident from its very first successful operation to demonstrate just how the machine-gun was central to its a role.

On the night of 14 December 1941, a small group of men led by Captain Paddy Mayne, a legendary figure in the history of the SAS, set out to destroy Italian aircraft at Tamit, on the Libyan coast close to Sirte. Transported to within striking distance by vehicles of the LRDG, Mayne's men infiltrated the airfield successfully and had achieved complete surprise when Mayne realized that the noise issuing from the one illuminated hut indicated that a party of some sort was under way there. Mayne was a big man, and had been a rugby player of some renown; he burst through the door of what proved to be the officers' mess with a Thompson sub-machine-gun, and expended an entire magazine – 30 rounds only; doubtless Mayne would have been delighted to have been able to have got his hands on one of the old 100-round drum magazines for his tommy gun, but they had been withdrawn long before – into the assembled men within, ending, apparently, by shooting out the lights and retiring in the resulting confusion. He posted a detachment to wait, like terriers outside a rabbit warren, for emerging survivors and proceeded to set demolition charges on twenty-three of the twenty-four aircraft dispersed around the field (the twenty-fourth he disabled with his bare hands, according to legend, having no bomb left for it). His methods may have owed more to the backstreets of Chicago than to the barracks at Caterham, but the point was well made, and established a ruthless *modus operandi* for L Detachment which its successors cheerfully continued.

Having relied, to begin with, on the LRDG for transportation, Stirling soon procured vehicles of his own – newly arrived American jeeps, rather than the Chevrolet or Ford trucks the LRDG favoured – and proceeded to cram into them as much weaponry as he could get his hands on, paired Vickers K guns, pintle-mounted, front and rear, being just the starting point. By the summer of 1942, the now self-contained SAS was raiding deep into enemy-held territory, and on a few famous occasions actually carrying out its missions by driving on to the enemy airfields and speeding up and down blasting everything in sight in a storm of machine-gun fire.

By no means all the operations which followed were as successful as the first, and some were disastrous, but Stirling and his men showed beyond doubt that, audaciously handled, the machine-gun was as devastating an offensive weapon as it had been in defence on the Western Front twenty-five years before. The armed jeeps which Stirling had put to such good use stayed in service with the SAS when the regiment moved to Europe; even when teams of SAS men were dropped by parachute behind enemy lines in France their jeeps went with them. 'The dropping of such vehicles simply required the establishment of a larger DZ [dropping zone]', says one account of the Regiment's activities, its tongue firmly in its cheek. The Regiment later switched to Land Rovers and also adopted other appropriate vehicles, among them stripped-out dune buggies, armed either with conventional machine-guns (usually Browning M2HBs), Miniguns or automatic belt-fed grenade launchers capable of about 300 rounds per minute.

The war on the Eastern Front was characterized by machine-gun duels at squad and platoon level, often at very close range. At first the Soviet tactics were crude repetitions of the worst of the 1914–18 war:

> Encircling an isolated bunch of Ivans doesn't mean a thing. There are millions more where they come from. As a substitute for tactics, their commanders sacrifice them without a thought. I have seen the Ruskies advancing in row upon row, when we were dug in outside Moscow. As they came within range, our machine-gunners mowed them down. Then more came, clambering over the dead, and we mowed them down, too; and more, and more, until great mounds of dead and dying men were piled high in front of our trenches. It only ended when our artillery found the range, and made further advance impossible. No soldier is proud of such fighting, but we have to survive.[1]

Later personal accounts from both sides are littered with references to desperate firefights in which sub-machine-guns as well as the heavier German MG34s and MG42s and Russian Maxims were used in both attack and defence, frequently on targets just a few metres away, their over-whelming firepower spelling the difference between survival and annihilation; as often as not the guns themselves were the objective, such was the importance of the extra firepower. A young soldier in the 93rd Panzer-Grenadier Regiment, Rudi Brasche – who had already taken part in the invasion of France and won the Iron Cross, Second Class, and was destined to win the coveted Knight's Cross for his bravery throughout the Russian war – was involved in clearing a brickworks close to the Mius river in December, 1941. This was urban combat at its hardest:

> Suddenly the night was torn apart in front of him in a wide semi-circle. Bursts of fire whipped towards the position from four or five directions. Figures jumped up not thirty metres in front and raced towards him ... Brasche fired a long burst at the approaching forms. Kneisel's machine-gun likewise opened fire. ... Brasche swung his weapon round in a rapid movement. His burst struck near an enemy gun in the chimney. Then he aimed at a position ten centimetres above the muzzle flash from the enemy weapon and fired again. A Russian emerged from behind the gun's protective shield [such shields had been a feature of Russian machine-guns since the days of the First World War]. He took three or four steps and fell as if he had been struck by lightning. ... Grenades went off in rapid succession. To his right, the gunfire rose to a climax. The enemy troops who had survived the hail of fire ran back, and disappeared into the snow as if the earth had swallowed them up. A moment later the silence was shattered by impacting rounds from Russian 'potato throwers'. The small mortars coughed all along a front of about 400 metres, and a rain of the dark objects fell and exploded, scattering fragments of steel.

'Looks like an entire mortar battalion, Herr Feldwebel,' said Brasche.

'Looks that way. We've gone from the frying pan in Rostov into the fire here, and—'

A terrible scream rang out from behind them and the hacking sound of a Russian sub-machine-gun caused the men to drop to the ground. Brasche was the first to speak.

'What was that?'

'The Russians have broken in!'

'Laupert squad follow me!' shouted Kneisel. 'Leave the machine-guns manned!'

Grunge crawled up next to Gambietz, behind the machine-gun. He readied a fresh belt of ammunition; however, no more enemy troops approached. The others returned an hour later.

'What happened?' he asked.

'They stabbed Bungertz and Kohler. Killed them with their bayonets. They took the machine-gun and Siebelhoff with them.'

'But you caught them?'

'They disappeared from the face of the earth without a trace. No sign of them.'

'This could become uncomfortable. . . .'

And things did become 'uncomfortable'. They became more than that. The next four nights saw whole machine-gun teams disappear . . .[2]

Through 1943 Soviet forces drove the invaders back and then, halfway through the year, the Allies began the reconquest of Western Europe via its 'soft underbelly' (which proved not to be soft at all) with an attack on Sicily, immediately using the island as the jumping-off point for an invasion of the Italian mainland. By then the best general-purpose machine-gun the world had ever seen had begun to make its mark on the battlefield, as the Wehrmacht proved as resolute in defence as it had been decisive in its lightning attacks. The gun was the MG42 – a more-than-worthy successor to the MG34 which had been the German infantry's main automatic weapon up until that point.

If fighting in the desert had been a far-ranging, ebbing-and-flowing affair, when the war reached Western Europe it proved to be very different. Outside the set-piece battles, each side constantly probed the other for weaknesses, getting drawn into fire-fights as a result. Inevitably, though they were characterized by sustained machine-gun fire, many of them served to do little more than liven up the day, as this account of an early-morning action at Ulipelli, near Salerno, on 17 September 1943, provided by Lt A. A. Blacoe, a platoon leader in the Cheshire Regiment, shows. The Cheshires were one of five infantry regiments of the British Army to be turned over to the fire-support role, armed with Vickers guns and, later, 4.2-inch mortars.

It was a few minutes after six, and the grey light of an early day was seeping through the trees. Suddenly a Bren gun over on my right broke the silence. I couldn't see any movement in front, but the answering spit of a Spandau resolved my doubts. It seemed to come from the other side of the open field, on the right edge of the trees, [but it soon became clear that] the Germans were there on both sides – they were in the tobacco plantation as well.

Section commanders didn't need any telling. Soon everything was firing – Vickers, Brens, 20mms, rifles and even the 2-inch mortars. For the next twenty minutes, there was quite a lot of noise! Gradually the firing died down. One could see very little of enemy movement, but there was not much doubt as to where they were. Some were still in the tobacco plantation, and so every three or four minutes the guns traversed its length, just in case. Rifle fire from both sides became intermittent, the Brens and Spandaus exchanged occasional courtesies, and our Vickers gave a comforting chatter every now and again . . .[3]

Meanwhile, on the other side of the globe, the Japanese were proving just as tenacious, and it was well into 1944 before the Allies made any real progress in recovering the huge tracts of territory Japan's own very effective form of blitzkrieg had gained her. Here, too, from the bare rock of the Pacific islands to the dense jungles of South-East Asia, the machine-gun ruled. Another platoon commander from a machine-gun battalion, this time from the Manchester Regiment, describes what must have been almost the perfect ambush, somewhere on a jungle road between Pyinzi and Natogyi in Burma, on 3 April 1944:

We occupied the ambush at 1730 hours, and at approximately 2345 the Jap column came along. Scarcely daring to breathe, we watched it pass into the killing area . . . Right in front of us, the head of the column halted and the tail closed right up; we thought we'd been seen, but apparently they were only checking up on the track.

The signal to open fire was to be the right-hand gun of B section opening up. Fire discipline was very good, and the sound of its first burst was drowned by gunfire and grenades, as everyone else opened up too. Each gun had a swinging traverse and as most of the Japs were between five and ten yards away, they were simply mown down. They had no chance of replying at all. A number managed to take cover actually behind our gun positions, but they had no idea where they were, and were only struggling blindly to get away. In doing so, they ran straight into the rifle pits and died there. Cpl Dickenson killed one by hitting him on the head with his Sten, having already emptied the magazine and having no time to replace it.

It was still five hours to daylight, and through the night there came the sound of isolated guns opening up on wounded Japs trying to crawl away. None of them got very far. When dawn came, the killing area was littered with dead and dying Japanese, over sixty of them altogether. We had first call on the booty; it included three 37mm guns, one MMG, two LMGs, two spigot mortars and two officers' swords.[4]

By that time, every infantry unit of every combatant nation – and every partisan band, too, from Norway to the Balkans – was clamouring for more automatic weapons, and factories all over Britain, the United States, Russia and Germany were producing them as fast as they could, together with the millions of rounds of ammunition they consumed each day in battle. Back in the early days of the machine-gun, when Hiram Maxim had demonstrated his 37mm pom-pom to the King of Denmark, the monarch enquired the cost of operating such a weapon. 'Each round costs six shillings and sixpence [£0.33], Your Majesty', Maxim told him. The King shook his head sadly. 'A most excellent gun, Mr Maxim,' he said, 'but its costly appetite would bankrupt my little kingdom in a few hours.' By early 1945 there must have been more than one Treasury bookkeeper with much the same thought in his head. In 1918 France alone produced seven million rifle-calibre rounds every day, but even such magnitude as that pales into insignificance when compared with the appetite the Second World War had for ammunition of every type, the machine-guns being by far the most greedy.

Much of the ammunition consumed by the machine-gun battalions was used up in 'pepper-potting' – a form of all-arms barrage which briefly preceded an infantry attack during the later phases of the Second World War. The object of a pepper-pot barrage, the *History of the Middlesex Regiment* tells us,

> was to make a fire plan with all the larger weapons of the Division which were not involved in the general artillery plan controlled by the Commander Royal Artillery [as each division's artillery chief was titled]. This consisted of the Bofors of the Light AA Regiment, the 17-pounders of the anti-tank regiments, the tanks' 75mms, the MMGs and 4.2-inch mortars of the support battalions and the 3-inch mortars of any infantry battalions not actually engaged in the attack. All these weapons were placed under the control of the machine-gun battalion commander. It was the intention that they should cover every inch of the ground over which a divisional attack was to pass, bullets, shells or bombs covering the area like pepper coming out of a pot.[5]

Unlike so many of the 'softening-up' barrages employed during the First World War, the 'pepper-pots' worked very well indeed, and became a major part of any offensive, but they certainly accounted for some ammunition: for instance, on the night of 3 August 1944, the 1st Manchesters fired 338,000 rounds of .303-inch Mark VIII ammunition through their Vickers guns, consuming over a score of barrels (and expended 5,700 4.2-inch mortar rounds, too), in support of an attack on a strong point between Caen and Evercy which lasted just seventy-seven minutes; during the move across the River Maas on 7 February 1945, the 1/8th Battalion fired 850,000 rounds (and over 8,000 mortar bombs) in a seven-hour period. At 0530 it was 'light enough to read a book' by the tracer rounds arching through the sky, one veteran recalled.

Chapter Thirteen

Significant guns of the Second World War

THE SECOND WORLD WAR was by far the most costly episode in mankind's history. One important effect of that cost was the introduction of austerity measures right across the board, even in such essential sectors as arms production, and that in turn meant both redesigning existing weapons to make them easier, and therefore cheaper, to manufacture, and also producing new, simpler designs, stripped of all but the most basic features. Perhaps the most famous of the wartime expedient designs was the British Sten, which embodied everything that is both good and bad about second-generation sub-machine-guns. The 9mm Sten first appeared in the summer of 1941, to almost universal derision. The 'Stench' gun, troops called it, and the 'Woolworth's Special' and the 'plumber's delight', but it saw use in every theatre of operations, in the hands of regular troops of all arms as well as by clandestine warriors and partisans, and over four million were to be produced before the end of the war, at an average cost of less than £3 each – about the cost of a suit or a good quality pair of shoes.

It was rough, certainly; it was scarcely tough (at one point during the fighting in the Western Desert, a particularly bad batch of magazines was issued, and promptly ordered destroyed. One young soldier attempted to carry out that order by smashing the magazine with the gun, and broke the gun instead. With some trepidation, he reported the incident to his sergeant, who tossed the damaged weapon aside contemptuously, saying that that was the sixth that week), but it did the job, and that was all that had been expected of it.

The Sten was a very crude weapon indeed; all its body parts were stamped out of sheet metal, formed to shape and roughly welded together, with no attempt made even to clean up the seams afterwards; its barrel was drawn steel tubing, secured to the receiver by a screw collar (when it was removable; that was not the case with the Mark 3, for example, the barrel and receiver of which were pressed together), and the butt was either a bent rod or a piece of tubing with a cross-plate welded to it. It only had one major fault – it was prone to misfeeds, as a result of a poorly designed single-feed magazine which also required a special filling tool. One of the most famous weapons malfunctions in history involved a Sten with a faulty magazine. On 17 May 1942 a Czech partisan calmly stepped in front of a car containing Reinhard Heydrich, the *Reichsprotektor* of Czechoslovakia, at a road junction, levelled his Sten and pulled the trigger, only to discover that compressed magazine lips had prevented it from feeding a round. His partner fatally wounded the SS General with a hand grenade instead.

The Sten – it took its name from the initials of its designers, R. V. Shepard and H. J. Turpin, and those of the RSAF at *En*field, where they worked – was the simplest possible blowback design with a fixed firing pin machined into the bolt head. It was cocked by pulling back on a bolt extension handle which emerged from the right-hand side of the receiver; when hooked upwards into a retaining niche, this served to lock the action safely. It was eventually produced in eight versions, two of them with integral silencers (the Mark 2(S) and the Mark 6) and in the last years of the war acquired a wooden butt-stock and pistol grip (and even, briefly, a vertical wooden fore grip, too, Thompson-style; it proved to be all too easily breakable, and was soon abandoned; users went back to gripping the gun by its magazine instead), in a vain attempt to make it more solid-looking. None of these tricks made it any more popular, we are widely assured, yet it survived in British service until the early 1960s. Like the rather more sophisticated German MP40, it was manufactured in component form (by a wide range of subcontractors more used to producing costume jewellery, lawn mowers, children's toys and dustbins, to name but a few) and assembled by a number of Royal Ordnance Factories and by BSA.

A shortened, lightened version was produced in small numbers for airborne troops, as was a variant called the Welgun, which used the Sten's barrel, magazine and main spring, the latter reversed and mounted around the barrel, pulling the bolt forward instead of pushing it, to reduce overall length. The Welgun had no bolt handle, and was cocked by inserting the finger and thumb of one hand in wide slots in the receiver, where the bolt itself was exposed, and pulling back on it; needless to say, those wide slots let in mud and dirt even more easily than they did fingers. Neither the Mark 4 Sten nor the Welgun was successful or popular, the paratroopers for whom they were intended preferring to beg, borrow or steal a Thompson whenever possible, and neither was made in more than token quantities.

Despite its somewhat exaggerated reputation for poor performance, the German Army paid the Sten the most sincere compliment possible when it began producing a gun copied directly from it, the MP3008, in late 1944, different only in having a vertical instead of a horizontal magazine. Difficult though it may be to believe, the German copies were even cruder than the British originals, despite their having been manufactured by engineering concerns of the stature of Mauser-Werke, Haenel, Erma and Blohm & Voss. Erma went on to make small quantities of an even shoddier gun, the EMP44, the barrel, body, butt and pistol grip of which were cut from identical pieces of tubing. It has been described as 'crude beyond belief'.

As well as the MP3008, which was intended for issue to last-ditch 'home guard' units, for reasons known only to itself the German High Command also commissioned exact copies of the Sten Mark 2 to be made, under conditions of great secrecy, by Mauser-Werke, for use by guerrilla 'stay-behind' units should Germany be driven from the territory she had occupied. Perhaps as many as 30,000 such guns were produced, but it is next to impossible to understand quite why the project was ever sanctioned at a time when every ounce of industrial productivity counted; after all, what difference could it possibly have made where an obviously pro-Nazi guerrilla unit's weapons ostensibly came from, except perhaps to give security forces an additional conundrum to mull over?

Not all the British sub-machine-guns of the war were 'cheap and cheerful' expedients. At about the same time as the Sten was going into production, a small independent British armaments manufacturer, Sterling Arms, began producing an altogether more traditional weapon, the Lanchester machine carbine. It carries the name of designer George Lanchester even though it was almost a direct copy of the Schmeisser MP28/II, chambered for the same 9mm Parabellum round, using similar furniture (though in this case adapted from that of the Lee-Enfield SMLE rifle, even down to the bayonet fixing lug). Most Lanchesters were issued to Royal Navy personnel, though few were actually used in action by naval ratings, the days of close-order fighting at sea being long gone. Their reliability made them favourites with anyone who could get his hands on one, though, and that included members of the LRDG.

A much more sophisticated British sub-machine-gun, the VAP or V42/V43, spent much of the war under development but the project was eventually abandoned before it reached production, at the end of the war in 1945. Its most significant feature was perhaps its double-column, double-capacity (i.e. 60-round) magazine, but it demonstrated a continuing concern for traditional engineering values and methods (it had wooden furniture and its components were machined), while at the same time managing to achieve a weight reduction of almost 20 per cent over the Sten. It also operated at a significantly higher 750 rounds per minute cyclic rate. Trials reports indicate that the weapon was reliable and effective, and popular with those who tested it, though how it would have performed under combat conditions is a matter of conjecture.

As we have seen, that other traditionally engineered weapon, the Thompson gun, was genuinely (if somewhat belatedly) popular all round, even if it was heavy and used sometimes-hard-to-come-by .45-inch ACP ammunition, but by 1942 Thompsons of any sort were increasingly difficult to find. Even in their 'austerity' M1A1 form, they were simply too expensive and time-consuming to manufacture, and the US Army's Ordnance Board had by then started looking for something new.

George Hyde – who had already produced the Hyde M2 –

and Frederick Sampson of General Motors, whose speciality was in mass-production methods, were given the task of designing an American equivalent to the Sten, and looked no further than Enfield for inspiration. Like its role model, the M3, as the resulting gun came to be designated when it was passed for service use in December 1942, was expressly designed to be produced by non-specialist engineering companies (in this case, predominantly the Guide Lamp Division of General Motors, better known, until then, for manufacturing car headlights). Also like the Sten, it was universally reviled by the soldiers to whom it was issued, immediately attracting the stigmatizing soubriquet 'grease gun' which was to remain with it all the days of its remarkably long life. It was certainly a 'quick and dirty' solution to the problem of producing cheap weapons, but in that context – and, once again, like the Sten it so resembled – it was actually a rather better gun than its reputation indicated.

It was notionally superseded by the even simpler M3A1 in December 1944. This was a cunningly designed piece, some of its components acting as tools to strip other parts. Like the Welgun, it did away with the bolt handle, being cocked by a finger acting on the bolt itself through a conveniently enlarged ejector port, the cover of which doubled as a safety catch when closed.

Both versions of the M3 were delivered chambered for the .45-inch ACP/M1911 round, but could be modified without tools, by swopping the bolt and barrel, and fitting a magazine adapter, to fire 9mm Parabellum rounds from the unreliable Sten magazine. No provision was made for anything but fully-automatic fire, but the cyclic rate was so slow – about 400 rounds per minute – that an experienced gunner could get off single shots by trigger pressure alone. By the end of the war, some 500,000 M3s and a little over 15,000

M3A1s had been produced, and a further 33,000 of the latter were made by Ithaca during the Korean War. Surplus stocks were later sold or given (they cost only $15 to produce, after all the same price as the Sten) to a variety of second-line US client states.

Germany, too, found itself running into problems maintaining its machine pistol production programme with the coming of war, and Erma was hastily ordered to simplify the design of the very successful MP38 so as to make it easier to manufacture. The result, which was substantially the same weapon in every essential, was the MP40. Despite adopting many of the same engineering practices used in the manufacture of the Sten, the MP40 always looked like a better-made gun, but the reasons for that can probably be traced to its having some residual elements of aesthetic appeal thanks to its pre-war ancestry The MP40 used very little high-grade steel, and where its predecessor had been machined and forged, it was stamped and spot-welded. Like the Sten, too, it was made up from sub-assemblies mass-produced by engineering factories quite unconnected to the armaments trade, to be assembled by Erma, Haenel and Steyr. In an attempt to increase the gun's firepower, a variant was produced in late 1943 which employed dual 32-round magazines, the second moving across into the charging position as soon as the first was exhausted.

The fourth major wartime expedient sub-machine-gun, and the one manufactured in the biggest quantities (though the Sten ran it a very close second during the war years themselves) was the *Pistolet-Pulemyot Shpagina obr.* 1941, better known as the PPSh41, designed by Georgii Shpagin and rushed into production in the late summer of 1941. Much simpler, and hence both cheaper and quicker to make, than the earlier Degtyarev designs, the PPSh41 differed from the other expedient weapons in that it always had wooden furniture and also in that it was widely used with a 71-round drum copied from a design by Lahti, while all the rest had box magazines of about 30 rounds capacity. It was chambered for the 7.62mm M30 pistol round which, while it was considerably lighter than the 9mm Parabellum loading fired by its European rivals, gave a rather higher muzzle velocity and a considerably greater cyclic rate – 900 rounds per minute. Its 26.5-cm (10.5-inch) barrel – which, rather surprisingly in a weapon designed to be as cheap as possible to manufacture, was always chromed internally – gave it considerably better range and accuracy, too. The M3's barrel was 20cm (8in) long; that of the Sten 6mm (.25in) shorter still.

The PPSh41 was in front-line Soviet service until the late 1950s, and was still current with the smaller Soviet client-states well into the 1970s. At least five million were produced by 1945, and whole units of Soviet infantry were armed with nothing else; it proved particularly effective in the savage street-fighting which characterized much of the combat of the battle for Germany in 1945.

Unusually, for it was Soviet policy to concentrate production on just one weapon of each type, a second machine pistol, the Sudaev-designed PPS43, also emerged from the war, this one as a direct result of conditions in Leningrad during the prolonged siege of the city, from September 1941 to the opening weeks of 1944. Also chambered for the M30 round, the PPS43 was manufactured locally to relieve a chronic weapons shortage. Extremely simple, it was an all-metal design with a folding butt-stock; perhaps one million were produced, all told, and examples were still to be found in service some years after the war's end. Of all the Soviet clients, only Poland was supplied with the PPS43, and later Fabrya Broni began making a version of its own in Warsaw, this time with a wooden stock, as the wz/43–52.

Italian gunmaker Beretta made a variety of sub-machine-guns during the war in its Gardone factory, all of them based on the successful pre-war *Modello* 38A but reverting to the more widely available though less powerful 9mm Parabellum cartridge. All the *Modello* 38/42s, /43s and /44s were fitted with full-length wooden furnishings, but as time went on their mechanical parts became less and less well executed, stamping and welding slowly replacing the traditional methods.

Fabbrica Nazionale d'Armi, Brescia, also produced a weapon, this time an all-steel gun (with the exception of a wooden pistol-grip) with a folding stock. Unusually for its time, the FNAB *Modello* 1943 was manufactured by traditional methods – that is, by forging and machining – and was operated by a considerably more complicated than necessary delayed blowback action using a two-piece bolt and integral retarder/accelerator. It was only ever produced in small numbers.

We have already remarked on the rather surprising tardiness of the Japanese in developing a sub-machine-gun of their own. It was, in fact, 1940 before a native design appeared, and then it was a well-made but less-than-successful anachronism, really more of a machine carbine than a machine pistol, chambered for the under-powered 8mm Taisho pistol round. The Type 100 sub-machine-gun (100 *Shiki Kikantanju*) was manufactured in two variants, some with full-length wooden furniture and others with folding metal butts. An improved model was produced in 1944, simplified to the extreme and very poorly finished. It is unlikely that more than 25,000 of all types were ever produced.

Sub-machine-gun designs were not the only ones subjected to drastic wartime cost-cutting exercises, of course, even if they were the most widely affected. The bigger light and medium machine-guns, too, were scrutinized to determine where savings in both time and materials could be made, but in most cases, little or no action was taken; the single and by far the most significant exception was the German MG42.

While its predecessor, the MG34, was unarguably an excellent weapon, both in terms of its quality and its performance, it was, also unarguably, a product of its time, and that meant that practically speaking, it was both over-specified and over-engineered. More critically, it was also over-complicated, and that was its crucial failing. As early as 1935 the German authorities had begun to doubt its ultimate serviceability (or, more accurately, the ability of the five factories responsible for assembling it to produce enough of the guns to satisfy demand) and eventually, in February 1937, three companies – Grossfuss of Doblen, Rheinmetall-Borsig of Sommerda and Stubgen of Erfurt – were asked for proposals for a new gun to replace it, specifying that accessories from the MG34 must be interchangeable, an aim which was imperfectly achieved, largely because of the different method of changing barrels which was eventually adopted.

The least likely of them, the Paul Kurt Johannes Grossfuss Metall- und Lackierwarenfabrik, which had no previous experience of weapons manufacture at all (the company's main product line was sheet-metal lanterns), submitted a demonstration model, which consisted of only two receiver side-walls and a novel breech-locking mechanism – which can be described as the rotating bolt-head and locking cams of the MG34 redesigned to operate on a flat plane – on 26 October 1937, and a working example in April 1938. Its barrel-changing method was unacceptable, as was its receiver construction, but its roller-locked breech mechanism (reportedly the work of one Dr Ing. Gruner, who had no more experience of weapons design than the company for which he worked) was clearly an inspired piece of design, both simple and relatively insensitive to dirt and dust, and as a result the proposals of the other two would-be manufacturers were eliminated then and there, and work on the MG39/41, as it was soon to be designated, went ahead at full speed. By late 1941, large-scale field trials were under way with around 1,500 of the new guns, and after favourable reports all round it was adopted as the MG42 early the following year. It first saw action in North Africa in May 1942.

We cannot be sure of the full extent of wartime production – many of the records pertaining to it were destroyed – but a total of around 400,000 units seems to be a fair approximation. Component parts of the gun were made in factories all over the Reich, final assembly being carried out in a number of locations including the Maget and Mauser-Werke plants in Berlin and by Steyr-Daimler-Puch, as well as by Grossfuss. It was to become, in the words of one expert, 'one of the greatest of the great weapons of the Second World War [and] proved its effectiveness alike in the burning sands of Africa and the frozen steppes of Russia'.

Long after the war was over, a fragment of one of the MG42's erstwhile manufacturers, Rheinmetall, put a slightly modified version of the gun, called first the MG42/58 and /59 and later the MG1, into production, in 7.62mm NATO calibre, and subsequently improved it further. The MG3, as it was by then known, became the German Army's standard general-purpose machine-gun, and perhaps a score of other nations also adopted either it or variants of the MG1, at least five obtaining licences for local manufacture. Elements of its design – particularly the way in which it handles ammunition feeding – found their way into the other two most widely distributed general-purpose machine-guns produced in the West, both of which we will examine in some detail later: the gas-operated Belgian FN, and the American M60, also gas-operated, which uses in addition the actuation method of another German design accepted for service in 1942, the FG42 assault rifle.

At roughly the same time that first deliveries of the new general-purpose gun were reaching the front-line troops, Kreighoff at Suhl and IC Wagner at Mulhausen were commencing production of this remarkable Louis Stange-designed hybrid weapon for the Luftwaffe's parachute troops. Designed as a lightweight assault rifle with a high cyclic rate of fire, the FG42 seemed to many to have achieved the impossible, in that it was a controllable selective-fire weapon which used full-power ammunition, in this case the 7.92mm × 57 *Gewehr Patrone* 98 round (though Stange himself is said to have wanted to employ the lighter 'Kurz' round instead). Magazine-fed, gas-operated from an open breech on automatic (and from a closed breech, for improved accuracy, on single-shot), the new rifle was immediately acclaimed by the airborne forces who were issued with it but it suffered from one major fault: it was expensive and time-consuming to manufacture. Less than 7,000 were ever produced, all told, and final, essential, development work was never carried out. None the less, the FG42 can claim to be the spiritual forerunner of all the assault rifles now in service all over the world.

The Schmeisser-designed MP43/44, an assault rifle which did use the shorter, lower-powered 7.92mm 'Kurz' round, found more favour, even though it was rather more conventional than the FG42, simply because it could be produced far more easily. Some of the later versions of the MP44 were produced in *vorsatz* form, with a curved barrel and mirror sights. Often billed as 'the gun which shoots round corners', no really credible reason for the development of the MPV44 has ever been unearthed, though one theory advanced suggests that it was for use from armoured vehicles to shoot attacking infantry who could not be reached by a conventionally aimed weapon because they were too close to the vehicle. It came in three versions, capable of turning the round it fired through 30, 40 or 90 degrees; only the first version, of which some 10,000 were said to have been ordered in 1944, was properly developed.

Of the other major powers, only the Soviet Union made any serious attempt to update its arsenal of medium machine-guns during the Second World War. The Red Army soldiered on with the PM1910 Maxim until then, despite its shortcomings in a more flexible tactical environment, the usually reliable Degtyarev having failed to meet the specification for a replacement with his Model DS of 1939. Goryunov took over the task in 1942, by which time the need for a new, easier-to-manufacture gun was becoming desperate. He used some of the elements of the unsuccessful DS, but completely redesigned the locking mechanism, using a tilting breech-block similar to that used in the vz26 and the Bren gun, but now turned on its side and locking into the receiver sidewall. Like the Bren (and the Vickers, of course), the SG43 (*Stankovyi Goryunova obr.* 1943) used rimmed ammunition (in this case, the old 7.62mm long cartridge) and this inevitably meant that the reciprocating action had to work on a long stroke, withdrawing the round from the belt backwards before feeding it into the chamber. This made for complications in the action but, nevertheless, the resulting gun proved to be reliable. It never entirely replaced the PM1910, which stayed in production right to the war's end, but went on to enjoy an extended life, remaining in front-line service with the Soviet Army and with its client states until the 1980s. Versions for mounting in tanks and soft-skinned vehicles were also produced. Like the heavy 12.7mm DShK, infantry versions of the SG43 were frequently mounted on light wheeled carriages very similar in general structure to the original which Sokolov designed for the Russian Maxims before the Great War.

The Red Army also took steps to improve the performance of the Degtyarev-designed DP, solving the problem of the recoil spring losing its temper by moving it out of the gas cylinder into a distinctive cylindrical housing at the rear of the receiver. Further modifications, including an improved barrel-changing mechanism and a heavier barrel, were not completed until after the war was over; they turned the gun into the belt-fed RP46, capable of sustained fire, though effectively it still qualifies as a light machine-gun by virtue of the fact that the feed mechanism was easily removable (in the field) and replaced with the flat pan magazine from the earlier gun.

The USSR's chief allies in the Great Patriotic War made no real effort to replace the ubiquitous Vickers, Bren and Browning guns with which their armies, navies and air forces were armed, and even fairly unremarkable development programmes were shelved in favour of increasing the rates of production of existing models, a state of affairs which had then to be addressed urgently after the war's end, when both Britain and the United States found their global roles changed beyond all recognition.

Chapter Fourteen

The machine-gun in the air and afloat

THERE ARE ENORMOUS and very obvious differences between a state-of-the-art fighter aircraft of 1918 and its counterpart in 1939; those two decades saw great strides made in the development of both airframes and engines. The new breed of aircraft were faster, of course, but were also capable of carrying greater loads, not least among which – for fighter aircraft, at least – was a battery of up to eight machine-guns, together with significantly increased supplies of ammunition. The guns themselves altered little in the intervening period, the most significant change being the disappearance of magazine feeds and the increasing predominance of larger calibres, reflecting the new realities of aerial combat at higher speeds and greater ranges. The problems of handling the guns, which had necessitated them being mounted within the pilot's reach (and hence, having perforce to fire through the arc of the propeller) were solved by improved reliability, and the use of metal for the aircraft's structural members permitted their migration out into the wings, where there was considerably more space for them.

Slowly but surely, Vickers guns began to disappear, even from British aircraft, to be replaced by the M2 Browning, the

American gun being preferred for its higher rate of fire as well as for its somewhat slimmer profile. It is perhaps significant that by 1938 fixed Vickers guns had been entirely superseded, even in the now much-enlarged company's own aircraft; the most successful of them all, the Spitfire (manufactured by the Supermarine Division of Vickers-Armstrong) had quad .303-inch M2 Brownings in each wing in the Mark I form, as did its partner in battle, the Hawker Hurricane. Later variants of both these aircraft lost four machine-guns and gained a pair of Hispano-Suiza 20mm cannon in their stead.

Ironically, the one nation which did continue to employ fixed Vickers guns in the air was soon to become an enemy: Japan. The Japanese Army and Navy Air Forces had acquired almost 2,000 Vickers Class 'E' guns up to 1937, and then began domestic manufacture as the Type 89 (for the Army) at the Kokura Arsenal and Type 97 (for the Navy) at the Yokosuka Naval Arsenal and at KK Nippon Seikosho (Japan Steelworks), in which Vickers had a large shareholding right up until the end of 1941. (The inconsistency in designation is common to Japanese weapons manufacture, and sometimes leads to considerable confusion.) The Type 97 was subsequently fitted into the most famous of the early Japanese warplanes, the Mitsubishi Zero, and was also employed in a remotely controlled flexible mount as a rear gun in some bomber aircraft. The Japanese Navy also adopted the gas-operated Class 'F' Vickers, which used Lewis-type magazines, and the .5-inch Class 'B' and Class 'D' in small quantities, as light AA guns aboard ship; there was no domestic production of these guns. As Dolf Goldsmith notes in his comprehensive history of the Vickers guns, *The Grand Old Lady of No Man's Land*: 'It does seem ironic that after so much work was done by Vickers on air service guns for Britain, the one country which benefited most from all this effort was Japan'.

Even before the start of the Second World War, it had become clear that the higher speeds aircraft could achieve drastically reduced the time available for an interception, and fighter pilots began to clamour for more powerful guns capable of destroying the enemy at increased range with fewer rounds. The arms manufacturers' first response was simply to up the calibre of the guns from around .3-inch to .5-inch but even this proved insufficient, and the next step was to redesign the weapons entirely, increasing the calibre to 20mm and beyond while decreasing the rate of fire somewhat, typically to around 450 rounds per minute instead of the by-then common 1,000 r.p.m. and upwards, both in the interests of economy of ammunition and to spare the airframe of the firing aircraft some of the battering it would inevitably receive from the guns' recoil. The intro- duction of the cannon, as the heavier automatic weapons came to be called, into aircraft spelt the demise of the machine-gun proper's brief dominance of aerial combat, although .50-calibre Brownings remained important with the US air forces in particular for a number of years. The cannon itself enjoyed an even briefer period of currency, being overtaken as the primary air-to-air weapon by the guided missile before the 1950s were out. Though the airborne gun, in various forms, was eventually to come back into vogue, as we shall see, it was to be in a very different role – and in a very different form.

Flexibly mounted machine-guns had virtually disap- peared from interceptor aircraft by 1939, but they were still to be found in the bigger, slower bombers. Indeed, until the development and introduction of long-range escort fighters, they were the bombers' only means of defence, and a poor enough one they were at that. The RAF fitted its heavy bomber aircraft with six, eight or even ten .303-calibre Brownings, mounted in pairs (quads in the tail) in power-operated turrets. A few magazine-fed Vickers K guns were to be found in RAF aircraft, too – usually where space was very limited, and there was no room for boxes of belted ammunition. The USAAF fitted even more defensive guns to its B–17 Fortresses and B–24 Liberators – sometimes as many as fourteen – and in the heavier .50-inch calibre, too. The much smaller, lighter bomber aircraft the German Luftwaffe operated were much more lightly armed, too, though later versions carried one or more 20mm cannon to supplement their 7.9mm MG17 and 13mm MG131 machine-guns. These same guns equipped the Messerschmitt and Focke-Wulf fighters of the early part of the period. Both were designed from the outset to be synchronizable with the propeller's revolutions, the heavier MG131 employing electric rather than percussion firing in order to improve the efficiency of the process. This firing method was adopted for all subsequent German machine-guns developed for aircraft mounting.

Later models of German interceptor aircraft, like their British and American counterparts, swapped some or all of their lighter machine-guns for 20mm guns, in this case the Mauser-manufactured MG151/20, which Rheinmetall-Borsig later tried unsuccessfully to supersede with the MG102, while right at the war's end the last variants of both the Bf109 and the Fw190 acquired 30mm *Maschinenkanone*, firstly the MK101/103 and latterly the much more advanced MK108, which had a true cyclic rate of over 500 r.p.m. and weighed only 59kg (130 pounds). Rheinmetall-Borsig also developed 37mm and 55mm cannon for aircraft mounting; the former was operational by 1941 – a late model of the Stuka, the

Ju87G–1, carried a pair in under-wing pods – but the bigger calibre gun never got past the prototype stage, though three different versions were built. A 5cm cannon, developed from a tank main gun, the KwK39, was used experimentally against American heavy bomber formations, while the 7.5cm Pak40 anti-tank gun (strictly speaking not a machine-gun at all, since it fired in semi-automatic mode only) was fitted to small numbers of Henschel Hs129s in place of the more common MK101 and used on the Eastern Front in 1945.

The fighter aircraft operated by the other two main combatant powers – Japan and the Soviet Union – followed a very similar development path over a basically similar time-scale, and the last generation of French interceptors produced before the country was overrun in 1940 looked set to follow the same pattern too. Only the Italian manufacturers – Caproni, FIAT and Macchi chief among them – were content to arm their aircraft more lightly than was the norm for the early years of the war: the Macchi MC202 *Folgore*, for example, which was comparable in every other way with a Messerschmitt Bf109E, say, or a Spitfire Mk II, had but two rifle-calibre machine-guns, though its successor, the MC205 Veltro, which went into service at the very end of 1942, did acquire two 20mm cannon to go along with them.

The most heavily armed aircraft for their size were the ground-attack fighter-bombers and the night fighters which came into their own in the last two years of the war. Both German and Allied night fighters were armed with literally as many fixed, forward-facing machine-guns and cannon as they could comfortably carry ammunition for: four 20mm cannon and six machine-guns in the case of the Bristol Beaufighter; six 20mm cannon and two machine-guns in the Junkers Ju88G–7; four 30mm cannon in the jet-propelled Messerschmitt Me262B–1.

Later ground-attack aircraft were even more heavily armed. Aircraft such as the Douglas A–26 Invader were routinely armed with up to a dozen guns, and some later models of the B–25 Mitchell had fourteen or sixteen machine-guns and a 75mm cannon, as well as carrying a ton and a half of bombs and underwing rocket-racks. Close-support aircraft were frequently used in the anti-shipping role, too, both in the European and Pacific theatres. This account, from the biography of an Australian newsreel cameraman, Damien Parer, describes a combined attack on a Japanese convoy carrying reinforcements and supplies from Rabaul to Lae and Salamaua, carried out by Australian and American aircraft in early March, 1943. Parer was aboard a Beaufighter of 30 Squadron:

The Beaufighters led the way. Behind them throbbed the B-25s, the Fortresses and the A-20s, while the Lightnings, high up at twelve thousand feet, weaved to and fro to keep the slower pace of the bomber armada.

The ships were spread out over fifteen miles. The decks of the transports were crowded with troops. There were four destroyers in line-astern to the south, and three warships leading, with two cruisers way out in front.

Flames suddenly spat from the warships as their guns opened up. The air filled with the smoke-puffs of bursting ack-ack shells to be followed, as the planes roared in closer, by the streaming fiery lines of the tracer. A dozen Zeros dived out of the clouds, bent on putting the leading planes off their runs. Lightnings pounced on them. There was cannon and machine-gun fire everywhere. Below, the Japanese destroyers swung round to meet the attack coming in from the south. This left the transports wide open. Swinging abruptly to starboard and knocking Parer off his feet, Uren [the Beaufighter pilot] avoided the warships and led his flight into the attack.

Parer scrambled back to his feet. . . . All he could see was the horizon streaking past the plane's nose, then a lot of water. Uren was coming down to mast level for his first strafing run. Parer was conscious of tracer from the destroyer whipping by, and shell bursts in the air, then there was the cargo ship in the sights. . . . And then there was a terrible stammering noise and a shock that jarred his feet; Uren had opened fire. Through his viewfinder, Parer followed the tracer down to the ship, saw orange and yellow flashes where the shells hit, then his stomach vaulted and his knees collapsed as Uren pulled back on the stick.

They made two more runs, on ships from which great billowing clouds of black smoke poured up into the sky [and then] Uren was diving low, on a burning transport. Parer saw soldiers jumping from her decks into the sea. A destroyer, steaming to her aid, crashed into her side. . . .

On his next run, on a badly listing transport, Uren had to run the gauntlet of ack-ack fire from a Japanese destroyer. There was a crash and an explosion. The men in the plane thought it had been hit; they waited tensely, but the Beaufighter held height. 'She seems okay,' said Uren, and everybody breathed easier. Turning to attack the next ship, he made a steep strafing run right through the curtain of tracer coming up from the ship's guns. Filming the run, Parer watched through the viewfinder [as] a Japanese gun-crew [was] swept from the deck by the blast of Uren's cannons. Then, out of ammunition after an action which had lasted barely thirty minutes, they turned for Port Moresby for a hasty lunch and to take on more. . . .[1]

But aircraft did not have it all their own way, by any means, when attacking surface targets, for the same up-grading in both the numbers and dimensions of defensive armament as happened in the air also took place at sea; even a big ship presents a relatively small target, and by the later days of the war was likely to be able to put up a very dense defensive barrage indeed.

In British coastal waters even the smallest merchant ships were armed to some degree against air attack, usually with light machine-guns left over from 1918. The Lewis gun was a firm favourite, but almost anything was better than nothing, and stocks of redundant (and obsolete) American Marlins also found their way on to British merchantmen. Small warships also relied on LMGs for anti-aircraft defence orig-inally, though they eventually received much more potent Oerlikon 20mm cannon and 40mm Bofors. Ships specifically tasked with air defence often had these in huge quantities There were also updated versions of the old Maxim pom-pom, now manufactured by Vickers in 40mm calibre and three chamberings, the most popular being for the so-called 2-pounder shell. Mounted in singles, pairs, fours or eights, the pom-pom finally found an important role to play, some sixty and more years after Maxim first unveiled it, as a significant component of the short-range defensive arma-ment of Royal Navy warships of all types, from battleships and aircraft-carriers down to lowly harbour defence launches, in which a single pom-pom often formed the main arma-ment. Full production records for the 2-pounder pom pom during the war have not been located, but during the period up to the end of 1943 Vickers supplied 3,375 Mark VIII guns.

The biggest aircraft carrier of the Second World War, the 72,000-ton Japanese *Shinano*, carried no less than 145 25mm cannon as well as 16 dual-purpose 5-inch guns in eight twin mounts. The USN's 60,000-ton *Midway* Class, which were commissioned just too late to see action, carried 18 5-inch DP guns, 84 40mms and 68 20mms.

At the other end of the scale from these sea-going airfields were the fast attack craft. They only ever played a very small part in any navy's offensive operations during the war, but proved able to punch far above their weight, usually by means of their torpedoes, but also by combining their superior speed with the firepower of automatic weapons. The best known of them were probably the German *Schnellbooten* (called E-Boats by the British) and the American Elco and Higgins Motor Torpedo Boats. These later lost their torpedo tubes as the war progressed, and gained more (and more powerful) guns instead.

By 1945, the armament configuration for 80-foot Elco boats operating in the Pacific included four .50-inch machine-guns, four 20mm cannon in a powered quad-mount and more pintle-mounted singles; a 37mm anti-tank gun or two, or single or twin 40mm Bofors; and twin eight-barrelled, spin-stabilised 5-inch rocket launchers, as well as either four 22.5-inch torpedoes in roll-off racks or depth-charge launchers. They were capable of 40 knots (80 k.p.h.) when new, which theoretically, at least, made them difficult to hit with any gun bigger than those they themselves carried. The British Fairmile D boats of the same period, while they were somewhat slower, were even more heavily armed, having a pair of 6-pounder quick-firing guns in addition to a similar number and mix of automatic weapons, while the German T Class fleet torpedo boats of the early years of the war carried up to a dozen 20mm cannon, four 37mm cannon as well as four 105mm QF guns, though by most criteria these would be reckoned ships, rather than boats. Like the contemporary fighter aircraft, these heavily armed motor gunboats, too, were to be a short-lived phenomenon, their gun armament eventually giving way to much more potent surface-to-surface and surface-to-air guided missiles.

Chapter Fifteen

Through Korea to Vietnam

THERE WERE CONSIDERABLE numbers of new automatic weapons under development at the end of the Second World War – some of them virtually ready to go into production – which never saw the light of day thereafter, but that does not mean that weapons production came to a stop with the end of hostilities, or even that it slowed down appreciably. Save for Germany and Austria, occupied and controlled by the victorious allies and much of what was left of their industrial base plundered for reparations, virtually every European nation continued to produce new weapons, particularly sub-machine-guns, at an astonishing rate.

The one major revision of the British infantryman's armoury, for example, in the decade after 1945, was to see the Sten slowly give way to the Machine Carbine, 9mm Sterling, L2A1, as it was known. This was an improved version of an earlier Sterling Arms Company design, the Patchett machine carbine, which had seen limited service at the very end of the war. Despite its no-frills appearance, the Sterling was actually rather better made than many of its contemporaries, with a higher proportion of machined parts, and was to prove outstandingly reliable, particularly in adverse conditions, thanks largely to a novel feature of the bolt: ribs were machined into it to clear away any debris which might find its way into the receiver before it could do any damage. A silenced version, the L34A1, was produced to replace the silenced Stens, and for the first time a police version, which operated in semi-automatic mode only, was also made available. Like the Sten, the Sterling's magazine was side-mounted, but unlike its predecessor, its ammunition feed system was well thought out and dependable. Unloaded it weighed just 2.7kg (six pounds), and was physically quite small and unobtrusive with its butt folded forward at a pivot located behind the pistol grip. The new SMG came into service with the British Army in 1953 and had completely replaced the Sten by the early 1960s; it was exported in large numbers.

Even though the sub-machine-gun has largely disappeared from the standard military inventory, having been replaced by the assault rifle, it soon found a new role in the unconventional terrorist wars which became a significant part of day-to-day life in many parts of the world during the last quarter of the twentieth century and at the same time went back to something resembling its roots in the United States of the twenties, as a tool of violent criminals. There was to be considerable cross-over between those two user-groups, with 'freedom fighters' turning to crime in order to finance their operations and so-called organized crime adopting the methods of terrorism.

Be that as it may, during the two decades after the end of the war, a rash of new sub-machine-guns appeared on the market, some of them clearly intended for military use, some equally clearly not. Among the Sterling's important contemporaries were an updated version of the ingenious Australian Owen, the F1, which retained the vertically mounted magazine and many other features of the wartime expedient gun and proved itself to be rugged and reliable in Vietnam and elsewhere; two Belgian guns (neither of them, for once, from FN), one of which, the Vigneron M2, was good enough to be accepted by the Belgian Army; four basically similar designs from Czechoslovakia, including the pioneering Samopal 23; a rather odd Danish design from DASI which unfolded into two halves around pins at the rear of the receiver and the base of the pistol grip by the simple expedient of unscrewing the barrel retaining nut; a Finnish weapon derived from a wartime copy of the Soviet PPS43; two French guns, one of them from Hotchkiss, the other the straightforward, conventional MAT 49, with its emphasis on safety interlocks, which was to arm the French Army through the disastrous Indo-Chinese and Algerian Wars; an entire range of guns from Beretta in Italy, based on the extraordinarily long-lived *Modello* 38 (itself derived, we may recall, from a 1918 design), some with folding metal stocks and some with quite handsome wooden furniture, which sold steadily to smaller nations with no arms manufacturing capability of their own; a rather rudimentary design from Carl Gustav in Sweden, the *Kulspruta* Pistol M/45; and no less than three guns from Switzerland. There was also the first offering from American designer Gordon Ingram, too: the M6. This was the only gun in this rather long list not exclusively chambered for the 9mm Parabellum round: it was also available in .45-inch ACP. American prejudices die hard. In fact, the M6 pays very clear homage to the Thompson, with its carved vertical fore grip and ribbed barrel, though the similarity ends right there. Germany and Austria are, of course, notable by their absence, though that was not to continue for long: you can't keep a good arms manufacturer down in a seller's market, as Heckler & Koch, Steyr and Walther would soon demonstrate.

All these weapons came from more-or-less established armaments houses, and most sold in large enough quantities to justify the expenditure incurred in putting them into production, but they were joined by a gun from a completely new source, and one which was to eclipse them all: the Uzi from the fledgling state of Israel. Uziel Gal was an ex-freedom fighter (the British called him a terrorist, and had jailed him for his activities) who had become a major in the Israeli Army when he put his mind to designing a machine pistol with as long a barrel as possible in a short overall length, an aim he achieved in much the same way as the British had with the Welgun, by mounting the main spring around the barrel. He also moved the gun's centre of balance forward by taking the main mass of the bolt forward of the breech; this he achieved by cutting away the bolt severely, so that it telescoped over the rear of the barrel. As well as shortening the weapon overall, this innovation allowed the magazine to be mounted within the pistol grip, where it was simple to find without looking or in the dark, on the principle that hand unerringly finds hand. The overall result was a well-balanced gun, easy to fire one-handed if necessary. Like the French MAT 49 it had a grip safety which prevented accidental discharge if the weapon was dropped – something to which the Sten and the American M3, among others, were very prone. While the gun was not an instant success outside Israel when it came on to the market in 1950, it soon earned a reputation as an accurate, reliable weapon in countless skirmishes and in war, and was eventually adopted by a score of countries for use by their armed services and in more clandestine applications. FN in Belgium acquired a licence, were the first to put it into production, and later manufactured it in parallel with Israeli Metal Industries.

A miniaturised version, the short-barrelled Mini-Uzi,

24cm (under 9.5in) long overall and weighing just 1.7kg (3.8 pounds) empty, but otherwise the equal of its big brother, came along in 1984 and earned an instant place for itself in popular mythology alongside the other sub-miniature third-generation weapons: the sub-calibre Czech Skorpion, the Ingram MAC–10 and the Steyr MPi–69, as well as the HK MP–5 and the Ruger MP–9, both of which were rather more sophisticated designs, firing from a closed bolt.

Save for the hollow bolt pioneered by the Czechs in the Samopal 23 (copied in this respect by the Uzi) and employed in all the third-generation sub-machine-guns, there was nothing basically new in this plethora of individual weapons. That so many should have appeared – and, clearly, been sold – is something of a phenomenon in itself, for there was certainly no shortage of sub-machine-guns, or heavier weapons, left over from the Second World War, and it is not as if new developments had rendered them obsolete or ammunition for them was hard to come by.

Not too surprisingly, the situation for medium and heavy machine-guns was rather more clear-cut during the late 1940s and '50s, if only because the weapons in question were more substantial and very much more expensive, both to produce and buy and to operate, though there was so much surplus ammunition on the market that that problem was a less significant factor then than at other times. The weapons which had served the victorious allies through the war (and which were only slightly modified, if at all, from those which had seen them safely through) continued to defy moves to supplant or even improve them, both for economic reasons and because they had been war-winningly effective. There was a very strong feeling of 'if it isn't broken, don't fix it' prevalent during the immediate postwar decade, though ultimately, everyone concerned had finally to admit that the

Vickers and the Browning actions were perhaps getting just a little long in the tooth, and that the improvements German designers had made during the 1930s did, after all, have merit and should be considered.

The difference between the types of ammunition the western allies had used during both the world wars had always created problems, and the establishment of the North Atlantic Treaty Organisation post-Second World War was clearly an appropriate reason to address that. Inevitably, the .303-inch and .30-inch calibres both disappeared in the re-shuffle, as did the German 7.92mm and, belatedly, the French 7.5mm, and in their place the NATO member states settled on a commercial round manufactured by Winchester in 7.62mm/.308-inch calibre, with a 51mm-long cartridge case, as a replacement.

The change-over was more traumatic for the British than for their allies across the ocean, since their infantry was still using a bolt-action rifle, together with an obsolescent fully-rimmed cartridge. This, as we have seen, was far from ideal for belt-fed applications since it had to be extracted back-wards from the carrier before it could be fed into the chamber and consequently required the action of any gun utilizing it to make a reciprocating stroke of at least twice the total length of the entire round, that is, over 15cm (6in) in the case of Mark VII and Mark VIII .303-inch ammunition. In the event, the Bren (having been designed with a rimless round in mind) proved easily convertible to the new standard, and the problems of designing and proving a new rifle were solved by buying a successful design from Belgium, the *Fusil Automatic Léger* and modifying it slightly to become the L1A1 Self-Loading Rifle (SLR). In this, Britain was not alone: something of the order of forty countries adopted the FN FAL for their armed services. It was – and remains – an excellent weapon. The version

British servicemen used fired single shots only, but others were capable of fully automatic fire, even though, being light, their muzzles tended to climb alarmingly after only a very few rounds had been expended. A version with a heavier barrel and a bipod was also available, for occasional use as an LMG, a modification many of its competitors also underwent but never with any real success, the assault rifle and the light machine-gun being two quite different types of weapon in reality, their apparent similarities notwithstanding.

This still left unaddressed the problem of introducing a new sustained-fire weapon to replace the Vickers guns, and in this, too, the British adopted a design produced in the Herstal-lez-Liège factory of Fabrique National, which, despite twice having been the victim of enemy occupation, had never looked back since first arriving at an understanding with John Browning in 1900. In the light of that long involvement with Browning, it comes as no surprise to learn that the basic actuation of the MAG (*Mitrailleuse d'Appui Général*, sometimes rendered as *Mitrailleur à Gaz*) which the British were to adopt as the L7 General-Purpose Machine-Gun in 1957 was similar to that of the BAR Browning had devised during the First World War.

FN inverted the bolt this time around and placed the locking shoulder in the floor of the receiver, in order to locate a roller on what was now the upper surface and use it to drive the belt advance mechanism. They added the ammunition feed path designed for the MG42 and finished up with a gun weighing in at a fraction over 10kg (22 pounds). This was equally at home stripped down in the LMG role; with its butt removed, fitted with a tangential sight and mounted on a tripod for use in indirect/sustained fire mode; or as a vehicle- or helicopter-mounted gun.

The barrel was located in the body of the gun by means

of an interrupted thread, and could be exchanged in a matter of seconds simply by turning the carrying handle through 90 degrees, releasing a catch and lifting the barrel and gas regulator free of the body and cylinder, rather in the manner of the Bren gun. It was not necessary to unload the gun in order to change the barrel; cocking it and making it safe (the safety is a very positive push-through plunger) was sufficient. The gas regulator was adjustable, more gas being progressively fed into the actuating cylinder either to compensate for the build-up of deposits or to regulate the gun's cyclic rate, which was thus variable between 600 and 1,000 rounds per minute in a clean gun. Heavy barrels with partial stellite coatings like that used in the M60 (see below) were tested for use in the sustained-fire role, but rather surprisingly were not adopted because of manufacturing difficulties. There were also enough detailed differences between the GPMGs manufactured by Royal Ordnance, the successors to the Royal Small Arms Factory, and the MAGs made by FN Nouvelle (likewise, the successors to Fabrique National d'Armes de Guerre) to render parts for the two guns non-interchangeable.

There should be no doubt of the stopping power of a modern machine-gun:

> During our skill-at-arms training at Folkestone ... our instructors demonstrated the power of our weapons. They prepared a box containing wood, brick, earth and sand. Then one of them fired at the box with an SLR from a hundred yards. When we looked at the box later, we saw that the round had sliced through the wood like butter, punched through the brick, ploughed through the earth and come to rest only in the sand. When they repeated the demonstration with the GPMG, a burst of fire cut the wood

and brick to shreds. 'Now imagine that's a human body', the instructor said.[1]

In action, the GPMG proved itself to be a deadly and accurate weapon. During the Falklands War, for example, it participated in many of the major engagements. 3 Battalion, The Parachute Regiment (3 Para) landed at San Carlos on 14 May 1982 and set out on foot to 'tab' across East Falkland toward the Argentine defences grouped in the low mountains west of Port Stanley, the capital. There, on 11/12 June, they fought the battle of Mount Longdon. L/Cpl Vincent Bramley was Number One on a General-Purpose Machine-Gun; he participated in the sustained-fire barrage which supported the assault on the Argentinian positions:

'Corporal B, stand by!' the Company Sergeant-Major screamed. The command to follow killed off all the cries and moaning. The weapon broke into a stream of fire at the Argentinian positions, three to five rounds bursting across the summit. The steady rate of fire continued as the CSM aimed across to change direction, using our tracer rounds as indicators. All six guns opened up. Our tracers ripped across the summit to the other end of the mountain, the bullets bouncing and ricocheting in all directions. 'Stop!' screamed the CSM. 'Corporal B, go right three clicks, up fifty mils.'

Bob removed his finger from the trigger and I quickly adjusted the weapon.

'On!' I screamed.

'Fire!'

I followed the CSM's orders and the gun burst into life once more. After about thirty or forty rounds, he screamed again. 'Stop!'

He shouted to all guns in place, 'All adjust to Corporal B's target area.'

Our platoon guns locked on to the targets across the hilltop.

'On, sir,' came every reply.

The CSM then shouted, 'Bramley, you will traverse right. Corporal's T and Cook, traverse left. Stand by, fire.

We all fired together. Tracer rounds could be seen passing left and right as we slowly moved the traversing drums in our respective directions. The flow of bullets parted like hair being combed. The summit came under a deadly stream of fire. Our gun rattled and thudded as the rounds were fed into the top slide. The bullets went to their targets and the empty cases fell below the tripod, the link spilled to the right of the gun and the cordite of the spent cases filled the air around us. The smoke whiffed off the barrels as we let about two hundred rounds pass through them.

'Stop. Everybody drop about sixty mils and go right seven, eight clicks.'

'On!' I shouted.

In the darkness I heard one of the team cry out, 'Stoppage!'

All was quieter for a few seconds, but my ears rang with the sounds of the GPMG. Then, once again, 'Fire!'

The barrel spat out the rounds again, the weapon fired steadily and with a good tempo. The empty cases piled up. . . .

The steady fire of the gun echoed around us. The bursts of fire had warmed the barrel so much that it glowed red-hot in the darkness. The CSM continued to correct our fire after long bursts. Sometimes we would hear him shout, 'Good shooting. Ah, that's got that lot. Right, quickly go

two clicks right, down thirty mils. Good, that's got that lot
– they're running all over the place.'

'Stoppage!' screamed Bob.

'OK, let's change barrels now.'

I cleared the weapon and we moved the barrel without
touching it. The glowing barrel sizzled as I placed it on the
frozen grass. We'd been firing across the hill for about forty
minutes. I can't remember the exact length of time – it could
have been longer. The ammo was going down rapidly. The
CSM screamed at us to get the gun firing again on our last
target. We resumed firing as soon as the gun was cocked.
Bob's finger was giving it max on the trigger, the gun
vibrating almost non-stop. I watched our tracer rounds
bouncing off the rocks about two hundred metres away.

'We've got them,' the CSM shouted.

Suddenly, the air around me seemed to disappear. I
heard a loud 'woosh', followed by a terrific explosion behind
me. The impact shook the ground . . . I lay there completely
stunned for a few seconds. I hadn't the slightest idea what
had happened. The air smelt of damp earth and cordite. I
turned round to face Bob and the platoon commander. We
all looked at each other wide-eyed, shock on our faces.

'But what' – Bob was the first to speak – 'the fuck was
that?'

'I think they fired a rocket, or something,' replied the
PC.

'Corporal B, get ready again!' screamed the CSM. All
three of us turned our heads back to the target.

'Ready, sir.'

The CSM shouted, 'Up fifty mils, go right four clicks and
fire.'

The gun erupted into life again and carried on firing. Its

noise drowned out everything around us but in the brief moments it stopped we could all hear the zipping sounds hitting the rock and ground to our left and front. We knew the enemy was still trying to get us, but we couldn't move. I was glad when the gun was firing; it took my mind off the snipers.

The ammo wasn't ours now, it was Argentinian. Some of the lads were searching empty bunkers now and bringing it to us. The Argies had fired one tracer round, one ball and one armour-piercing bullet in every three rounds they fired. We had had one tracer and four normal (i.e., ball) rounds in every five.

The CSM shouted, 'Stop! Stop!'

Worn out, we rested our heads on the ground. The battle had now been going on for some eleven hours. How long we had lain there firing, I did not know. The CSM came over.

'Well done. A Company are moving through to our left now. We've given them all the help we could give. The rest is up to them. We can't fire any more – it'd get them, it's too close now. It'll be light in an hour or so. Pull the gun back and dismount it.'

'Sir, did we get any?' asked Bob.

'More than enough,' he replied and walked away.

Had we killed? We must have. I felt nothing afterwards – just relaxed. I hadn't seen our target: they had been hidden in the darkness. We hadn't killed at the end of a bayonet, or through a rifle sight. We had killed with a spray of machine-gun bullets. It didn't seem personal. It was as if the enemy hadn't existed at all.[2]

Experts consider the MAG/GPMG to have been the best of the third-generation medium machine-guns, outstripping the German M3 (and the other MG42 derivatives), the Heckler & Koch HK21 (easily), the Swiss SIG 710 and the French AAT 52 and a surprisingly large number of other weapons manufactured all over the world around that time, as well as the much overrated American M60 and the Russian PK (*Pulemyot Kalashnikova*) series. In terms of market penetration (which is probably a good indicator of both its popularity and its efficacy), it was more widely disseminated than even its British predecessor, the Vickers gun, being purchased by some seventy-five national governments. Forty years after its introduction it was still in production in India, Israel, Sweden and the USA, as well as in Belgium and Britain.

To pass from a great gun to one which, in its original form at least, was little better than mediocre, we need look no further than NATO's most powerful member. A great deal of rubbish has been written in praise of the M60 machine-gun, mostly by contrasting it only with the M1919 Browning it replaced in the US Army's inventory, and ignoring its modern peers. It was never the great gun these descriptions alleged it to be and, in its early form, was barely usable in combat. The gun's early defects had little or nothing to do with its basic design, which was a sound adaptation of that first seen in the German FG42 assault rifle, midway through the Second World War, with the addition of the belt advance mechanism from the contemporary MG42; rather, it was the detailed arrangement of the gun's furnishings which were poorly thought out.

That is not to say that the M60 in its original form was flawed through and through; some aspects of the gun – the stellite lining, for example, in the first 15cm (6in) of the barrel (the remainder is chromed), which permits the gun to continue firing without causing lasting damage even when it is glowing red hot – were excellent, and well worth emulating. Stellite – a patented nonferrous amalgam of cobalt, chromium, molybdenum and tungsten, bound together by a polymer – was developed by the Haynes Stellite Corporation, and represented an important step forward in firearms metallurgy. One very rigorous test, which took place at Fort Benning, Georgia, in 1967, saw a standard off-the-shelf M60 fire a 50m belt of ammunition in a single burst; the barrel became red-white hot and each of the last few hundred rounds fired caused showers of sparks to radiate from its outer surface. On later examination, the gun was found to be substantially undamaged.

The inordinate strength and resistance to distortion of the barrel liner was, the gun's critics would say, probably just as well, since changing the barrel of the early M60 was not the sort of task one wanted to undertake in combat. Firstly, there was no barrel handle (the carrying handle, which in any event proved too flimsy for its purpose, was receiver-mounted), which meant that the Number 2 had to grasp the barrel itself, using the asbestos mitten thoughtfully provided (at considerable expense) in the gun's spares kit and almost invariably mislaid, and secondly, the bipod on which the gun rested was integral with the barrel (as was the forward portion of the gas cylinder), so the gun either had to be held up in the air (hardly to be recommended on tactical grounds) while the change-over was accomplished, or laid on the ground, with all the attendant risk that entailed of dirt and debris fouling the ammunition feed mechanism and even the receiver itself. This poor piece of functional design (a result of wishing to get the bipod as far forward as possible, for reasons of stability) was also present in the French AAT 52 and the Russian PM, though overall, that latter gun at least was rated as easier to use and more reliable than the M60 by American infantrymen who test-fired it.

The M60 had a long development history, the first steps toward replacing the ageing Browning M1919 having been taken in 1944, when engineers at the Springfield Armoury mated the ammunition feed system of the MG42 with the action of the FG42 to produce an experimental gun known eventually as the T44, retaining the 7.92mm × 57 chambering of the originals. However, the new gun was to have no user-adjustable means of regulating gas flow – an unusual solution to a problem which plagued the designers of gas-operated guns from the outset. The gas passages of such a gun rapidly become fouled with the by-products of combustion, and it is normally necessary to introduce a regulator to compensate, allowing more gas into the actuating cylinder as the system becomes constricted. The FG42 dispensed with this necessity by a form of demand regulation known as the constant pressure system: the gas enters the cylinder through a drilling connecting it with the bore (as usual) but via a second drilling in the long hollow head of the piston within. When sufficient pressure has been built up to overcome inertia (this occurs in a matter of milliseconds, of course, during the interval between the round clearing the bore drilling and leaving the muzzle) the piston is pushed backwards to begin the actuating stroke, the first effect of which is to move the drilling in the piston head out of alignment with the one from the bore into the cylinder, shutting off the gas supply. In theory, such a system is foolproof, but in practice it is not dirt- and dust-proof, and this aspect of the M60 has proved to be extremely sensitive to contamination by foreign bodies.

These (and other) drawbacks aside, the T44 was passed to the Bridge Tool and Die Co for development, a long process which saw many modifications to little real benefit. Eventually, a version known as the T161E3 was produced, chambered for the 7.62mm × 51 NATO cartridge, and it was this gun which became the M60, being authorized for issue in 1959. As if to add insult to injury, the M60 in its basic form cost over four times as much as its rather better contemporary, the MG42/59, when it was finally adopted. It saw action throughout the Vietnam war and, as a result of shortcomings observed in combat, no less than twelve major modifications (including a complete redesign of the gun's front end) were necessary to turn it into a practical infantry weapon, but before the modified gun (known as the M60E1) could be brought into general service, the entire concept of the 7.62mm-calibre infantry machine-gun came under review by the US Army and was rejected, whereupon the M60 was phased out, from 1986, in favour of a switch to 5.56mm calibre and the Squad Automatic Weapon (SAW).

The M60 stayed in service as a tripod-mounted fire-support weapon, and in a number of variants designed for fixed or flexible mounting in vehicles and helicopters. The US Marine Corps, which has always considered its role to be rather different from that of the US Army, did adopt the Echo variant, but in a version developed privately by one of the M60's civilian constructors, Saco Defense: the lightened (by almost 2kg/4.4 pounds) M60E3. Saco also produced a heavy-barrel version of their modified gun, which incorporated all the desirable features of the abandoned M60E1 together with a further set of improvements including provision of a vertical fore grip, notionally to make the gun more manageable as an assault weapon.

In terms of performance in the field, the most significant modification incorporated into the M60E3 rectified a howling design fault in its predecessor. Originally, the M60's foresight was a simple blade, with no protection and no provision for adjustment; thus, the gun had to be re-zeroed at the rear sights whenever the barrel was changed. Naturally enough, few gun teams ever bothered (and it is a safe bet that none did under fire), and accepted the consequent loss of accuracy, even though that effectively invalidated the gun as a long-range fire-support weapon. The M60E3 barrels produced by Saco had foresights adjustable for both windage and elevation, so that all barrels allocated to a particular gun body could be pre-zeroed together with it, eliminating this source of inaccuracy, at least. Needless to say, M60E3 barrels were not interchangeable with those of early-model M60s.

Unsurprisingly, considering its poor overall performance, export customers for the M60 were relatively few in number, and were really restricted to those client states of the US Government who received weaponry at well below its par value, such as South Korea and Taiwan, though Australia also procured small numbers. The Taiwanese, who began manufacturing the gun themselves in 1968 as the Type 57, later switched to a modified FN MAG designated the Type 74, even though they had to pay the market price for it.

Only in absolutely the last resort have the French armed forces ever been equipped with weapons designed or manufactured outside France itself – notable exceptions occurred during the First World War, when Darne manufactured Lewis guns under licence at St Etienne, and the state arsenal at Chatellerault manufactured some thousands of air-cooled Vickers guns, and during the second global conflict, when the Free French Army and Air Force had no resources of their own. With the Second World War over, France soon reverted to her policy of self-sufficiency, and produced, in quick succession, a new sub-machine-gun, the MAT 49; a new self-loading rifle, the MAS 49, using a rather idiosyncratic method of gas operation which dispensed with a conventional piston and cylinder, the gases acting directly on the bolt-face instead, with all the problems that caused in terms of fouling; and three years later the *Arme Automatique Transformable, Modèle '52*. Usually known as the AAT 52, this was a general-purpose machine-gun which, like the M60, drew heavily on German experience, the action this time being derived from the unfinished StG45 self-loading assault rifle Mauser-Werke was developing when the war came to an end, which was chambered for the reduced-power Kurz round. The ammunition handling method was, once again, a modified version of that developed for the MG42.

There have to be doubts as to the applicability of the assault rifle's action at this level. Unusually for a modern general-purpose machine-gun – or even an LMG, come to that – the AAT 52 used a delayed two-stage blowback action which frankly would have been more at home in a weapon using a less powerful cartridge than either the 7.5mm × 54 M1929 for which it was originally chambered or the 7.62mm NATO round for which it was modified in the 1960s, France's partial departure from NATO notwithstanding. Most experts agree that it was operating at the very limits of the safe capability of its action, and it is certainly true that headspace adjustment (the clearance between the bolt-head and the rear face of the chamber) was critical; even when it was correctly adjusted, the AAT 52 tended to split its cartridge cases, resulting in frequent jams. None the less, it was also available with a heavy barrel for use, tripod-mounted, in the sustained-fire role. When the original 7.5mm version was superseded in French service by the new version firing 7.62mm NATO ammunition, it was redesignated the AAT 52/ Mle' NF–1.

Not all assault rifle mechanisms are incapable of translation to a heavier weapon, however. The action M.T. Kalashnikov designed (in 1947, while on convalescent leave from the Red Army), for the series of Soviet assault rifles and sub-machine-guns which bears his name was surely the small-arms success story of the latter part of the twentieth century, not just in terms of global diffusion (though it would certainly win that contest in a walk-over) but also in respect of its wholly appropriate technology. Specified for the reduced-power 7.62mm × 39 M1934 round, the AK (*Avtomat Kalashnikova*), the AKM (*AK Modernizirovanni*) and the AKMS (*AKM Skladyvayushchimsya* 'folding stock') became the standard infantry small arms not just for the armed forces of ex-Soviet Union members and the old Warsaw Pact nations, but for much of the Communist world, including the People's Republic of China, North Korea and Vietnam, as well as the weapons of choice for guerrilla fighters the world over. Strictly speaking, though they did retain the capacity for automatic fire, and were quite comfortable and controllable in that role, the AK and AKM (a lightened, more easily manufactured version) fall outside the scope of this work, though the shortened AKMS, which largely replaced the sub-machine-gun in the old eastern bloc, equally falls within it, such are the vagaries of modern weapons classification. For our purposes, it is the gas-management system and the two-part rotating bolt-action Kalashnikov conceived which are of primary interest, since they were also employed in the RPK (*Ruchnoy Pulemyot Kalashnikova*) light machine-gun and in the general-purpose PK (*Pulemyot Kalashnikova*) which, despite their similarity of names, were actually distinctly different guns.

The Kalashnikov system derives its gas from a tapping towards the muzzle-end of the barrel, just as all gas-actuation systems do, but there was no regulator employed in the fixed-barrel RPK, excess gas being vented through a row of small holes. The gas acts on a piston which is an actual extension of the bolt carrier, pushing it back no more than 8mm (0.3in), during which travel a cam causes the bolt itself to rotate through 35 degrees, releasing the lugs which lock it to the barrel during firing. By that time the gas pressure in the chamber has been reduced to a safe level, and the bolt and carrier begin their rearward travel, a large ejector claw on the bolt head withdrawing the spent cartridge case in the process. The motion is then reversed by the recoil spring, the bolt and carrier pick up a new round on their way forward and chamber it, and as the carrier completes the last 8mm of its travel, the cam pin rotates the bolt and locks it once more. In the RPK, which is fed by an under-slung 30- or 40-round box magazine, the gas cylinder and piston were located above the barrel (as they were on the AK assault rifles), while the situation was reversed in the belt-fed PK series. The other main distinction between the two lay in the ammunition: the RPK, which had many parts interchangeable with the AKs, and accepted AK magazines, was naturally chambered for the short M43 reduced-power 7.62mm round, while the PKs reverted to the long 1891-pattern round of the same calibre. The PK's ammunition feed system was a modified version of that found in the SG43 and its derivatives.

The RPK replaced a not-entirely-successful (though that did not prevent it from being made and issued in huge quantities) Degtyarev design, the RPD (*Ruchnoy Pulemyot Degtyareva*), introduced in 1953 as the squad-level support weapon. The RPD went through five distinct versions, the major modifications made all affecting the piston and gas cylinder. It was belt-fed from a drum clipped below the receiver, and the ammunition feed mechanism therefore had to lift the belt unaided. There is every reason to believe that the short M43 round for which the gun was chambered barely developed enough power to accomplish this, and that it was this deficiency which spurred the many modifications the gun underwent. The RPD was not capable of sustained fire inasmuch as the barrel, like that of the RPK, was not interchangeable; much of a Russian squad machine-gunner's training was geared to ensuring that he fired short bursts.

It is by no means coincidental that much of the engineering design of post-Second World War general-purpose machine-guns has its roots in Germany; had it not been for an almost universal desire to switch over from recoil operation to gas actuation, there is little doubt that anyone would have bothered to design a new gun at all, but would simply have copied and modified the MG42. That is, of course, exactly what Rheinmetall did when the slimmed-down company re-entered the armaments market in the late fifties.

The MG42 never went completely out of use after 1945, for guns recovered from the Wehrmacht and the Waffen-SS were reissued widely (to the re-established German Army, for example, which had to purchase them from other countries), but it did go out of production (in Germany) and worse still, from a would-be manufacturer's point of view, the master drawings of it were lost. The fact that the MG42 went into production in Yugoslavia as the Model 53, soon after the war's end, perhaps gives a clue as to their whereabouts.

In the process of re-creating the drawings from an existing gun, Rheinmetall made a few detailed changes (and added more later) but adhered very strictly to the basic operating procedure. The most important changes concerned the bolt group. Firstly, there was the need to prevent improper field assembly: the original components could be assembled with the bolt head and the bolt housing inverted in relation to one another; the gun would seemingly go together correctly but would not function. A simple change prevented that. The second was the addition of a bolt catch inside the bolt housing to prevent (very uncommon) premature unlocking, about the only operating fault of any magnitude identified in the original design. This improvement had been contemplated as early as 1944, and may have been put into effect; the records in question have been lost. Conversion to 7.62mm NATO chambering apart, the most important new modification – and it was not applied to all variants – allowed the operator to alter the gun's rate of fire by changing the bolt and buffer: the V550 bolt (its weight 550gm = 20ozs) and the Type N buffer produced a fire-rate of between 1,150 and 1,350 rounds per minute, depending on the condition of the gun and the ammunition used, while the V950 (950gm/33.5ozs) bolt and Type R buffer gave a more economical cyclic rate of between 750 and 950 r.p.m.

The remodelled gun went into production as the MG42/ 58, and the new German Army promptly redesignated it MG1. From that time on, it has been variously described as the MG42/59 (by Rheinmetall), and MG2 and then MG3 (by the Bundeswehr), which added sub-designators (-A1, -A2 and so on) as further detailed changes were made. As well as at Rheinmetall's factory in Düsseldorf, production of one or other version was established in Iran, Italy, Pakistan, Spain and Turkey. A very similar gun, itself developed directly from the original MG42, was produced in Switzerland by the Federal Arms Factory at Bern, and adopted by the Swiss Army as the MG51, in 7.5mm × 54 Swiss calibre, while two other Swiss manufacturers, Hispano-Suiza and SIG also produced versions. The latter's MG710, in 7.62mm NATO calibre, was an unsuccessful competitor for the British Army's GPMG contract which went to the FN MAG.

Despite the all-round excellence of the MG1/MG3, elsewhere in Germany three former Mauser employees who styled themselves Heckler & Koch GmbH – which was to become a significant force in the arms industry, later to be acquired by the British Royal Ordnance plc – continued to work on the StG45 design (which also, we may recall, formed the basis of the French AAT 52) in collaboration with designers from the Spanish Government's Centro de Estudios Technicos de Materiales Especiales, commonly known as CETME. The first fruit of this collaboration was to be the Fusil d'Assalto Modello 58, which later evolved into the G3 assault rifle accepted for the Bundeswehr, but neither CETME nor Heckler & Koch were finished with the design yet. In succession, they produced the HK 11, a magazine-fed LMG (essentially, a G3 with an exchangeable barrel) firing the 7.62mm NATO round; the HK 12, a similar LMG chambered for the Soviet 7.62mm short cartridge and the HK 13, which is chambered for the 5.56mm × 45 round which was to become the new *de facto* NATO standard. They also produced belt-fed variants of these guns (the designation has a 2 in place of the original 1, hence HK 21, HK 22 and HK 23) which are supplied with tripods for sustained firing. Experts generally rate these guns as inferior even to the M60.

CETME also experimented with the locking device of an unfinished variant of the original MG42 design (called tentatively the MG45; work on it began as a means off counteracting the MG42's occasional tendency to unlock prematurely, but evolved into a completely new action), and produced an experimental gun known as the Mauser-CETME light machine-gun, in 7.62mm NATO chambering, and the CETME-SPAM (Special Purpose Assault Machine-gun, also known as the AMELI, an acronym of the Spanish for light machine-gun, *ametrallador ligera*), which is chambered for the 5.56mm round.

The adoption of this round for military use, beginning with the appearance in the late fifties of the Armalite AR–15, which was to become the M16, was to have lasting ramifications for the further development of the general-purpose machine-gun. We have already noted how important it is for infantry assault and support weapons to use the same ammunition, and the necessity for that certainly did not diminish with the adoption of a much smaller round; instead, it led, as we shall see, to the development of a new generation of still more flexible GPMGs.

Chapter Sixteen

The return of the Gatling gun

BY THE END of the Second World War news of the imminent demise of the piston-engined fighter aircraft was writ large upon the wall, and it was clear that within a very few years jet-powered aircraft would have taken over the air defence/interdiction role entirely, and boosted combat speeds by up to 50 per cent in the process. To the tactician, this meant just one thing: the period of time spent in combat – already measured in seconds – would inevitably become still shorter, and that led to renewed demands for guns with an increased cyclic rate. The resultant research forced weapons designers to conclude that the conventional reciprocating machine-gun action had reached the peak of its development with the .50-inch Browning AN-M2/AN-M3, with its cyclic rate of about 1,200 rounds per minute.

Now, this was in fact no faster than a manually operated Gatling gun of mid-1880s vintage could achieve, albeit only for limited periods, and that realization caused researchers to re-examine the final stages of Richard Jordan Gatling's work from the last decade of the nineteenth century, just as his manual guns were being eclipsed by Hiram Maxim's automatic weapons, and in particular to reappraise the electrical machine-gun he patented in 1893.

Trials conducted by the US Navy in conjunction with the Crocker-Wheeler Motor Company in 1890 produced excellent results from a Gatling modified only by the addition of an electric motor to drive the barrel-and-cylinder assembly by means of a simple belt and pulley. Over the three years which followed, Gatling himself, using a gun chambered for the new US Army rifle calibre, .30-inch Krag-Jorgenson ammunition, doubled the test gun's rate of fire to 3,000 r.p.m. over short periods, and then added water-cooling to allow that rate to be sustained. Such a rate of fire was unheard-of, but it was also entirely without purpose at that time, and in any event, the manual machine-gun was rapidly losing favour. Even in its most compact form, the Gatling was too heavy and cumbersome to compete with the Maxim. The results of Gatling's work were noted, and then lay largely forgotten.

With the realization that any significant improvement on the performance of existing heavy machine-guns would require a radical re-think in their design, Gatling's work was reappraised, and as the Second World War drew to a close, the US Government commissioned Johnson Automatics, Inc., a small private arms manufacturer set up by a retired Marine Corps colonel, to look into the possibilities of updating Gatling's design. Johnson located a Model 1883 gun in .45-inch chambering in working order, together with a supply of usable ammunition. He repeated Gatling's own work almost step for step, but thanks to the improved performance of electric motors, bettered his results considerably: the modified gun fired 50-round bursts at a cyclic rate calculated to be equal to 5,800 rounds per minute.

As a result of Johnson's work, the US Army awarded a

development contract to the armaments division of the General Electric Corporation in June 1945, and early in the following year Project Vulcan resulted in a prototype gun known as the T45, which varied hardly at all from the operating principle Gatling had established eighty years earlier (the main distinction is in the firing method: Gatling used percussion caps, while the Vulcan employs electric ignition). It was to take a further decade to put the gun, now designated the M61 Vulcan, into production, firstly in 20mm calibre, but it rapidly became the standard by which others were measured (while acquiring its share of imitators) as well as forming the basis for an entire new family of super-fast externally powered machine-guns in everything from 5.56mm to 30mm calibre.

The 20mm M61 Vulcan went into service with the USAF in 1956 in the Lockheed F–104 Starfighter, and later versions are now standard equipment for US aircraft and will remain in service beyond the end of the century. It also won the approval of both the US Army and the US Navy, the Army adopting it as the M168 to form the basis of a towed or vehicle-mounted air defence system and the Navy commissioning GE to build the autonomous Phalanx close-in weapons system around it, to defend ships against missile attack at short range, and also using it in the EX–84 Universal Mount aboard light craft. A lighter, three-barrelled version of the gun, called the M197, was employed by both the US Army and the Marine Corps to arm Cobra attack helicopters and by the Air Force in fixed-wing gunships.

The essence of the M61 Vulcan cannon is its simplicity. In fact, the most complex feature of the entire gun is the way in which up to a hundred rounds every second are presented to its multiple breeches; quite an engineering undertaking in itself. When ammunition is delivered to the gun mount in standard disintegrating-link belts, they pass through a de-linker and into a drum. Individual rounds are then transported from the drum to the gun itself by means of an Archimedes screw. In other applications, 'loose' ammunition is fed directly from a large-capacity drum, once again by means of a helical screw.

With the M61 cannon in series production, development engineers at General Electric began to examine the possibilities of constructing a similar gun in rifle calibre. The US Air Force-funded project got underway in 1960, and by late 1962 a prototype was under test; two years later the GAU–2B Minigun, firing the 7.62mm × 51 NATO round, was adopted. The Miniguns were mounted in SUU–11 pods designed to be slung beneath the wings of aircraft or on the undercarriage of helicopters, but the first combat operations in which they participated saw three of them mounted transversely inside the fuselage of an antiquated C–47 Dakota, firing out through what had originally been the aftermost cabin windows and the cargo door while the pilot executed a tight 'pylon turn' around a ground target below. Widely known as Spooky or Puff the Magic Dragon, from a song popular at the time, the AC–47s soon proved to be effective ground attack aircraft, and the concept was expanded and extended, firstly into Shadow and Stinger and subsequently into Specter, converted C–130 Hercules, initially armed with four Miniguns, two of which were later removed and replaced by a pair of 40mm Bofors or occasionally, in the Pave Aegis version, by one Bofors and a specially adapted M102 105mm howitzer.

The next step General Electric took was to reduce the concept still further, and produce a prototype multi-barrelled externally powered gun in 5.56mm calibre, but this time the US Government proved to be less than enthusiastic. The

Microgun was in fact rather more flexible than its bigger-calibre counterparts, for while they could fire selectively at one, two, three, four or six thousand rounds per minute (a simple matter of controlling the speed of the drive motor) it was infinitely variable between 400 and 10,000 rounds per minute, the higher maximum figure being due to the reduced revolving weight of the much smaller gun. Ammunition for the Microgun was contained in a pair of factory-packed 500-round cassettes, mounted one each side of the gun; as the last round in a cassette was expended, the feed automatically switched over to the full cassette, while the empty was ejected and replaced. The gun was regularly demonstrated to be able to fire 2,500 rounds in a single burst at a rate of 4,000 r.p.m. Though it was tested under the designation XM214, the Microgun was never adopted by the US Armed Services, and the project was later suspended. As one commentator put it, the Microgun 'appears to have been an example of a weapon produced to meet a tactical requirement that has yet to emerge', and given the practical limitations on its role imposed by its ammunition, that is scarcely surprising.

There was still a gap to be filled, however – between the 7.62mm Minigun and the 20mm rotary cannon – and GE promptly stepped into it with a rotary multi-barrel gun firing the tried-and-tested 12.7mm/.50-inch round. The original intention was to use 12.7mm calibre ammunition as a test-bed, and to produce a gun chambered for a new 10mm round which was to be developed simultaneously, but in the event, the planned new calibre was abandoned, and instead, development of the GECAL 50, as the gun came to be called, went ahead in 12.7mm form.

The first prototype, the GAU–6, was a six-barrelled gun, limited to a cyclic rate of 4,500 by the strength of the individual links in its ammunition belt. Production-model

GECAL 50s later appeared in two forms: a six-barrelled gun firing up to 8,000 rounds per minute and a lighter, three-barrelled gun capable of half that. Mounts for both helicopters and light vehicles were produced as interest developed in a gun which combined relatively low weight and the proven hitting-power of the .50-inch round. There was an even bigger variant, too – the GAU–8A 30mm cannon which formed the basis of the A–10 Thunderbolt ground-attack aircraft. The GAU–8A was a remarkable gun in many ways, and soon passed into the mythology out-of-the-ordinary weapons create for themselves, but there was nothing artificial about its performance. Firing rounds of solid shot composed of tungsten and depleted uranium, which destroyed armoured vehicles by kinetic energy alone, at a cyclic rate of 4,200 rounds per minute, the gun actually generated more thrust than the A–10's main engines – and it acted in the opposite direction!

Richard Gatling's rotating-barrel-and-chamber method was not the only one examined in the course of trying to improve further the performance of the heavy machine-gun. A relative newcomer to the world of armaments manufacture, the Hughes Tool Company, set out in 1970 to develop a 7.62mm machine-gun with the same overall dimensions as the 'conventional' (though very complicated) recoil-operated M79/M219 gun adopted in 1960 as the co-axial gun for the M60 main battle tank. A prototype called the Externally Powered Armored Vehicle Machine Gun (thankfully reduced immediately to the rather handier EPAM) was produced, its action driven and regulated by a gearbox and a series of cams. It worked well enough on test, but was very clearly over-complicated for a weapon which would inevitably have to be serviced in the field, and a comprehensive rethink produced a far simpler action driven by an industrial roller chain such as those used to drive most motorcycles.

An endless loop of chain provides both the motive power for the gun and times its operation. It passes over four sprockets arranged in a rectangular pattern, one of which drives it and another of which takes off power to supply the ammunition feed system; the other two are idlers, there to provide the necessary geometry and maintain tension. One link of the chain, known as the master link, contains a cam follower, which is permanently engaged with a slide acting in a transverse slot in the lower surface of the bolt carrier, which carries the bolt itself (and the integral extractor) backwards and forwards as the chain passes around its sprockets. The resulting gun is much less complex than the rotary cannon, and considerably smaller and lighter (its rate of fire does not approach theirs, but it was never meant to), but shares with them the inherent reliability of an externally powered gun – thus the very failing which Maxim used to justify the ascendancy of the automatic, self-powered gun over its manual rivals eventually turned into an asset after all.

By 1972 Hughes Tool was producing a Chain Gun (the term was registered as a trade mark) in 30mm calibre which was adopted by the American Army as the M230 in 1976, and became the main gun armament of the AH–64 Apache attack helicopter, mounted in a chin pod and controlled by a computerized link with the pilot's helmet. A second model, this time in 25mm calibre, became the M252 Bushmaster cannon mounted on the M2/M3 Bradley AFV and elsewhere, while a 7.62mm version known as the EX–34 was adopted as the co-axial machine-gun for the M1 Abrams MBT and the British Challenger II MBT and Warrior AFV.

A solution to the problem of dealing with spent cartridge cases also harks back to the very earliest days of the machine-gun. We noted that in one respect the introduction of the brass cartridge case was a retrograde step, in that its predecessor, the paper cartridge, was entirely consumed, and had no need to be ejected when spent. Late twentieth-century materials technology held out the hope of a return to that state of affairs, the propellent charge itself being formed into a durable, handlable entity, with its projectile encapsulated within it. By the early nineties, at least one firearms manufacturer had unveiled a design study for a light automatic weapon utilizing this ammunition technology in the square-section 4.85mm × 33 caseless format developed to prototype stage by the Dynamit Nobel company in Germany. Similar research also took place in the United States. Other research topics in the last decade of the twentieth century included the replacement of conventional projectiles by saboted sub-calibre flechettes or darts, and the emulation of experiments already well advanced in artillery pieces with a view to substituting liquid propellent charges for solid, whether encased in plastic or traditional metal, or caseless. The ubiquitous micro-processor found employment, too, in matching the physical performance of the machine-gun with environmental variables such as windage, humidity and temperature, in an effort to ensure that more rounds were first-time hits in the direct-fire role, once again replicating new technology already introduced into the world of heavy artillery.

Chapter Seventeen

The world turned upside-down

THERE IS A famous British march, dating from the eighteenth century, called 'The world turned upside-down'; it could well have served as the International Anthem of the second half of the twentieth century. The period was characterized by drastic, often violent, change in the way the world was organized, particularly in terms of who ruled where and how, if not why. Not unnaturally, since the changes in question were not always bilaterally consensual, the process often manifested itself in the employment of weaponry of all sorts; and since the machine-gun provides the most bangs for any given buck, to quote a common Americanism, it comes as no surprise to find it well to the fore, together with its ever-closer cousin, the assault rifle. The period may well have been called the cold war, but for all that, it was ruled by a succession of hot guns.

Guerrilla warfare became the norm for the wars of liberation. It relied heavily on individual firepower, and in the provision of that, of course, the machine-gun in all its various guises excels. As a result, automatic weapons proliferated, and arms dealers with access to 'surplus' stocks from the Second World War grew obscenely rich selling them on a cash-and-carry basis. This fire-sale clear-out was just what the arms producers of the first (and second) world countries needed, of course, for it allowed them to develop new product, using new technology, to restock the now-depleted inventories, and that, more than any other factor, fuelled the upsurge in military small-arms development during the period.

Little more than five years after the end of the Second World War United Nations forces tried to prevent the Communist Chinese client, North Korea, from devouring its neighbour to the south. That 'police action', as it was known for legal reasons, has often been characterized as exhibiting a return to the massed assault/human wave offensive theory which died, both literally and metaphorically, with the adoption of the machine-gun. It is true that there were such incidents – the assault on positions held by the US Eighth Army's 23rd Infantry Regiment, near Chipyong-ni in early February 1951, for example, where Communist attackers came on *en masse* and were cut down in their ranks almost to a man – but that was an isolated occurrence and seldom repeated.

More commonly, CCF (Communist Chinese Forces) made good use of the broken terrain which covered much of the combat zone and employed fieldcraft and subterfuge to get within 15–20m (roughly 50–60ft) of the Allied Main Line of Resistance (MLR) before revealing themselves, by which time the defenders clearly had a close-order battle on their hands and little opportunity to employ heavier support weapons such as MMGs. The UN troops who faced them knew from the outset that they would have to depend on automatic weapons, and came to rely heavily on the BARs and Brens which were the squad support weapons of the day – a

264

significant condemnation of the sub-machine-gun, which should have excelled in such circumstances, having been designed with close combat in mind. The M3A1 in particular was so poorly regarded that it scarcely figures in any weapons usage analysis.

But no matter which weapon was successful, this sort of fighting was a bloody business:

PFC Navarro met the Chinese attack with machine-gun fire, but got off only one short burst. The enemy went straight for the gun. Navarro and his assistant were shot to death by a Chinese with a tommy gun, standing directly over them. A grenade landed hard against Sgt Hawkins, lying in the shadow beside Lt Burch. The explosion lifted him bodily and blew him across Burch; his leg was shattered. PFC Brinkman, already wounded, was struck by a second bullet. Cpl Barry, who had been trying to dress his wound, was also shot down. Someone yelled, 'The BAR's jammed!'

Burch shook loose from Hawkins and jumped to his feet. Now he could see from 75 to 100 Chinese in a wide semi-circle so close upon him that he could have dented any part of the line with a well-thrown rock.

He knew that his own position was no good. From the higher cone on the right, the Chinese could look right into his ground, and their fire would take him in the flank even if he could beat back the line closing round his front. He shouted the order, 'Fall back on the Company!' and as his survivors took off at a run, he stood his ground – one man, covering their retreat with the fire of his carbine.

It worked beautifully – full automatic as long as he continued to pull the trigger. At less than five yards range he killed two Chinese who tried to take him in a rush. The rest hesitated long enough. His men got away without a shot being fired at them. He turned his back, and followed them down the path.[1]

The US Army's inventory had changed scarcely at all between the end of the Second World War and the beginning of the war to rebuff the invasion of South Korea: US infantrymen carried M1 carbines, BARs and Browning M1919s, just as they had six years earlier. The well-tried weapons continued to give good service, but for the first time in the increasingly detailed after-action reports we begin to detect an absolute, blind reliance on the ability of the automatic weapons to lay down a constant blanket of fire, and to hear the first tentative, almost plaintive, enquiries as to what happens when the ammunition runs out.

'From repetition', says US military historian General S. L. A. Marshall, 'it was well indicated that when the BARs and machine-guns fire excessively and exhaust ammunition supply in the early stages of the fight [a circumstance which he attributes coolly – and probably accurately – to "panic firing"], the position becomes bankrupt. . . .' And was often, he has no need to add, overrun as a result, both in Korea and later, with a slightly different weapons mix, in Vietnam.

The same thing occurred when the squad's automatic weapon was put out of action: 'The loss of the BAR at that point came near to folding up the whole position', or a similar phrase, is a common recurrence. Not that any of the individual machine-gunners Marshall interviewed (he was in a unique position, given the virtual freedom of the battlefield to compile on-the-spot after-action reports; that is why his work is so important, and why we shall have cause to refer to it again) ever admitted to firing wildly (or to anything but rigorous self-control, in fact), though it soon became clear that a gunner's idea of firing 'short bursts' was to release the trigger occasionally, rather than resting the gun whenever there was no compelling tactical reason to fire (contrast this with the disciplined approach of the machine-gunners of fifty years before). For a variety of easily understandable reasons, the machine-gunner's personal role in the US Army had come to be that of providing constant, indiscriminate 'covering' fire, and whether much of it was at all effective is open to serious doubt. It was perhaps the first sign of a growing readiness within the US Army to commit technology rather than soldiery to battle, though it was to be by no means the last.

That was by way of being a direct contrast to the basic ethos of the CCF, for whom life and the war had a different meaning from that it had for the GIs fighting far from home. The initial success of CCF tactics was due in no small measure to their willingness to die to order. Discussing their machine-gunners, Marshall noted: 'CCF operations are characterized by simplicity of fire means, centring around maximum use of the machine-gun. The expendability of this force's human material is one of the enabling factors toward this end. When Chinese MG crews can be committed repeatedly to situations permitting no escape, the weapon *ipso facto* is given a chance to score heavily prior to liquidation,' he wrote in a battlefield analysis of infantry weapons published while the war was at its height. To most Americans, it would be unthinkable for their leaders to demand such actions of US servicemen under such conditions; that is no reflection on the individual fighting man's personal courage or commitment, but rather on the 'mindless' fanaticism of many of the CCF troops. American soldiers in Vietnam, a generation later, were to encounter the same suicidal courage in the Viet Cong or North Vietnamese Army (NVA), just as their great-grand-fathers had discovered it in the Philippines around the turn of the century.

The following account from the Vietnam War graphically illustrates the above points with near-continuous machine-gun fire only just, in this instance, prevailing over a reckless attack:

I pulled the trigger. Orange tracers spiralled away from me. My first target exploded backward, arms and legs flailing. I laid on the trigger for what seemed like an eternity. Frantic screams screeched from the rice paddy, piercing even the explosions. I could feel the screams more than I could hear them. The NVA scrambled for cover that wasn't there. Some ran from the machine-gun fire and directly into the row of M16s, while those at the front of the column retreated into a shower of lead from the M60. The crossfire was a human lawn mower.

I swept the machine-gun from one end of the column to the bottom of the mountains. The phosphorous ends of the tracer rounds broke off the bullets and sizzled like miniature sparklers as they found their mark.

Chan changed clips [*sic*] in his rifle as fast as he could. The barrel of the M60 glowed red then white. Adrenalin and fear pushed me, while my whole body vibrated to the rhythm of the gun; I became one with my weapon and we were killing. The barrel became transparent from the heat of continuous fire as I poured another hundred rounds into the rice paddy.

A fluorescent lamp couldn't have pinpointed my position any better than that glowing barrel. I knew the barrel might melt and jam, but I couldn't stop. I felt like I did in my first fist-fight, scared to stop swinging for fear of getting hit.

Chan dropped his rifle and started frantically feeding ammunition into the gun with both hands. ... A flare sizzled into the dark sky, arcing over the paddy, then popping into a tiny sun and drifting down. The lights were on. The miniature red sun added a 3-D effect to an already bloody picture. ... Chan screamed and reached for his rifle. Three gooks were running at us, bobbing and weaving in a suicidal charge to knock out the gun. They fired full automatic, spraying bullets all around us. They were screaming. I swept the stream of tracers from left to right, bearing down on them like a sputtering laser beam. A ChiCom grenade blew up ten feet in front of us, stealing my night vision. Incoming bullets kicked dirt into my eyes and mouth. The barrel melted. The gun jammed. The sweeping laser stopped along with my breathing.

I fumbled for my pistol like a drunk in a shoot-out. My vision turned spotty. I heard Chan firing. The grunts on my left opened up full automatic. Blurred images of men came through the spots in my eyes. Their heads jerked back like poorly manned puppets, legs crumbling last, not knowing the upper half was lifeless.

Silence. The loudest silence of my life. My heart pounded the breath out of me faster than I could bring it in. The bloodlust evaporated into the gunpowder air. Payback. The frustration turned into fatigue. . . .[2]

Even when the gunner had taken care to study his craft the demands of sustained fighting could prove to be too much for the M60:

The pig [as the M60 was known] belonged to the guy with experience, the guy who could keep cool in a fire-fight, a guy that knew what he was doing, and not to a guy that was green. It was the only major firepower in our entire platoon. Your automatic weapons fire was your heavy artillery; the pig had greater range. It was your heavy heavy. If a man panicked and really didn't know how to handle the heavy heavy, you really didn't have too much. A lot of guys didn't want to carry it because it was very heavy and it was lethal – meaning it was lethal both to you and to Charlie [the Viet Cong or North Vietnamese]. Obviously, Charlie tried to knock you out first. They tried to hit you with RPGs [Rocket-Propelled Grenades]. Their first target of interest was the guy with the machine-gun. If they knocked out that machine-gun, they could easily overrun the platoon. Then the only thing they had to contend with was just light weapons. . . .

The fault of a lot of guys with the M–60 and the reason why they used to get wiped out was because they would fire the M–60 wildly. Like Young was doing that day, clips flying all over the place. He had his eyes shut, just pulling the trigger. Shit, the lead was all going up in the God damn treetops. Charlie was just sitting down there on the ground waiting to beam our ass. So I kept the forearm weight on it to hold it level. I took aim through the big sight right on the end of the barrel. I had to ignore the vibration, watch the sight, keep it leveled downward. I used to keep it leveled at where a man's waist would be. That was how I would decipher how low I was going to shoot it. If I thought a man was up in the treetops, I'd level it right where I thought that treetop was, and I'd shoot down just about a foot and I would be lethal. I'd blow the guy out of there.

When I saw the sergeant was really taking an interest in me, I asked him all kinds of questions about the weapon. He taught me how to fire on the run, in a crouch position, laying on my back, falling down, anyway I wanted to. He

just told me all kinds of tricks about firing this weapon. . . .
He knew his shit, mechanically. Maybe he was an M–60
specialist, I don't know. The guy knew the weapon, though.
I got that information from him, and after that I developed
a reputation very, very fast. The guys started getting confi-
dence in me. . . .

A gunner needed an ammo bearer that was not so
worried about his own head that he couldn't effectively
feed the gunner the ammo. I would be blowing lead out of
that pig so quick I'd go through a belt in ten seconds,
needed a man to be able to hand me the ammo. He didn't
have to stick it in the weapon. I did that. He just simply
handed it to me and I flopped it in there. I could do it faster
than he could, anyway . . . I was at the dike, firing like hell
with Emory right with me, just handing me that lead. He
said,

'Hey, Goff, I'm out of lead. What do you want me to
do?'

'Don't worry, I've got enough right down here,' and I
was still firing. 'What I want you to do is go and get all the
ammo from the other guys down at the other end of the
company. Find anybody that's got ammo, just get it.'

So this kid, on his hands and knees, crawled along in
back of the dike, collecting ammo and bringing it back up
to me, and I was firing like hell. I probably went through
two thousand rounds. Everybody was depending on Goff
right then; Goff was the firepower. And I knew I was
quieting that area, because my firepower was very effective.
As I was running I was steadily blowing out lead. I saw these
guys moving around in the woodline [the objective of this
particular assault]. But primarily I wasn't looking at the guys;
I was only looking at the angling of my weapon and where
my firepower was going. That was the only thing I was

worrying about. And as I was going, I was steadily laying down my firepower so effectively that I was just not getting hit myself. That's the only explanation I can come up with.

Emory and I were running up and down this rice paddy firing. The guys would tell me, 'Hey, Goff, right here, right in there, man.' I would sit down between two guys and blow out where they thought they were getting a heavy concentration of fire. Then Emory and I would run into another area along the dike. Sergeant Needham hollered, 'Goff, Goff, over here, man, I got thirty or forty of them, right here . . .' Those were the thirty or forty NVA I am accredited with in that area. . . .

We were in the middle of the paddy at the first dike, which we went over. We cut down that body of men so well, knocked out their firepower, that we could move now on toward the second dike at the end of the paddy, firing steadily. After we got to the second dike, I went on firing for about fifteen more minutes, then my pig fell apart. It just blew up in the air. The barrel did fine, but the pins came out of the side of the weapon. It just got too hot, and when it expanded, the pins and the locks and the keys which held it in place were no longer workable, and the pig just came apart. It came apart in my hands. The top of the tray popped up; it was sprung, and I couldn't keep it down. I couldn't fire without the tray being down. By that time there was hardly any activity. I was still staring at the woodline and the guys saw how it was.

'Goff, are you all right?' Emory said. 'Are you all right, man?'

'Yeah, I'm fine, man.'

Just exhausted as hell. I could hardly talk, my whole mouth was so dry. I was slumped on my knees at the second dike, just staring. The second dike was almost at the woodline. With us being at the woodline and me sitting there exhausted, and with the area completely quieted, a few of the other squads started to run into the woodline, crouched, searching, looking, weapons at the ready.

They started taking a body count. That was when the CO went into the woodline – to see if they could find any prisoners or whatever. But I'd done most of the work. The rest of the guys were sitting. I'd been doing all the running, so I was dead to the world. The guys just told me to sit there, because my pig was out of action. They told me to sit there while they went to take a body count, which they did. I just sat there.[3]

There is a clear similarity between the Korean War and the two wars fought in Vietnam. In both theatres, artillery was to be the dominating factor on the ground, though machine-guns still claimed their share of victims, too. In the other, less well-known conflicts of the 1950s and '60s – the wars of independence in Africa, in the Middle East and elsewhere in Asia, which were true guerrilla conflicts – artillery was totally inappropriate and was seldom, if ever, employed. Instead, troops on both sides relied on machine-guns and light mortars for their firepower, and on superior tradecraft and intelligence analysis to bring the enemy to battle.

In such conflicts, the well-mounted, well-sprung ambush became a tactical imperative, as did the need to maintain a defensive system capable of containing a sudden, unexpected attack for long enough for the entire fighting force to get into position and into action, and here the disproportionate firepower of the machine-gun came into its own – but it did not always have things entirely its own way:

The weather got worse, rain and wind slapping through the brush so that speaking voices were drowned out, and a blanket of fog cutting visibility down to zero. It was half an hour before ten that night, and the grunts were shivering miserably under ponchos in their mudholes, when a burst of fire broke out from the Second Platoon side of the line. About a dozen North Vietnamese had crept up through the wind, rain and fog to assault the platoon's M60 position.

When the NVA moved on the M60 foxhole, Stahl and another grunt crawled from their holes towards the shooting, Stahl shouting back, 'Doc, someone is hurt over here!' Wheeler [the platoon medic] pushed through the elephant grass on his stomach, whispering that he was coming. He was five feet from them when the NVA suddenly flung satchel charges and grenades around the M60. Everything went off at once. Mud and shrapnel sprayed all around Wheeler as Stahl and his companion collapsed. Wheeler rolled to them. Stahl had been hit in the chest by shrapnel. Both men had been killed instantly.

The enemy tormented Charlie Company for the rest of the night, moving unseen through the brush. They snatched the M60 from the perimeter. At each rustle around them, the grunts threw hand frags [grenades] and fired LAWs [light anti-armour weapons] and M–79 grenade launchers. Artillery illumination burst overhead, serving only to reveal company positions to the enemy who stayed hidden in the thick undergrowth. Each time the flares burned out, the NVA tossed more grenades into the lines . . .

Come the morning, five GIs were dead, and four wounded.[4]

The BAR, the Bren and the DP had all, quite literally, had their day by the 1960s, and were replaced, along with the heavier PM 1910, Vickers Mark 1 and M1919 Browning, by the GPMG, the M60 and the PK, as we have seen. The increase in firepower these new weapons gave to the infantry squads was reflected in their tactics, and particularly in the increasing reliance placed on them, continuing the trend which had become obvious in Korea. As well as bringing new flexibility to the infantry, the new generation of lighter automatic weapons also found a new home in the helicopter, which soon turned into a new weapons platform, a three-dimensional fighting vehicle, the helicopter gunship.

The first helicopters saw limited service during the latter part of the Second World War, particularly for observation purposes at sea, and were used for that task and for casualty evacuation in Korea. It was 1956, during the invasion of Egypt by Britain, France and Israel, before they were used as a means of delivering troops into the battle zone, but by the time of the American involvement in Vietnam that had become established practice. Soon, along with the troop-carriers, were going armed helicopters, whose job was to 'sanitize' the landing zone and offer some immediate protection to the infantrymen at one of the most dangerous moments of their mission (and to repeat the exercise during the potentially no-less-lethal extraction). M60 machine-guns in both fixed and flexible mounts came to characterize this form of operation, and very soon all other capable nations followed suit, not only in arming what had been designed as transport/utility helicopters but also constructing purpose-built gunships such as the American AH–1 Cobra and the Soviet Mi–8 Hind. By then, of course, the firepower of the conventional machine-gun had been deemed insufficient for the task at hand, and a new generation of revolvers and chain guns had replaced them not only aboard the attack helicopters but also in terrestrial fighting vehicles.

275

Both the conventional and the newer types of machine-gun could be fitted to quite a variety of vehicles:

> Convoys went well, protected by ... APCs [armoured personnel carriers], and most importantly, the gun trucks. They were an example of battlefield improvisation which had developed because simply mounting a machine-gun, as per army regulations, did not protect a thin-skinned truck. The solution was to reinforce a five-ton truck with steel planking [normally used to create instant roadways or airstrips]. Some had APC hulls fitted atop the bed. Then put three or four soldiers in the cargo bed, arming them with whatever [automatic weapons] could be scrounged together: .50 calibers, grenade launchers, numerous M60s, even an occasional minigun. All of the gun-truckers were volunteers. If a convoy was ambushed, it was the gun truck which was hauled into the fire, engaged the enemy, and extracted the truck drivers. The sight of gun trucks in a convoy probably deterred many North Vietnamese ambushers on Route 9.[5]

Paradoxically, the switch over to bell-fed squad support weapons caused its own problems for the infantry. The US Army soon discovered in Vietnam that – especially in the hands of non-professional, conscripted soldiers, who had undergone only the briefest training and who had very little discipline under fire – because the M60 could put down something like sustained fire, it was expected to do so at all times; that inevitably meant that a vast amount of ammunition was going to be expended in any contact no matter whether it was firm, and led to real action, or not. And all that ammunition had to be carried.

There were other problems of mobility and vulnerability as well:

No one wanted it [the M60]. The pig position was the one attacked by the enemy after the company commander and the radio man. If they could, they wanted to take out the machine-gun because that was where the firepower was coming from. Everybody knew that, even in training. But back at Fort Lewis, in the qualifying tests with the M–60, I'd shot the best in the division. So I humped it. First thing was that I had to get used to the extra twenty-four pounds. Once you were humping, the pig man was more likely to get hung up in the brush. Everybody got hung up, but the pig barrel is long and the weapon is bulkier. You were carrying tripods, too. The weapon has so many different side pieces that it was easy to get hung up. It was tucked under your arm in the ready position with the strap for support across your neck. You were going through all that brush and you can't imagine how thick it was. Except for the Vietnamese, my main foe was the wait-a-minute vines. I could be walking along and all of a sudden the vine took the gun from me. I was tearing at the vine, trying to kick it, and it was raining. I was wet and I was mad. One time I was walking along and the vine completely pulled the gun out of my hands, and the barrel stuck in the mud. I had to clean it, then and there. There were days like that. Anyway, old-timers didn't want no part of that gun, but they wanted somebody on it who could use it.[6]

Before long every member of the rifle squad was carrying belts of ammunition for the machine-gun, but that was not at all a satisfactory situation in combat, for how was the ammunition to reach the gun from the sort of tactical positions the riflemen themselves ought to adopt or would adopt as soon as the squad came under effective fire? All too often, the distribution of the machine-gun's ammunition around the squad members was an open invitation to them to bunch together (which was their natural reaction anyway, and one which would have been trained out of professional soldiers) and a means for the individual riflemen to busy themselves with something other than laying down effective fire themselves, also a very present phenomenon. S. L. A. Marshall's work revealed that during the Second World War only 15 per cent of American riflemen could be depended on to fire at the enemy in battle; the figure had increased a little by the time of Vietnam, but not by much. For the machine-gunner, of course, there was no such opportunity, if only because the contribution he made to any fire-fight was so obvious and spectacular.

As in other wars throughout history there are outstanding examples of just what such an individual contribution could achieve:

Lozada and three other grunts were staked out 360yds from the company perimeter, an outpost to warn of enemy approach. The rest of the 2nd Battalion were starting up Hill 875 when they ran into a bunch of entrenched NVA regulars who poured out a stream of fire from well-concealed fighting positions. Company A, near the base of the hill, became exposed. As an NVA company moved along a trail near Lozada's outpost, he sounded the alarm and then opened fire with his M60. Twenty North Vietnamese went down, and the attack was broken up.

But the battle was far from over. Other NVA units were enveloping the company, and Lozada's outpost was ordered to move back into the perimeter. By now it was too late, as the NVA pressed another assault against the beleaguered men. Lozada broke up the attack on one side of the trail and then leapt across it with his M60 to take on another group of NVA soldiers. His wounded comrades were being pulled back inside the company perimeter, which was now threatened with imminent destruction.

Lozada must have realized that if he withdrew from his position, the way would be open for the enemy to over-whelm his company. Urging his wounded comrades to work their way back to safety, he held off the NVA on three sides, cutting down waves of enemy troops as they charged to within yards of his position.

Company A was badly mauled that day, but its survivors were able to make their way back into the beleaguered battalion perimeter, thanks to Lozada's courage and skill with the M60. On the next day, a relief force from the 4th Battalion, 503rd Infantry, found scores of NVA bodies littering the trail where Lozada made his stand. His body lay face up, his hands crossed on his chest, M60 at his side.[7]

The tendency to avoid actually killing the enemy is much less prevalent in professional armies, and certainly there was no sign of it among the British soldiers sent to drive the invading Argentinian Army (once again, a body composed largely of conscripts) out of the Falklands Islands in 1981. Here, two similarly equipped armies faced each other over an otherwise almost-empty battlefield and superior training and professionalism won out over numerical superiority. Once again, ammunition supply was a crucial factor, not least because the men of the Parachute Regiment and the Royal Marines marched cross-country carrying all their weaponry and equipment with them in order to fight the battles which led to the capitulation of the Argentinian forces in Port Stanley. Weaponry at the time was in 7.62mm calibre – FN rifles and GPMGs – and the loads were correspondingly heavier (and smaller in terms of the number of rounds of ammunition available) than they were only a decade later, at the time of the invasion of Iraq, by which time the change-over to 5.56mm calibre had been completed.

The sheer physical effort required to move useful amounts of ammunition in battle is clear:

The RSM appeared. 'Load up with ammo, as much as you can carry; they need every bullet!' We were going forward to A Company. It was only about 1,500 metres, just follow the track. Some GPMGs were next to the ammo pile, so I took one and about 1,000 rounds of belted ammo. I stowed my SMG in my rucksack. Each medic now carried about 200 pounds altogether. It wasn't far, but we had overdone it with the ammo. Bit by bit as it slowed us down it was being left behind. We were about half way there when a Pucara light attack aircraft flew low over the ridge towards us. I let rip from the hip with the GPMG. I was getting a bad feed and having to recock. I screamed at Gibo to come and feed the belt. As he raced towards me, he dropped like a stone. I thought he was hit, but continued to fire. Gibo lay under his enormous rucksack, arms and legs straining, trying to get a grip. I had to laugh; he looked like a tortoise on its back.[8]

Just how important also is good fire control is amply illustrated by the following two incidents recollected from the Falklands conflict. In one the failure is by the Argentinians and in the second by their British opponents, who are, however, able to deploy further machine-gun power to retrieve their position.

When he realized that A Company's advance had become bogged down, Colonel 'H' Jones determined that the best way to get them going again was to take charge himself, so 'Tac 1' – battalion headquarters – set off at a fast pace, but soon came under enemy MG fire. Happily, it was ineffective, and the incident illustrates the need for machine-gunners, in particular, to get it right first time:

The amount of fire that came down on us in that first few seconds was thousands of rounds. By firing high in the first burst they gave us time to get to ground. Once they realized their mistake, nobody was standing up. Again they brought down fire. We were behind little tufties and in an inlet, so the fire never hit anybody. The CO stood up and said, 'Right, we can't stay here all day,' and went into the inlet and, with a mixture of crawling, running, sprinting and diving we all got out of the killing ground and into the inlet and the protection of a bank.[9]

The British failure was one of communication also:

Misunderstandings happen in wartime just as they do in time of peace, the main difference then is in the speed with which events can unfold, and the deadly effect which that unfolding can have.

By the end of twelve hours of solid fighting, with darkness fast approaching, C and D Companies found themselves in action together – quite by accident – as they approached the school which controlled the northern approach to the settlement of Goose Green. Lieutenant

Barry's 12 Platoon had begun its advance up the slope, over open ground, towards the flagpole to the right of the school itself, two sections up and one back, when Barry saw a white flag waving, and – almost unaccountably, and against his Company Commander's standing instructions – decided to accept the Argentinians' surrender. In the circumstances, and with the Paras' own Support Company within machine-gun range from behind, but unable to distinguish friend from foe in the gathering darkness, it was a fatal error of judgement:

'There was a group of three or four Argles with a white cloth wanting to surrender. They definitely wanted to pack it in, I've no doubt about this group. They were less than 100 metres from us, but the ground was open like a football field. They were up this slope by a fence with a gap in it. Mr Barry and his radio operator, Geordie Knight, were in the lead, with myself a short distance behind, then came Corporal Sullivan's section in support. When we got to the top I saw there were more Argies in trenches nearby. The first group still seemed to want to give up, but I was worried about the others as they were not leaving their trenches.

'Mr Barry went right up to the fence, only a few feet from the Argies. I was about twenty feet behind him. He started to demonstrate to the Argies that they were to surrender by putting down their weapons. He went through the motions of putting down his own. I reckon we were there only a matter of seconds, less than a minute, when this long burst of SF [sustained fire, i.e. machine-gun fire] came cracking overhead from behind. Suddenly there were bullets everywhere. All the Argies opened up. Mr Barry was hit at point-blank range by the Argies in front of him.

'I fell flat. There was fire from everywhere, I could see rounds striking the ground all around; a lot was coming from the trenches. I was in a bit of a state as the strap of my medical bag was wrapped around my neck. My rifle barrel was stuck in the dirt. A bullet went through my sling and another through the heel of my boot. After a bit I sort-of sprinted sideways and dived into a rut made by tractor tyres. It was only a foot deep. Corporal Sullivan's section was firing ... and Brummie Mountford was firing his GPMG. The next thing I knew was Sergeant Meredith coming up with another machine-gun. After that, we seemed to get the better of the Argies ...'

This incident clearly illustrates the problems the poor siting and control of a sustained-fire support weapon can produce. In a perfect world, the gun should clearly have been moved forward from its position back on Darwin Hill so that it could have provided covering fire from the flank (though it is difficult to imagine how this could actually have been achieved in the time available). In this particular instance, the fault lay with a decision to centralize Support Company's heavy weapons and a failure to maintain adequate radio communication between them and the assault platoons, with the result that the sustained-fire crews had no clear idea of exactly who they were firing at, or why, but were laying down indiscriminate fire instead.[10]

At the other end of the scale, there was not nearly such urgency to seek replacements for the Browning M2HB heavy machine-gun, though there were a significant number of improved designs under development by then, as well as new types of ammunition in the familiar 12.7mm/.5-inch calibre to supplement the jacketed ball round. One such uses technology developed for tank main guns, and consists of a sub-calibre dart mounted in a discardable full-calibre guide which falls away soon after the round leaves the muzzle.

These so-called SLAP (Saboted Light Armour Penetrating) rounds are fully capable of defeating the protection of armoured personnel carriers out to a range of a kilometre and more. An alternative, developed in Norway, is a remarkable combination of armour piercing, incendiary and fragmentation round.

The adoption of these specialized ammunition types caused an additional problem, however – they were less effective than conventional jacketed rounds against infantry targets, while at the same time being very considerably more expensive. The American AAI Corporation, working in conjunction with the US Army's Armament Research and Development Command, solved the problems of having the two types of ammunition ready to hand with a gun known generically as the general-purpose heavy machine-gun (GPHMG) but usually called the Dover Devil after the town in New Jersey where it was developed. Building on experimental work carried out during and since the Second World War in heavier calibres than 12.7mm, the Dover Devil incorporated twin ammunition feed-paths, one from each side of the receiver, permitting two quite different types of ammunition to be available, selectable by a simple switch. The Dover Devil was lighter and much simpler in operation than the M2HB it was designed to replace, with fewer moving parts, but after protracted tests, the US Army decided that it did not offer significant enough advantages over the older gun to warrant the change, and the project was shelved. AAI tried to continue to develop the gun on its own, but with no market in sight, eventually cancelled the project completely. A gun developed in Singapore by the state-owned Chartered Industries (CIS), which also produced the 5.56mm Ultimax 100, clearly owed a great deal to the GPHMG project. The 50MG, as the gun was called, was a modular design comprising five basic group assemblies and like the Dover Devil it was capable of taking its ammunition from either side. It went into production, but failed to find export markets.

Such procurement as there was of new 12.7mm HMGs tended to go to traditional sources of Browning M2HB guns, licensees such as Saco and Ramo in the USA and FN in Belgium. Both the American companies developed light-weight versions of the venerable gun – the unloaded weight of their new models was around 26kg (57 pounds) against 38kg (84 pounds) for the original – but surprisingly enough, not even the added provision in both cases of a quick-change barrel system persuaded customers to switch their allegiance from the original.

The Dover Devil started life in 20mm calibre, and was not the only would-be infantry weapon to deviate from the 12.7mm standard. In Belgium, FN – which showed itself quite prepared to pioneer the development of new ammu-nition types where necessary – also opted for a bigger, heavier projectile, this time in 15mm × 115 form, but was deterred by excessive barrel wear in the prototypes and subsequently adopted a 15.5mm × 106 round for the gun which was to become the BRG–15. This time, the novel feature of the new projectile was the addition of a plastic driving band – a device common to artillery, but previously unknown in an infantry weapon. A variety of ammunition types including PB-AP (plastic banded – armour piercing), which can penetrate 19mm (0.75in.) of armour plate at a range of 800 metres (0.5 mile), and PB-HEPI (plastic banded – high explosive penetrat-ing incendiary) were produced, as were saboted sub-calibre AP rounds. Like the 50MG and the Dover Devil, the BRG–15 was equipped with a dual-feed mechanism to facilitate the change-over from one ammunition type to another. A heavy gun, at 60kg (132 pounds) unloaded, it was nevertheless capable of deployment from nothing more robust than the tripod and pintle mounts normally employed for the M2, thanks to an internal recoil buffer system.

The development costs for the BRG–15, while they were not a matter of public record, clearly put an intolerable strain on the financing of FN, for mid-way through the project, control of the company passed into foreign hands, and the successor, Fabrique National Nouvelle Herstal, FNNH, became a subsidiary of the French state-controlled arms maker GIAT.

The projectile weight of the various types of load used in the 15.5mm round varies considerably but the kinetic energy contained in such a projectile travelling at a velocity in excess of 1,000 metres per second is enormous. Only one ammunition type in use by machine-guns, as opposed to cannon, in the last part of the twentieth century came even close to it in performance: the 14.5mm × 114 round employed by the Russian KPV (*Krupnokakilbernyi Pulemyot Vladimirovna*), a simple, almost crude weapon devised in the years immediately following the Great Patriotic War. The KPV was widely deployed in both the anti-vehicle and anti-aircraft roles, in the latter in towed or vehicle-borne single, twin or quad mounts styled ZPU (*Zenitnaya Pulemyotanya Ustanovka*). It was extensively deployed in North Vietnam during the war there. This gun is clearly too heavy for unmounted infantry purposes, and in that role, the ex-Soviet forces replaced the DShK by a 12.7mm gun employing the Kalashnikov rotary-bolt action known, after its designers G.I. Nikitin, J.M. Sokolov and V.I. Volkov, as the NSV. Available in tripod- or vehicle-mounted versions, the NSV was effective out to 2,000m (1.25 miles), and was otherwise comparable in every way with the Browning M2HB.

Chapter Eighteen

Minimizing the threat

HARDLY HAD THE North Atlantic Treaty Organisation established the 7.62mm × 51 cartridge as its standard for infantry assault and light support weapons in 1953 than the Americans, who had bullied their allies into accepting it despite its various shortcomings, issued a specification for an assault rifle using a much smaller, lighter round with what one expert has called 'a fortuitous combination of bullet mass and stability, which resulted in a projectile which tumbled rapidly when it struck its target and delivered up its energy in massive fashion rather than . . . passing through the target with minimal energy transfer'. The round in question, the 5.56mm × 45 which Remington had previously sold commercially as the .222/.223-inch, combined a projectile weighing just 3.56gm (55 grains) with a 1.55gm (24 grain) charge in a proportionally smaller cartridge case than that of the 9.7/3.0gm (150/47 grain) M59 ball round (the US NATO standard), and was thus under half its weight – a very important consideration indeed for the individual infantryman, effectively doubling the amount of ammunition he could carry without increasing his load.

The first purpose-built military weapon chambered for

the new round, the AR15, was designed by Eugene Stoner while working for the Armalite Division of the Fairchild Engine and Airplane Corporation. It was modelled very closely on his earlier Armalite AR10, a lightweight assault rifle firing the 7.62mm round, which had been an unsuccessful contender for the US Army contract finally awarded to the short-lived, M1 Garand-derived M14 in 1957.

Like its larger-calibre brother, Stoner's Armalite AR15 used a simple system of gas actuation not dissimilar to that developed in Sweden by Ljungmann or the one used in the French MAS 49 rifle, gas tapped off from the barrel acting directly on the bolt carrier to operate a front-locking rotating bolt. The AR15 – which became the M16 and then, in improved form, the M16A2 – is only of passing interest here even though it did have a full auto-fire capability. Stoner's subsequent work, and in particular the M63A1 weapons system which he designed, is of greater significance to this study, as are offshoots such as the Colt HBAR and CMG–1 projects. The HBAR never quite made it (it incorporated a heavier barrel and other modifications to create a light support weapon) and the CMG (with further changes) was still-born.

Meanwhile, Stoner had formed an association with Cadillac Gage, a company better known for light armoured vehicles than for small arms, and had started work on a modular lightweight weapon which he called System 63. It was to comprise fifteen assemblies in all, and encompass an SMG, a short-barrelled carbine, an assault rifle, an LMG and a sustained-fire machine-gun, all of which shared a basic body group to which could be added different barrels, butts and ammunition feed mechanisms for box magazines or ammunition belts as well as a bipod or a tripod. Not surprisingly, the Stoner M63 uses the simple rotating bolt from the

AR10/15 series, but this time with a more conventional piston-and-cylinder gas actuation arrangement. Both the United States Navy and the US Marine Corps purchased examples, the former as the Mk 23, the Marines as the XM207, and put them through a protracted evaluation process in Vietnam. The US Navy's SEAL special forces teams, in particular, were most enthusiastic about the gun, especially in its LMG form, but despite that support, no large order was forthcoming then, and none has been since.

Eugene Stoner was not alone in thinking that the 5.56mm round was adequate for a lightweight fire support weapon; designers Ernest Vervier and Maurice Bourlet at Herstal-lez-Liège, too, went to work on a belt-fed light machine-gun in that calibre, with considerably better results. FN's first offering in the miniature calibre was a version of the FAL assault rifle, known as the CAL (Carabine Automatique Légère), which was never a startling commercial success but did provide considerable data on the behaviour of a new 5.56mm round which the Belgians were promoting as an alternative to the American M109 round which Stoner had adopted. Externally, the SS 109, as the new round came to be known, was identical with the American, but its ballistic characteristics were quite different; the M109 was optimized for performance at up to 400m/440yds (though even by that point, the drop in the bullet's trajectory was excessive, at around 76cm/30in), while the SS 109 was considerably better at longer ranges. At that time, NATO had yet to make up its mind about an ammunition standard to supersede the 7.62mm round: Britain was pushing for a 4.85mm round; Germany for one of 4.6mm calibre, while France (then still a full member) and Belgium, as well as the USA, urged a 5.56mm round of some description. The 5.56mm round was always a distinct favourite, and despite the considerable political muscle of the US armaments industry, it was the Belgian version which was adopted. That not unnaturally gave a considerable fillip to the prospects for the light machine-gun which was being developed to fire it.

The FN Minimi prototypes were produced during 1974, and since they were the first real attempt to produce a weapon capable of anything like sustained fire in the 5.56mm calibre, they aroused considerable interest. However, the development process went slowly, even for the notoriously conservative weapons industry, and it was 1982 before volume production began. That said, it is worth noting that the Minimi came to the commercial market as a properly developed design, finished and complete in every sense; a telling contrast to the history of the M60, for example. It was light enough, in theory anyway, at slightly under seven kg (15.5 pounds) 'dry', to function as an assault weapon, and with that in mind, was equipped from the outset to accommodate both conventional box magazines (it accepted FN's own and those from the M16) and belted ammunition, the latter either being fed free or contained in a lightweight plastic box. There was no modification necessary to switch between belt and magazine. The Minimi came equipped with a conventional rigid skeleton stock, or with an even lighter extensible version, and the quick-change barrel, which utilized a system much akin to that of the MAG, was available in two lengths. Its kinship with the MAG was also manifested in the tripod and accessory sights used in the sustained-fire role.

Despite the US Army's considerable chauvinism, the Minimi, slightly modified to meet US production methods, was adopted the same year it went into series production. The US Government made an initial order for 68,000 units, and the Belgian gun (manufactured by the company's US subsidiary) entered the inventory as the M249 Squad Automatic Weapon or SAW, a new classification which sat – rather uncomfortably at first – between the sustained-fire M60 and the M16, taking over the former's role as squad fire support weapon. The only serious problem the American military encountered related to the continued use of M109 ammunition instead of the more powerful SS 109 round; specifically, there were occasional problems in pulling the ammunition belt through into the action, and the cyclic rate when magazine-fed (when that problem is naturally eliminated) was deemed to be too high. Not surprisingly, a switch to SS 109 ammunition solved the problems entirely, and a new version of the M16, the M16A2, was also developed to use the more powerful round, improving that gun's characteristics considerably, too.

By the time it had celebrated ten years in series production, the Minimi had been adopted by a dozen nations, and had spawned at least two clones, the South Korean K3 and the Taiwanese Type 75. It also had competition, in the shape of the Ultimax 100 from Singapore, which had actually appeared on the international market at around the same time as the Belgian gun, and the Israeli Negev, the latter being very similar indeed to the Minimi in both its basic character and operating characteristics and in the extent of its versatility. Elsewhere, a selection of lighter selective-fire weapons chambered for the 5.56mm round came on to the market during the 1980s (and at least one chambered for the slightly smaller 5.45mm round adopted by the Soviet Army at about the same time, though that was really no more than a rejigged variant of the RPK, just as the new AK–74 was a revamp of the original AK–47).

Royal Ordnance in Britain produced a new bull-pup rifle in the mid-1970s, designed with the 4.85mm × 49 round in mind, and though the ammunition was unsuccessful in the 1977–80 NATO trials, it stuck to its gun, quite literally, and put it into production as the SA–80, in 5.56mm calibre. It was adopted for British Army service as the L85A1, accompanied by a heavier-barrelled version, complete with bipod, known as the L86A1 Light Support Weapon (LSW), the two having 80 per cent of their components in common. Like the Minimi, the LSW was accurate and effective out to 800 metres. Germany and Spain made contributions, as we have already noted, in the form of guns from both Heckler & Koch and CETME; they were joined by Beretta from Italy with a more rugged version of the AR 70/90 assault rifle, the AS 70/90, complete with the obligatory heavy barrel and bipod, but otherwise little modified. Steyr in Austria also produced a support weapon variant of its futuristic AUG assault rifle.

These new so-called 'machine rifles' had a considerable effect on infantry tactics, of course, since they boosted individual and small-unit firepower considerably. British infantry battalions issued two LSWs and six IWs (Individual Weapons) to every eight riflemen. The new genre of light automatic weapons had shortcomings, certainly, and chief among them was their reduced hitting power at medium to long range, though the Belgian-developed 5.56mm round is lethal out to well beyond the 800 metres quoted as the maximum effective range for the Minimi. There were also well-founded misgivings as to the real ability of weapons such as the HK 13, the LSW and the AS 70/90 to lay down enough fire to support either offensive or defensive operations effectively, given their fixed, relatively lightweight barrels. Certainly, in that respect they are far removed from their spiritual ancestors, the LMGs of the Second World War era.

Be that as it may, in the right hands weapons such as the

Minimi have proved themselves excellent machine-guns in battle. During the 1991 Gulf War against Iraq, for example, it was used by British SAS teams behind the lines to great effect. The eight-man SAS team codenamed 'Bravo Two Zero' was equipped with four Minimis. The leader of the team, Sergeant 'Andy McNab', gave the reasons: 'The weapon is so light that it can be used in the attack like a rifle, as well as giving support fire, and it has a fearsome rate of fire. It has a bipod to guarantee good, accurate automatic fire if needed.'

When the patrol engaged Iraqi forces during its mission in January 1991 the Minimis put up a good show, and McNab's account of a firefight with the enemy illustrates the mobility that is possible with one of the new generation of squad automatic weapons:

The [Iraqi] APC stopped. I couldn't believe my eyes. It was using the machine-gun as a fire base instead of coming forward with the infantry and overwhelming us, which was wonderful.

Everybody was getting the rounds down. The Minimis were fired in bursts of 3–5 rounds. Ammunition had to be managed. Two 66s [American 66mm light anti-tank weapons] were fired at the truck and found their target. There was a massive shudder of high-explosive. It must have been very demoralizing for them.

Decisions. After this initial contact, what are you going to do? Are you going to stay there all the time, are you going to move back, are you going to move forward?

Everybody knew what had to be done. We psyched ourselves up. It's unnatural to go forward into something like that. It's not at all what your vulnerable flesh and bone wants to do. It just wants to close its eyes and open them again much later and find that everything is fine.

'Everything OK?'

Whether people actually heard further down the line didn't matter, they knew something was going to happen, and they knew the chances were that we were going to go forward and attack this force that vastly outnumbered us.

Without thinking, I changed my magazine. I had no idea how many rounds I had left in it. It was still fairly heavy, I might have only fired two or three rounds out of it. I threw it down the front of my smock for later on.

Stan gave the thumbs up and stepped up the fire-rate on the Minimi to initiate the move.

I was on my hands and knees, looking up. I took deep breaths and then up I got and ran forward.

'Fuck it! Fuck it!'

People put down a fearsome amount of covering fire. You don't fire on the move. It slows you up. All you have to do is get forward, get down and get firing so that the others can move up. As soon as you get down on the ground your lungs are heaving and your torso is moving up and down, you're looking around for the enemy but you've got sweat in your eyes. You wipe it away, your rifle is moving up and down in your shoulder. You want to get down in a nice firing position like you do on the range, but it isn't happening that way. You're trying to calm yourself down to see what you're doing, but you want to do everything at once. You want to stop this heavy breathing so you can hold the weapon properly and bring it to bear. You want to get rid of the sweat so you can see your targets, but you don't want to move your arm to rub your eye because you've got it in the fire position and you want to be firing to cover the move of the others as they come forward.

I jumped up and ran forward another fifteen metres – a far longer bound than the textbooks say you should. The longer you are up the longer you are a target. However, it is quite hard to hit a fast-moving man and we were pumped up on adrenalin.

You're immersed in your own little world. Me and Chris running forward, Stan and Mark backing us up with the Minimi. Fire and manoeuvre. The others were doing the same, legging it forward. The rag-heads must have thought we were crazy but they had put us in the situation and this was the only way out.[1]

There is no doubt that 'force multipliers' – squad automatic weapons – have changed the character of warfare once again, just as their predecessors did during the First World War, if perhaps not to quite the same degree. In the immediate future it seems that most armies will be using some form of 5.56mm machine-gun at squad level, be it a box-fed LSW or belt-fed SAW. If there is a cloud on the horizon where modern light machine-guns are concerned it is that they are not powerful enough for long-range work, or for penetrating cover and light armour. Nevertheless, the new generation of light machine-guns will remain in use well into the next century, not least because they are popular with the soldiers who operate them, the machine-gunners. Likewise, there will still be a place for the heavier GPMG, which does have the range and the 'punch' that the LSW lacks.

Machine-guns themselves have become much lighter, and their operating principles both more secure and more efficient; the ammunition they use has shrunk to a quarter of its original size and become almost 100 per cent reliable. The one important thing which has not changed dramatically is the human component; the attitude with which man faces the prospect of death in battle, and how he prepares himself to face that possibility quite deliberately, for it was the original invention of the machine-gun which reformed that. More than any other single 'advance' in weapons technology, the machine-gun allowed an individual (or actually, a small team of men) to dominate a sector of the battlefield. They had an inhuman advantage which simply had to be exploited if they were to be on the winning side, whether their opponents were Zulus, Sioux or Dervishes, or other industrialized nations to be beaten into last place in the race toward economic supremacy. Whether the machine-gun has been as important, in any sense at all of the word, as its near-contemporary, the internal combustion engine – or even, dare one say it, the bicycle or the sewing machine – is still to be decided, but there is one clear, irrefutable fact connected with its short history: it has killed tens of millions of men, women and children and blighted the lives of tens of millions more.

We cannot lay the responsibility for the existence of the machine-gun at any one individual's door; we cannot round off this history with a neat reference to a chance remark made in Vienna, or to the unconscious stimulation of the inventive genius of a Yankee from Maine transplanted to Europe by the insecurity of a competitor, for nothing is more sure than that had Hiram Stevens Maxim not invented the automatic machine-gun, someone else would have done so. That the 'phantom other' would have been somewhat more or somewhat less efficient is likewise neither here nor there, for the genre has seen huge ingenuity and vast inventive genius lavished upon it in the course of its development. No matter where or what the starting point was, the successor products would likewise have had all their faults analysed and examined time and again, corrected time and again and been reappraised and subsequently redesigned time and again, and we would doubtless still be in possession of a straightforward man-portable firearm capable of killing, maiming and wounding at the rate of thousands per hour. We call this progress, but perhaps that is what we will always call the inevitability of human nature. Death comes in many shapes and forms, and who are we to know how and when we will meet the Grim Reaper?

Sources

Chapter One: The manual machine-gun

1 Brochure published by the Cooper Firearms Manufacturing Co of Philadelphia, 1865
2 Captain J. F. Owen, RA, *Compound Guns, Many-barrelled Rifle Batteries, Machine-Guns or Mitrailleurs*, London, 1874 (reprinted by Partizan Press, Leigh-on-Sea, 1988)
3 Ibid.

Chapter Two: Richard Gatling's gun goes to war

1 Graham Seton Hutchinson, *Machine-guns: Their History and Tactical Employment*, Macmillan, London, 1938
2 Quoted in P. Wahl and D. R. Toppel, *The Gatling Gun*, Herbert Jenkins, London, 1966
3 Quoted in Hutchinson, op. cit.
4 Ibid.
5 Theodore Roosevelt, *The Rough Riders*, Charles Scribner, 1899

Chapter Three: 'A quiet, scientific gentleman living in Kent'

1 A lecture to the Royal United Services Institution delivered in 1896, quoted in Dolf Goldsmith, *The Devil's Paintbrush*, Collector's Grade Publications Inc, Toronto, 1989

2   An address given to the Institution of Mechanical Engineers in
     1885, quoted in Goldsmith, op. cit.
3   Sir Hiram Stevens Maxim, *My Life*, Methuen, London, 1915
4   Ibid.

Chapter Four: 'Whatever happens . . .' The Maxim gun in Africa, 1890–1905

1   A letter from R. C. Batley Esq. to the Maxim Nordenfelt Guns &
     Ammunition Co Ltd, published in a booklet on the Matabele and
     Chitral campaigns. Quoted in Goldsmith, op. cit.
2   Quoted in Hutchinson, op. cit.
3   T. Ranger, *Revolt in Southern Rhodesia 1896–7*, Heinemann, London,
     1967
4   Catholic Missionary Society *Evidencer*, quoted in Thomas Paken-
     ham, *The Scramble for Africa*, Weidenfeld & Nicolson, London,
     1991
5   Quoted in Goldsmith, op. cit.
6   Ibid.
7   Ibid.
8   Dialogue betwen Rudyard Kipling and Bennet Burleigh of *The
     Daily Telegraph* at Karee Siding near Bloemfontein, March, 1900,
     from Kipling's unfinished autobiographical fragment, *Something
     of Myself*, quoted in *Rudyard Kipling* by Charles Carrington,
     Macmillan, London, 1955

Chapter Five: Towards the Great War – developments up to 1914

1   Quoted in Goldsmith, op. cit.
2   Quoted in Hutchinson, op. cit.
3   Ibid.
4   Quoted in Goldsmith, op. cit.
5   Quoted in C. H. B. Pridham, *Superiority of Fire*, Hutchinson,
     London, 1945
6   Quoted in Pridham, op. cit.

7 Ian Macdougall (ed.), *Voices from the Spanish Civil War*, Polygon, Edinburgh, 1986.

Chapter Six: The war to end war, Part One

1 Lyn Macdonald, *Somme*, Papermac, London, 1984
2 Hutchinson, op. cit.
3 Captain R. V. K. Applin, DSO, addressing the United Services Institute, October 1909. Quoted in Pridham, op. cit.
4 David Lloyd George, *War Memoirs*, London, 1933–36
5 Macdonald, op. cit.
6 G. S. Hutchinson, *History and Memoir of the 33rd Battalion, Machine-Gun Corps*

Chapter Seven: New tools to finish the job

1 Jim Thompson, *Machine-Guns: A Pictorial, Tactical and Practical History*, Greenhill Books, Lionel Leventhal Ltd, London, 1990

Chapter Ten: The birth of the light machine-gun

1 Anon, *The Book of the XV International Brigade*, Frank Graham, Newcastle, 1975 (reprint of the original published in Madrid, 1938)
2 Ian MacDougall (ed.), op. cit.

Chapter Eleven: Heavy machine-gun developments between the wars

1 Mark Baker, *Nam*, Sphere Books, London, 1981

Chapter Twelve: Blitzkrieg: The mechanization of war

1 Bruce Lewis, *Four Men Went to War*, Leo Cooper, London, 1987

2   Franz Kurowski, *Infanterie Aces*, J. J. Fedorowicz Publishing Inc., Manitoba, 1994
3   Regimental History, The Cheshire Regiment
4   Regimental History, The Manchester Regiment
5   Regimental History, The Middlesex Regiment

Chapter Fourteen: The machine-gun in the air and afloat

1   Frank Legg, *The Eyes of Damien Parer*, Rigby, Adelaide, 1953

Chapter Fifteen: Through Korea to Vietnam

1   Michael Asher, *Shoot to Kill*, Viking, London, 1990
2   Vincent Bramley, *Excursion to Hell*, Pan, London, 1992

Chapter Seventeen: The world turned upside-down

1   S. L. A. Marshall, *Battlefield Analysis of Infantry Weapons (Korean War)*, Desert Publications, Cornville, Arizona, 1984
2   John Clark, *Guns Up*, Ballantine Books, New York
3   Stanley Goff, *Brothers*, Presidio Press, Novato, 1982
    Stan Goff served with the 196th Light Infantry Brigade's Bravo Company, 2nd Platoon, in Vietnam, 1968–69. He was awarded the Distinguished Service Cross for bravery under fire
4   William Nolan, *Into Laos*, Presidio Press, Novato, 1986
5   Ibid.
6   Robert Sanders, from Stanley Goff, *Brothers*, Presidio Press, Novato, 1982
7   Cliff Berry, *Fighting with the Pig*, Orbis, London, 1987
8, 9, 10   Mark Adkin, *Goose Green*, Leo Cooper, London, 1992

Chapter Eighteen: Minimizing the threat

1   Andy McNab, *Bravo Two Zero*, Bantam Press, London, 1993

Index

Boxer, Colonel E.M., 4
Boxer Rebellion (1900), 74
Bramley, L/Cpl Vincent, 239–42
Brasche, Rudi, 200–201
Bren gun, 163–4, 166–7, 236
British Army,
  Bren gun, 164, 166–7, 236
  colonial wars, 18–19, 20–21, 22,
    45–58
  distribution of machine-guns, 55,
    59, 83
  First World War
    Machine-Gun Corps, 96–8,
      101–2, 127
    musketry skills, 98
    number of machine-guns, 95,
      100
    tactics, 96–7
  Gatling gun
    Ashanti War, 18–19
    purchases of, 6, 17–18, 61–2
    Zulu War (1879), 20–21
  Lewis gun, 113
  machine-guns
    as kettles, 88–9
    underestimated, 55
  Maxim gun, 37
  Sten gun, 207–9, 231–2
  tactical use of machine-guns, 66
  see also Falklands War; Gulf War;
    Special Air Service; Second
    World War
Brno, Czechoslovakia, 163, 167, 188
Broadwell drum magazine, 16
Browning, John Moses, 115, 182–6
Browning gun,
  and USA, 184
Browning guns,
  action, 35, 115
  airborne machine-guns
    AN-M2/AN-M3, 255
    M2, 162, 221–2
  ammunition, 119, 147–8

BAR (Browning automatic rifle),
  157–8
'fifty-cal', 185–6
heavy machine-gun development,
  182–6
M1917 and modifications, 183–6
M2HB, 283, 286
Bruce, L.F., 16
Buffalo Automatic Arms, 119
Bulldog Gatling gun, 25
Burke, Fred, 148–9
Burma, 45
Butler, General Benjamin F., 5

CAL (Carabine Automatique Légère)
  assault rifle, 289
CETME assault-rifle, 253
CETME-SPAM, 253
CRSG (Fusil Mitrailleur Modèle
  1915), 115–16
Cadillac Gage, 288
Cambrai, Battle of, 128
Capon, Alphonse, 148
Carl Gustav, Sweden, 158, 233
cartridges, see ammunition
Chain Gun, 261
Chandler, Captain Charles, 119
Chartered British South Africa
  Company, 45, 51
Chartered Industries (CIS), 284
Chatellerault light machine-gun, 163,
  247
Chauchat,
  Fusil Mitrailleur Modèle 1915,
    115–16, 163
  M1918, 77
Chelmsford, Frederic Thesiger, 2nd
  Baron, 20–21
China: arms industry, 90–91, 174
Churchill, Winston, 123
Clark, Sir Andrew, 34
Claxton (hand-cranked machine-
  gun), 2, 10
Colenso, Battle of (1899), 56
Colorado Fuel and Iron Company, 26

Star S135, 153–4
Sten, 207–9, 231–2
Sterling, 231–2
Steyr-Solothurn (S1–100), 142
UZI, 234–5
VAP (V42/V43), 211
Vigneron, 233
Welgun, 209
ZK383, 142
see also Thompson gun
submarines, 13
Sudan, 51–4
Swebilius, Carl, 68
Sweden,
  arms manufacturers, 11, 86, 169
  Carl Gustav Mle'30, 158
  Nordenfelt trials, 11–12
Swinton, Lieutenant-Colonel Ernest,
    123, 124
Switzerland, 37–9, 142, 158, 169–70,
    177, 252
Symon, Randolph R., 36
System 63, 288–9

T.u.F. (Tank und Flieger) gun, 118
tactical use of machine-guns,
  artillery role, 81–2
  beaten zone, 127
  Blitzkrieg tactics, 192–6
  British, 66
  enfilading dead ground, 84
  fire teams, 195
  First World War, 96–103
  German, 65–6
  indirect role, 103, 127–8
  'pepper-potting', 205
  special forces, 196–9
  static defence, 82
  supporting assaults, 84
  sustained-fire role, 73
  training, 101–2
Tanganyika (Tanzania), 50, 57
tanks,
  armament, 124, 196, 260–61
  introduction of, 101, 123–5, 128

Tel-el Kebir, Battle of (1882), 22–3
Thompson, Colonel John T., 144–5
Thompson, Jim, 88
Thompson (Tommy) gun,
  action, 150–51
  cost of, 151
  development of, 144–5
  imitators, 152
  sales
    Britain in the Second World War,
      151
    gangsters' weapon, 146–9
    IRA, 149
    marketing, 145–6
    police use, 145–6
    US forces, 150, 151–2
  semi-automatic versions, 152
  types, 151
Thorneycroft, Lieutenant-Colonel, 62
Thun, Switzerland, 37–9
Tikkakoski factory, Finland, 143
Tokarev, Feydor, 174
Transvaal, 51, 54–8
Triton, William, 123–4
Trotha, General von, 50
Tuchman, Barbara, 93–4
Turkey, 21–2
Turpin, H.J., 208

Uganda, 49–50
Ultimax 100, 291
Ulundi, Battle of (1879), 20–21
Unge, E., 11
Union Gun (hand-cranked machine-
    gun), 2–3
United States of America,
  BAR (Browning automatic rifle),
    158
  Civil War (1861–65), 1–2
  Colt machine-guns, 68
  First World War
    captured German weapons, 175
    fighting in Europe, 128–9, 132
    lack of weapons, 71
    machine-guns, 115–16